Achieving Peak Performance in Music

D1590663

Achieving Peak Performance in Music: Psychological Strategies for Optimal Flow is a unique and comprehensive exploration of flow in music performance. It describes the optimal performance experiences of great musicians and outlines ten psychological steps that can be implemented to facilitate and enhance optimal experience.

Achieving Peak Performance in Music reveals strategies used by experts to prepare themselves emotionally, cognitively, and physically for performance. Combining this information with research carried out amongst professional performers and knowledge gained from decades of study and research by psychologists on how to achieve a positive experience, the book guides readers on a pathway towards optimal performance. Using everyday language, it presents invaluable practical guidance and a toolbox of strategies to help with all aspects of performance, including memorisation, visualisation, focus, performance anxiety, thought management, motivation, and pre-performance routines.

Based on psychological research, the book shares practical knowledge invaluable to music students, parents, and amateur and professional musicians. The strategies on performance provided are applicable to every type of performance, from a student exam to a gig or a concert, making *Achieving Peak Performance in Music* a significant resource for anyone looking to achieve peak performance.

Sarah Sinnamon, Ph.D., psychologist and musician, is a performance consultant actively involved in performance psychology and coaching as practitioner, researcher, and lecturer. She was lecturer in psychology in All Hallows College DCU, in performance psychology in Griffith College Dublin, and was assistant violin teacher in Yehudi Menuhin School, UK.

Clare McLeod
603 339 7193
cmcleod @berklee.edu

"This is a must-read for any performer, in any field, who wants to understand the processes that underlie and govern their experiences on stage."
—*Simon Fischer, Violinist, Pedagogue, and Author of* Basics, Practice, *and* Warming Up

Achieving Peak Performance in Music

Psychological Strategies for Optimal Flow

Sarah Sinnamon

LONDON AND NEW YORK

First published 2021
by Routledge
2 Park Square, Milton Park, Abingdon, Oxon OX14 4RN

and by Routledge
52 Vanderbilt Avenue, New York, NY 10017

Routledge is an imprint of the Taylor & Francis Group, an informa business

British Library Cataloguing-in-Publication Data
A catalogue record for this book is available from the British Library

Library of Congress Cataloging-in-Publication Data
Names: Sinnamon, Sarah, 1971– author.
Title: Achieving peak performance in music: psychological
strategies for optimal flow / Sarah Sinnamon.
Description: [1.] | New York City : Routledge, 2020. |
Includes bibliographical references and index.
Identifiers: LCCN 2020017556 (print) | LCCN 2020017557 (ebook) |
ISBN 9780367480639 (hardback) | ISBN 9780367480622 (paperback) |
ISBN 9781003037804 (ebook)
Subjects: LCSH: Music Performance Psychological aspects.
Classification: LCC ML3838 .S53 2020 (print) |
LCC ML3838 (ebook) | DDC 781.4/3111 dc23
LC record available at https://lccn.loc.gov/2020017556
LC ebook record available at https://lccn.loc.gov/2020017557

ISBN: 978-0-367-48063-9 (hbk)
ISBN: 978-0-367-48062-2 (pbk)
ISBN: 978-1-003-03780-4 (ebk)

Typeset in Baskerville
by Newgen Publishing UK

For Lola and Tadhg –

My source of fun and wacky-ness, challenge, and inspiration

Brief contents

Contents

Figures

Tables

Introduction

Is it peak performance, optimal experience, or in the zone?

There are many terms used to label and describe what can be called 'optimal experience' both in research and in everyday contexts. In psychology, peak experience was first described by Abraham Maslow,[1] and the concept of 'flow' has been pioneered by Mihalyi Csikszentmihalyi,[2] with a vast amount of research on flow carried out in the domain of sport by Susan Jackson.[3] The term 'in the zone' has been popularised in mainstream sport culture, and so it's one that most people have heard of. There is also the 'paratelic state' which was put forward in Apter's Reversal theory;[4] 'trance' has been described by Becker[5] and Rouget[6] in the field of ethnomusicology and the jazz pianist Kenny Werner[7] wrote about 'effortless mastery'.

There are some differences in the detail of descriptions by various academics, but for the purposes of this book, I will refer to the experience of flow, peak experience, and optimal experience as similar experiences because these are the psychological terms that are often used by musicians to label or describe what they have experienced. Musicians tend to use words such as 'buzz', 'rush', or 'zone' to describe flow in everyday language – I won't use these ambiguously defined terms in the book.

Musicians' descriptions of flow are strikingly similar, even when compared across different types of music, different genres, different instruments, and different performance settings. One of the key outcomes of flow seems to be that when experiencing flow, people play their best, they play at their peak.

We'll read more about this in Chapter 1, but for now I want to emphasise that whilst flow happens and can be experienced by any musician under the right conditions, peak performance does not have to and does not always incorporate an optimal experience such as flow. Expert, professional musicians perform at their peak consistently, but they may not experience flow every time or indeed, any time. When in flow, people perform at their peak, however, performing at your peak does not automatically result in a peak experience. Mostly, performing at your peak, is plain hard work. When in flow, musicians describe performing at their peak as performing with effortlessness and ease.

To put it more simply: there is flow, there is peak performance, and there are positive experiences of performances (even if not peak or flow). This book aims to show you how expert musicians prepare for peak performance *and* for flow. Whether they experience one or both, by preparing the way they do, they certainly enjoy more positive experiences of performance. By passing on their methods of preparation, their guidelines, the strategies they use, combined with what we've learnt from psychological research on how best to use these strategies, I hope that you too can enjoy more positive experiences of performance, more peak perform- ance, and as an added bonus you may even experience flow more often.

Sport psychology and music performance psychology

In many ways, sport and music performance are clearly very different activ- ities; but whilst there are indeed differences – the artistic production of sound and the expression of emotion in music being the most obvious – there are also many similarities. Performance in these activities requires similar mental skills, long hours of practice, and a great deal of motivation and persistence over years of training.[8] Some sports have more in common with music performance than others. For example, figure skating, synchronised swimming and some gymnastics include such features as the conveyance of emotion and communication with the audience, as well as the memorisation and execution of complex skills and pre- ordained routines combined with improvisation. Both sport and music involve an audience, although the actual experience of the audience in sport has not always been considered an essential ingredient of the overall performance as it is in music. Having said that, recently, during the early stages of the pandemic of COVID-19, empty sports arenas have affected the enjoyment of the sport. Research has yet to be carried out on how players felt about this and the impact of it on their game and performance.

The execution of coordinated complex skill that is performed at a particular moment in time in front of an audience is the key factor that is common to sport and music; it requires similar mental skills and psychological strategies in the prep- aration and execution of performance in each of the domains.

Therefore, what musicians do and what athletes do in psychological prepar- ation for performance are often similar and the research in either domain can benefit the other. The current research and knowledge in sport psychology on how best to carry out the (shared) strategies is beneficial to musicians.

In interviews with expert professional musicians, they described how they pre- pare for performance, and they actually talked about many of the techniques that are used by athletes and recommended by sport psychologists.

Another vital factor that is common to both sportsmen/women and expert musicians is the hours and years of training and practise that they carry out. The '10,000 hours'[9] rule or ten years of training, that was proposed by Anders Ericsson and popularised by Malcolm Gladwell in Outliers,[10] and 'deliberate practice',[11] also put forward by Anders Ericsson, has been shown by a body of evidence to be well founded not just in sport and music, but also in many other domains.

The psychological strategies that are discussed in this book will only be effective when the necessary practise and training have been done. Musicians speak about 'no stone unturned'; in order to effectively employ the strategies in the book, it is necessary to have done the work with your music and your instrument first. No amount of psychological strategies can take the place of the practising and preparation of music that is necessary before a performance.

The research this book is based on

This book is based on and inspired by the research that I carried out with expert professional musicians for a PhD thesis.[12] In carrying out the research under the supervision of sport psychologist Prof. Aidan Moran,[13] a few years were spent designing and deploying a survey of 200 student musicians, carrying out and analysing interviews with over 100 professional musicians, testing the effectiveness of a program for musicians, having discussions and focus groups with expert professional musicians, music psychologists, and sport psychologists, giving seminars and talks, publishing and presenting parts of the research at conferences.

Through analyses of the interviews with musicians, I drew together thousands of statements made by the musicians, and categorised them systematically into themes. From this lengthy and complex type of analysis, the factors that were most often talked about by the expert musicians became evident and I was able to compile the top ten steps that experts take in order to prepare for performance.

I myself was a musician, a violinist, and I performed and taught violin for over ten years before becoming a psychologist. It was when working as an assistant violin teacher at the Yehudi Menuhin School (a specialist music school in the UK),[14] that I became fascinated with the ways in which the students there were taught, and learned how to perform at their best with the aid of psychological strategies. That led me to my research investigating music performance – peak performance and flow, the experiences of expert and novice musicians and the strategies that expert musicians use to prepare for performance.

The musicians

During my research, in interviews I asked musicians about their most recent favourite and best performance. They responded by describing performances that were inspiring and approaches to preparation for performance that were intriguing, intelligent, detailed, enlightening, and personal.

The musicians who took part in interviews and gave generously of their time and shared their personal experiences, were all expert musicians who had been performing professionally at an elite level for over ten years; many were recording and touring performing artists. The musicians were recommended for the research by other performing musicians, therefore their reputation in the music domain and amongst other musicians was important for the validity of the research, rather than their level of public acclaim. They shared their personal experiences of performances, and described in detail how they prepare for performances, and what they've learnt over the years, about themselves and about performing.

Who is this book for?

This book is for music performance students, music teachers, parents of aspiring musicians, amateur musicians, and professional musicians. I would also say that anyone who ever finds themselves having to perform in their job or personal life (at meetings, pitches, and public speaking of any kind), will find the psychology and performance strategies in this book extremely helpful.

To parents and teachers: how to use this book

You could assist your young student musician(s) with the reading of this book, with understanding the information if required, with putting strategies into practise and, as you are already doing, with your compassionate and informed support.

Read the strategies and *ask* your aspiring musician(s) how you can *help* with employing strategies. You may be able to help with specific strategies such as challenging their thoughts *if* they are negative, engaging in positive self-talk (Chapter 5), and helping them to create their own mantra (Chapters 5 and 10). You can assist them in finding their individual zone of optimal performance (Chapter 4). You can read about motivation and then support them in maintaining their love of music and performing. Assist them in feeling like they are competent, that they belong in music or to music groups by supporting them in other musical activities, and by helping them to feel they have some control over their musical development (see Chapter 6). You can help with applying strategies for focusing and with limiting distractions (Chapter 7). You can help them with memorising and support them in trying to carry out mental practice and visualisation techniques (Chapter 8). You can support them in experimenting with breathing exercises and mindfulness meditation (Chapter 9) and you can help them put together a pre-performance plan for the day of an upcoming performance (Chapter 10).

Gently encourage them to try strategies and to identify strategies that would be useful for them to implement into daily routines. None of the strategies have to be carried out during designated practising time, although they can be and it's a good idea to start building them into practise time. However, you can also support your young musician(s) by helping them to carry out strategies at times when they feel relaxed or have nothing else to do.

Your compassionate help and support are crucial to your young musician's development. It's not a coincidence that some research has shown that children with exceptional ability tend to be first children or the baby of the family, children for whom parents tend to have more time, resources, financial resources, patience, and energy. I have to accompany that by saying exceptional ability is not necessarily something you should desire for your young musician – in adulthood typically progressing children achieve as much or more and are as happy or happier than adults who showed exceptional ability as children. Children with exceptional abilities tend to 'plateau' in their early 20s, whilst typically developing children who show an early interest in their domain tend to catch up and even overtake them. Mental health and wellbeing are critical factors to be appreciated and supported in all children, whatever their level of progression and enjoyment.

Musicians: how to use this book

Read all the strategies. Try all of them. Decide which strategies are most useful to your needs, and tailor them to your own individual needs.

Make a plan, and factor the strategies into your everyday routine. Different strategies will be relevant for you at different points in the performance schedule and at different times of your life. Set aside time to implement strategies into your daily routine.

Strategies must be used daily. They must be part of your daily practice schedule. They are as important as the physical practice that you carry out every day. Strategies are not useful if only used on the day of a performance and if they haven't been practised prior to that day. Even though you know all the 'notes' in a piece of music, you still need to practise and plan putting them all together in a musical, technically proficient manner with fluent execution of motor skills and in an emotionally expressive way. Likewise, mental strategies have to be tried out, tested, planned, and practised, so that they can also be executed proficiently and fluently on the day of a performance.

This might seem like a lot of hard work on top of the work you already have to do. But it could also be fun! It is a psychologist-recommended, scheduled time for you to think about yourself and look after yourself a little, amidst all the hard work you do when preparing for performance.

1   Music performance

Flow, being in the zone, peak experience – these are all words to describe the same thing, the same experience. This description by jazz pianist Kenny Werner sums up how it can feel for the performer:

> The first time it happened is something I will never forget … I put my hands on the piano and they played! I mean that they actually played by themselves while I watched! And what they played was blowing my mind and everyone else's. Not only was it good, it was so much better than I usually played.
>
> Kenny Werner, jazz pianist[1]

Sounds good, doesn't it?

Musicians performing

Performing involves a range of experiences from amazing, satisfying, and rewarding to anxiety provoking and scary, with relaxed, calm, unconcerned, even ordinary, run-of-the-mill, and boring experiences in-between. The performer has a lot to do. It is always a complex emotional, cognitive and physical phenomenon, from time to time it is automatic, and from time to time it is *transcendent*.

When we think of performing at our best in any domain, we don't usually relate it to out-of-body experiences, or transcendence, or overwhelming joy, or freedom, or euphoria, or altered states of consciousness.

But these are some of the words that are often used to describe flow, optimal experience, peak experience, peak performance, or being in the zone by athletes, musicians, and psychologists.

We know very little about what it takes for a musician to perform at their very best. There has been some research and dissemination of information on performance anxiety or 'stage fright' during music performance. But very little is known or written about the other extreme experience of performance – that of flow and peak performance. Musicians tend to talk only briefly about amazing experiences or awful experiences of performance. Actually musicians tend to not talk about their amazing experiences of performance in any detail. Likewise, they tend not to talk about their awful experiences in detail either. Perhaps musicians just don't like to talk much about performance and the details of performing or the details of preparing for performance.

So we haven't known, until now, about the great experiences of performance, how musicians describe their peak performances, what they feel like during peak experiences of performance and most importantly, we haven't known *how* they make those great experiences happen.

We haven't known the steps taken by musicians to perform at their best, how they practise, the strategies they use, the psychological thought management, the emotion management, the psyching up or calming down, the routines or rituals they carry out.

This book describes the optimal performance experiences of musicians, how they prepare for performance and the strategies they use to perform at their best.

It describes the extremes of performance – the great performance experiences and also the more harrowing performance experiences. It describes the intense emotions involved in music performance and how great performances are created. It shows how even great performances can occur when musicians use all their skills to turn negative emotions and negative thoughts into positive.

Perhaps one of the most enlightening things that is revealed by musicians in this book is that sometimes their best performances happened when they were most scared. Powerful, negative emotions can be harnessed to become powerful, positive experiences.

Great musicians have strategies that they use to prepare themselves emotionally, cognitively, and physically for performance. This book reveals what those strategies are. It combines those strategies with the knowledge that has been gained from psychologists' decades of work and research on how best to use performance strategies.

Flow

Flow is actually an altered state of consciousness;[2] the kind of experience that people usually speak about with awe and amazement. It can be described as an effortless coming together of mind and body that occurs when the person is totally absorbed in an activity. When in flow, there is total ease, absolute self-confidence, a sense of control, total focus, loss of self-consciousness, and body and mind seem to work totally in synch. People who have experienced flow describe feeling almost in awe of what is happening, feeling like they can do anything, that they are totally in control and able to take risks in their performance; they describe performing at their best with ease and effortlessness, they describe an amazing experience that feels great and is quite different to their usual experiences of performance.

When optimal experiences such as flow happen during performance, they can be life changing. For some, flow is something they have been experiencing in some way, some of the time, since they began playing music. For others, it happens out of the blue, suddenly, intensely, and unexpectedly, just like Werner describes in the quote above.

Musicians' descriptions of their experiences of flow are fascinating. They describe an experience that made them feel empowered, invincible, free, absorbed, joyous, happy, satisfied, creative, inspired, free from self-consciousness.

> *"Amazing, powerful experience", "an incredible high", "had to hold back the tears after", "I felt a high velocity energy", "very alive", "you're captivated yourself by what is going on", "I was in complete control", "everything just worked", "I was able to do exactly what I wanted", "I felt invincible", "I was aware of the audience, but not aware at the same time", "you're free from worry, free from any concerns", "you're right in the moment", "totally absorbed", "free to create on the spot", "it was no effort", "it felt easy", "slightly out of body", "you're watching the stuff pour out of you", "something just clicked", "it was like a spark".*

You can see from these descriptions the extraordinary and unusual quality of the optimal experience of flow. Sounds amazing! Does it sound familiar? Possibly you've had experiences like this yourself.

People experience flow in all areas of life and at all levels of skill.[3] Flow varies in its level of intensity, depending on factors such as the person themselves, the situation, the challenge, the level of emotion involved. So flow might not always have the high intensity that those short descriptions convey – perhaps it is not always a 'life-changing' experience – but it is always of a similar quality, it is always satisfying, motivating and empowering.

Peak experiences in music performance encompass all of the above descriptions and more. Musicians described feeling their body and mind working together effortlessly, being able to do and play exactly what and how they wanted, feeling totally absorbed, feeling free from worries, concerns, or awareness of any negativity, knowing exactly what they wanted to do, being able to respond easily and effectively to any new ideas or errors, or co-performers, not having full awareness of time, feeling highly challenged and even taking a risk(s), and feeling a sense of joy, fulfilment, achievement, satisfaction.

This is just what has been found in research in sport, music, writing, education, creative pursuits, work, computer use, and other areas.[4]

Nine dimensions of flow

There are nine aspects of experience that come together during flow and optimal experiences.[5]

1. The 'challenge–skill balance' – this is a balance between feeling challenged but knowing that you have the skill to take on that challenge.
2. Total focus and absorption – this is an easy focus that just happens when flow happens.
3. A merging of action and awareness – this is one of the most distinctive features of flow. The body and mind work together effortlessly, the body doing exactly

what the mind wants. It is often described as that sense of being 'at one' with the instrument, the violin, the trombone, the guitar, the throat, the bike, the racket, the car, whatever the object of conveyance is.

4. Clear goals – the player or singer knows exactly what they have to do and what they want to do.

5. Unambiguous feedback – the player/singer is feeling, seeing, hearing clearly, totally aware of what is happening in their body, mind, and music. With this clear feedback comes the ability to respond to new ideas they might have, to respond quickly and easily to errors or mistakes that they or others might make.

6. A sense of control – this is a kind of control that is not experienced at other times. There is a feeling of being able to do anything and that nothing can go wrong. This is often described as invincibility and even 'unshatterable self-esteem'.

7. Loss of self-consciousness – this is another highly distinctive aspect of flow that is rarely experienced at other times. The sense of self and concern for the self disappears. People describe feeling free from worries or from self-consciousness, and even describe a feeling of not caring about anything at all. This brings about a remarkable feeling of freedom, freedom from the ordinary worries of the day, freedom from nervousness, anxiety, doubt, or any negativity. This is not a loss of consciousness, or a loss of self; but rather a loss of the concept of self. It is an altered state of consciousness, one that is sometimes sought out through mind-altering drug use. The result of this loss of self-consciousness during flow is that the self is expanded, there is a feeling of transcendence and of the boundaries of the self having been pushed to their extreme.

8. Time transformation – this is where the concept of time seems to speed up or slow down. This is not always described by musicians, perhaps because time, tempo, rhythm are part of the essence of music. But musicians do often describe feeling some kind of alteration of time.

9. 'Autotelic experience' – this feeling occurs when we do something purely for the enjoyment of it. There is a feeling of total satisfaction and fulfilment, happiness and joy, with no concern for extrinsic rewards such as praise, applause, winning, or financial reward.

When all these factors come together, flow happens! An amazing, rare, and illusive experience. When in flow, people perform at their peak, due to the sense of control, the loss of self-consciousness, the merging of action and awareness, the clear feedback, and total absorption.

Musicians describe having performed to the best of their ability during flow experiences. They even describe performing better than they ever knew they could or better than they had in rehearsals, bringing off difficult passages, sequences or creative inspirations in the moment, and to a level they hadn't previously achieved.

All this makes flow a highly motivating and maybe even addictive experience. Feeling great joy, achievement, and fulfilment is certainly not something anyone wants to go out of their way to avoid. Flow may be the reason we continue to do anything. During flow we get a glimpse of our 'best selves', of freedom, of growth, of fulfilment, and satisfaction. We get to push ourselves to our boundaries, out of our comfort zone, and we get to experience a naturally induced altered state of self; it is highly fulfilling and empowering.

Many musicians have described experiencing flow during their practise sessions. It seems to come about in a different way, perhaps more through repetition and focus, than through the high level of challenge and emotion involved in performance. And so, musicians describe experiencing flow to varying levels of intensity and for varying lengths of time.

Flow is for everyone

The next chapter illustrates musicians' actual experiences of flow. Their descriptions are based on their most significant, intense, and memorable experiences of flow. This might give the impression that flow is out of the normal bounds of our everyday experience. But it is not. Flow is for everyone.

Flow can be experienced by anyone at any level of skill. It can be experienced during performance, yes, but it can also be experienced when we are on our own when practising,[6] or in small groups, or large groups. It can be experienced when we are at work, when we are walking, when we are writing, thinking, cleaning, entertaining, playing computer games, interacting with children, interacting with others. As long as the prerequisites for flow are in place, flow can be achieved by anyone, doing anything.

The three main prerequisites, the musts, for flow to occur are – first, that you are doing something you love to do, something you enjoy. Second, that there is a challenge – whether that is performance-related, skill-related, time-related, or experience-related. And third, you must believe you have the skills to meet that challenge.[7] Together the second and third prerequisites here are known as the 'challenge–skill balance' (Chapter 2 has more on this).

Performance

What's involved in music performance?

Music performance is complex – emotionally, cognitively, and physically. It involves a long list of skills and processes. There is the expression of emotion, the co-ordination of physical skill, the production of sound, improvisation, communication and rapport with co-performers, communication and rapport with the audience, technical skill, motivation, memorisation, a deep and intimate knowledge of the music, planning, decision making, concentration, persistence, co-ordination of the senses, adaptation to new and unfamiliar situations, physiological change, the use of psychological or mental skills, the articulation of musical ideas, there is meaning and there is entertainment.

The components of music performance can be separated into four main categories. First, emotion – there is expression of emotion, the performer's own emotion state, the arousal of emotion in others. Second, cognition and cognitive aspects – there is memorisation, the planning of musical goals, execution of skill and technical aspects of the music, mental skills and strategies, sight reading, the co-ordination of the visual, auditory and kinaesthetic (physical) senses, adaptation to changes or mistakes, on-the-spot decision making, coping. Third, there are physiological components – the execution of technical skill, co-ordination of complex motor skills, physiological preparedness, physiological response of the body. And there is communication – communication with the audience, communication with co-performers, adapting and responding to co-performers, adapting and responding to the audience.[8]

The two extremes of performing are linked – fear and exhilaration

There are good experiences, bad experiences, and in-between. At the two extremes of performance experience, there is peak performance and flow, whilst at the other extreme there is performance anxiety. Ironically, these two experiences are firmly linked. Performance anxiety can actually 'flip' into peak experience.

Many musicians have described feeling apprehensive, nervous, even terrified before performing at their best. Their feelings of fear were not a coincidence or not something they overcame or ignored in order to perform their best. Those feelings of fear can actually be used to create great performances and may be essential for some people to experience in order to heighten the components involved in performance.

The emotions, thoughts, and behaviours that musicians experience prior to performance are what play a key role in their performance experience, in managing and coping with challenge, stress, and anxiety, and even 'flipping' those nerves into peak performance experiences.

There are many factors in performance that are outside of the performer's control, but emotions, cognitions, and behaviours can be managed, trained, and harnessed to create great experiences and better performances.

Peak experience is experienced by some people some of the time. It is not essential to experience it – but having knowledge about the antecedents to peak experience, knowing what musicians do to prepare for peak performances, knowing the strategies that other musicians use, provides a great model for finding your own way to having more satisfying performances and for learning to cope with pre-performance anxiety. And an added bonus – flow might just occur too.

What cannot be controlled?

The many factors outside of the performer's control include co-performers, technical aspects such as acoustics, sometimes the instrument provided, the venue, the audience, often the music to be played, the people around you – peers, teachers, parents, critics. When you are a professional performer, you may have more control over the music you are going to play and the venues you play in, but actually this is not always the case – the more people want to hear your music, the more audience a performer has, and the more famous you become, the more expectations there are on you and the more people there are involved in selling your music, organising your concerts, and managing your career. There are managers making decisions, tour managers, promoters, PR people, venue managers, sometimes hair and make-up, producers, and many more, all of whom are relying on your performances to sell your music and pay their salaries. This impacts on your music, your ability to perform, the pressure and expectations on you, the amount of travel you do, where you play, where you stay, even what you eat.

Anything can happen with these external sources of stress, so the performer needs to become very aware and knowledgeable about what they *can* control and *how* to do it.

Can we make flow happen?

What we all want to know about optimal experiences – does this often talked-about 'buzz' come together in very special circumstances that are completely out of our control? Or can we create the circumstances, can we set up the conditions and make peak experiences happen for ourselves?

My research with expert musicians has shown that there are a number of factors in place prior to peak experiences and great performance experiences that may be controlled. Musicians can control many of these factors and this book outlines what these controllable factors are, so you can work towards managing them and learn how to make it happen for yourself.

It will also let you know what the uncontrollable forces are … so that on the occasions when you're not having those amazing performance experiences, you can give yourself a break, not beat yourself up. Sometimes, however, it just isn't going to happen. So even when you have done everything you can, other people, environmental circumstances can get in the way and disrupt great performance experiences and in those circumstances there is very little the musician or performer can do about it. Still, of course, you can have a very positive performance experience.

Is it important to experience flow?

In order to be a musician or a great performer it is absolutely *not* necessary to experience flow. Performers create great experiences for themselves and audiences all the time without experiencing flow. But since flow does occur, and performers often chase that 'buzz', it is possible to create the conditions to make flow happen if you would like to. We now know the factors and conditions that need to be in place in order for flow to occur and we know the strategies that other expert musicians use in order to facilitate its occurrence.

Knowing what expert musicians do prior to great performances is beneficial to all aspiring musicians and experts in the making. The knowledge of what experts do prior to good performances is a great tool-kit for any student, novice or amateur who wants to perform well and enjoy performance.

Many performers experience performance anxiety, but using the conditions and strategies that other expert musicians use to turn anxiety into great performance experiences can show aspiring performers and musicians that performance anxiety is controllable and that we all have within our reach, the tools for easing the anxiety and creating great performance experiences for ourselves.

Flow might be what drives musicians to work as hard as they do

Many people, musicians, artists, and athletes believe in talent. Psychological research has shown mixed results on talent and there are various theories that explain skill acquisition. There are intelligence tests telling us how good, or not, we are at maths or spelling or memorising or reasoning. Musical talent is difficult to test and there are discussions and controversies, analyses and conclusions argued in research that contribute to an international 'nature versus nurture' debate, and that span many capacities, abilities, and intelligences.

In the psychological research, the theory of 'deliberate practice' proposes that the level of achievement reached by anyone is a direct result of the amount of deliberate and purposeful practice that is carried out.[9] The theory has strengths and weaknesses in its argument. It is controversial to many, but common sense to many others.

Although there is evidence for the idea that the amount of practice predicts the level of achievement, there are many factors that influence why some people practise more than others. And this is one of the big questions that psychologists want to answer. *What makes some people practise more than others?* The answer to this includes a number of factors, which are discussed throughout this book; they include motivational orientation, support from parents, teachers and peers, available resources, growth mindset, beliefs about ability, self-efficacy, self-confidence, to name a few (see Chapter 6 for more on these).

All of these factors are changeable, all allow the individual some element of control, and none of them are fixed in the idea of innate ability; none of them can be attributed to 'talent'.

We do know for sure that if you don't practise it doesn't matter how 'talented' you are, your talent will not come to fruition. Ask any expert or elite performer how they got to where they are, and the common answer will be 'a lot of persistent hard work'. There is also the now popular notion that without making mistakes and without experiencing failures along the way, great achievement and success is not possible. A lot of experts give testimony to that idea. Yet there is still widespread use of the word 'talent' in the performing arts.

Our standard of performance is impacted greatly, not just by our level of preparation, and some might say talent, but also by the thoughts and feelings that we have about ourselves. What can be difficult to ascertain from experts, is just how much of their hard work involves mental skill training.

A great deal of research has been carried out on the psychological side of performance and expertise in the world of sport. Research has found that expert and elite performers in sport use a range of strategies and techniques in order to advance their performance. There is also a large body of work and years of advancement in sport psychology research that has sought to improve and refine the psychological strategies used in elite sport in order to improve performance. The thoughts and feelings involved in performance can be managed and harnessed by the performer in order to create better performance and more positive performance experiences.

Expert musicians use strategies in order to manage their thoughts and feelings, to manage their psychological state prior to performance and to prepare cognitively and emotionally for performance. Furthermore, they have found ways to prepare for peak experience during performance, ways to manage and control their performance experiences and to make peak experiences happen during performance.

Before exploring the strategies that musicians use to make flow and peak performance happen, we will see how musicians describe their experiences of flow and peak performance, in the next chapter.

2 What flow feels like

How musicians describe being in flow

"Everything just seemed to click into place … All the practice and preparation, it just worked. I felt like the instrument was part of me almost. I didn't know what it was but it felt good. I felt in control, I felt like I could do anything. And I felt totally in it … and yet at the same time my body was just doing it. I remember it seemed like my arms and fingers were just doing everything that I wanted … And at one point I remember I wondered would I come out of this thing, I didn't know what it was, but it just kept going. So I was even thinking, seeing people in the audience, but it didn't matter … at the same time I was totally involved in the music. I expressed all the emotion, all the music … It just worked, easily, no problem. Fluid, gorgeous."

From a vast amount of research on peoples' experiences of flow in various domains, but particularly in sport, we know that there are nine key factors, nine 'dimensions' that occur together when we are in 'flow'[1] or when we experience what athletes might call being 'in the zone'.

Expert musicians' descriptions of their peak experiences of performance align exactly with athletes' descriptions. As in sport, musicians' descriptions outline nine factors that come together to create the peak experience of flow.[2]

These are a challenge–skill balance, a merging of action and awareness, concentration, sense of control, loss of self-consciousness, clear feedback, clear goals, time transformation, and autotelic experience.

The nine dimensions of flow: as described by musicians

The challenge–skill balance

The challenge–skill balance is central to the experience of flow and is often experienced just before the actual state of being in flow.[3] This is because in order for flow to occur, there must first be a perceived challenge to be undertaken by the player, which is generally recognised well in advance of an actual performance, and the performer must perceive that they have the skills to meet the challenge. It is actually ideal if the level of challenge is just beyond the reach of the perceived skill. Therefore, this stretches us to the limits of our capacity, outside of our comfort zone. It may well be that it is this stretch that takes us out of our usual level of awareness and propels us into what can be described as an altered state of consciousness, i.e., into the state of flow.

Expert musicians talked about having a sense of challenge that they looked forward to, as something they needed or was good for them.

> *"I was very glad of the challenge", "it was new, it was exciting, the kind of thing that makes you feel I'm stretching myself here and that's a good thing", "the challenges were delightful", "the bigger the challenge, the bigger the high", "it's a very, very challenging thing".*

An important point here is that it is *subjective perception* of challenge and skill that colours the flow experience. The word 'perceive' is used because we all have our own 'perception' of what constitutes challenge and also we have our own 'perception' of our level of skill. It is not the actual or real challenge or skill level that is important, but rather that we *believe* we have the skill to meet the challenge we *believe* we are facing. Each one of us can find the balance of challenge that matches our own skill level. This means that peak experiences can occur for any one at any skill level in any domain. It is not something that is just for the experts.

Furthermore, it is relevant to point out that overt physical movements need not be involved and the necessary skills do not need to be physical; flow can occur when reading, surfing the internet, thinking, or even socialising, so long as there is a challenge and the appropriate skills to meet the challenge of the endeavour.

Merging of action and awareness

This may be one of the two most distinctive features of flow and the one that is most often described by both athletes and musicians when talking about flow experiences.

According to people's reports, the mind and body seem to work together as one with a sense of effortlessness and ease. Musicians described feeling as though they were very much connected with the music, and also 'at one with' or in harmony with the instrument, as if the instrument felt like it was part of them.

Expert musicians described this as feeling:

> *"Totally connected to the instrument", "there was a harmony between me and my instrument", "the instrument is really working for you", "everything is fluid and gorgeous", "there were no obstacles and nothing getting in the way".*

Athletes have made similar comments. Speaking about his gold medal triumph in the 1968 Olympic Games, David Hemery said, "I felt in such condition that my mind and body worked as one".[4]

There is a feeling of automaticity, spontaneity, flow, and a sense of oneness with the activity that comes about from the merging of the mind with the physical process.

Musicians also described a sense of ease and effortlessness during flow, which comes about as a result of this merging of mind and body, action and awareness. Technically difficult passages suddenly seem easy, and musical ideas flow. New creative or musical ideas can easily be put into action and performed successfully.

"It was so easy", "you're playing and everything that's going on in your head, it all comes out", "it's like the music is a place and you're both right there, melding together", "sometimes you have an idea and then you realise that this was what you had been trying to find for months", "stuff comes out that you never even thought before", "it was easy, no effort".

With this easy, effortless production of ideas, expression, and technique, musicians are able to play their best, even playing better than ever before. It just happens and they know it.

"I knew I sang really well", "I just knew it was good ... knew they liked it", "you know yourself that it was great", "you've taken it to a different level".

Concentration

During flow, there is a heightened concentration and focus experienced. And what's really interesting is that like other aspects of flow, once in flow, this concentration is effortless, it just happens. There is an easiness about it. No one has to try really hard to focus, when in flow.

People have described an 'unshakeable' focus and concentration on the task. There is total immersion and absorption in the activity, with no thought of anything else. The famous Formula One racing champion Ayrton Senna once said, "I felt as though I was driving in a tunnel ... I had reached such a high level of concentration, that it was as if the car and I had become one".[5]

When musicians were asked about their peak performance experiences, they said they felt:

"Totally in it and loving it", "I was very focused but it was no effort at all", "you lose yourself", "you're right in the moment", "you're oblivious to distraction".

This feeling of being fully in the moment and completely absorbed even allows for awareness of external distractions, like an audience member coughing, or fainting, or a cheering crowd, or a siren on the periphery. There is an intense focus but with an awareness of what is going on in the surroundings. However, this awareness doesn't seem to disrupt focus or flow in any way, but rather it adds to it.

In flow, the awareness of something that would, on other occasions, be a distraction doesn't indicate a lack of focus, but instead shows that the player is so in tune with the activity, with what they are doing and the moment they are in, that there is a sense of all occupants and goings-on being part of the total experience of flow.

One musician said, "nothing else got in the way of what I was doing". A singer spoke about how at a very quiet moment a member of the audience was taken out to an ambulance and she said, "the whole audience could have been taken out in an ambulance and I wouldn't have noticed". Clearly, she did notice this happening – or she wouldn't have been able to describe it – however it did not shake her focus, put her off, or distract her in any way.

The focus experienced during flow doesn't just eliminate external distractions, but also the distractions we create ourselves, in our own heads, during performance. One of the greatest challenges for performers is staying in the moment, and not ruminating about past mistakes or worrying about upcoming challenges. It can be really difficult for the performer to stop themselves from thinking about what went wrong along the way, or that one bit that didn't go as planned musically or technically, the thinking, critical head stuck in the last bar, phrase, song.

It's refreshing and freeing in flow to not even have to try to not ruminate on what's gone. There are no worries or concerns during flow. As one musician said, "what I was able to do was get out of the way". Others said, "there's a sort of blankness involved", "I wasn't intellectually involved", "you're not thinking at all, it's just there".

For some, this sense of focus is the key aspect or the most memorable aspect of flow – "the greatest sense of the thing is being in the moment", "being in the moment – that's all!".

Sense of control

People have described feeling an unusually strong sense of control and even "unshatterable self-esteem".[6] There is a feeling of invincibility and that nothing can go wrong. Footballer Pelé (three times World Cup winner) said: "I felt I could run all day without tiring, that I could dribble through any of their team or all of them, that I could almost pass through them physically. I felt I could not be hurt. It was a very strange feeling … strange feeling of invincibility."[7]

Musicians' descriptions of this feeling are similar. They said:

> *"I was in complete control", "I was able to communicate exactly what I wanted", "I felt free to create, I was able to do new things".*

Musicians also described a sense of invincibility,

> *"I felt I could do anything", "nothing was a problem", "I had a feeling of invincibility".*

With that feeling of invincibility comes an ability to take risk or a confidence that enabled risks to be taken. For example, musicians said,

> *"You take more risks", "you just go for something in that moment, not knowing how you will pull it off".*

So it seems that due to this feeling of invincibility, risks can be taken, new expressions of creativity and spontaneity can occur with the perception that anything can be done, anything is possible.

Loss of self-consciousness

Loss of self-consciousness is possibly the most striking feature of flow and also the most controversial and difficult to measure within the research on flow.[8] It gives rise to a feeling that is highly unusual, certainly in our everyday levels of awareness, and has an immensely powerful impact when experienced. Our usual sense of self and concern for the self seems to completely disappear and people have described feeling totally free of worry and of feelings of self-consciousness.

This loss of self-consciousness does not mean that we become unaware of ourselves or others or that control is lost. We do not lose 'consciousness' but rather we can become devoid of interference of the ego or the concept of the self. Whilst perfectly aware that there are people watching, listening, that there is an audience, the loss of self-consciousness brings about an amazing lack of concern and a sense of freedom from the worries of performance or even of everyday concerns. The result is a feeling of transcendence and of the boundaries of the self being pushed to their extreme.

Musicians described this feeling like:

"You've gone beyond being judged, you're not inhibited", "I wasn't worried about anything at all".

They described a feeling of being aware but at the same time unaware. For example, they said, "I was aware of the audience, but I was in my own space", and "I was conscious that I was on stage but not of the audience". About the feeling of freedom associated, people said "I felt completely free!", and "it is escapism!".

With the loss of self-consciousness, musicians describe a feeling of detachment. One musician said that when in flow "you feel slightly detached from yourself", another said that it's "like you're outside of the physical act of playing". Other descriptions of this were "it's like you're at a distance from yourself" and "it's as if you're watching yourself from a distance". This is like a transcendence that is experienced in altered states of consciousness.

When this feeling of freedom and loss of self-consciousness is added to feeling invincible (the sense of control experienced in flow), and to the feeling of being at one with your body and your instrument (as is felt with the merging of action and awareness), and to the feeling of supreme focus, it is easy to see how this becomes a very powerful experience, that can be emotional and intense and one that is chased, once experienced.

Clear goals and unambiguous feedback

In order to experience flow, it's important to have a good knowledge of what you have to do, what you want to do in the music. It is important to have clearly set goals. This might seem quite an obvious concept, since to perform a piece of music or a song one has to know the music, the words, the notes, rehearse with other players or an accompanist, and so on. But there are varying degrees in the extent to which different people know what they have to do and to which 'goals' might be known or learnt. To experience flow, the musical goals must be very clear, known inside out, to the extent that no stone is left unturned – as we will see in Chapter 3 when we find out more about how expert musicians prepare for performances prior to experiencing flow.

Once in flow, individuals have described that their musical goals and creative or expressive plans are exceptionally clear. The player knows exactly what they have to do, what they want to do, and how they are going to do it.

Athletes have described knowing with great clarity what it was they were trying to achieve in every moment and with every movement. Likewise, musicians have said:

> *"I knew exactly what I wanted to do", "you have the feeling of being able to say exactly what you want in the music", "you have a plan, and you execute it", "you have a plan and you produce it".*

There is a feeling of experiencing very clear feedback from the mind and body about how tasks and goals have been carried out. Feedback can take the form of awareness of movements, of ideal performance skills, or awareness and know-ledge of the situation and context, or of other people taking part.

In music performance, this acute feedback during flow also extends to responding to the physical and musical feedback from executing new ideas, new creative insights, and trying new things. The player is able to respond quickly and effectively to feedback from other musicians, their co-performers. There is a fluid adaptability and responsiveness during flow that is not usually present. Musicians described this feeling as,

> *"You're able to listen and respond quickly", "you have a tolerance for small mistakes", "you have fabulous interactions with the other players", "it's fantastic when you play with someone and then they do something different and you catch it … You feel very connected".*

Time transformation

In flow the perception of time is often transformed. When absorbed in the enjoy-ment of an activity, time can seem to fly by or alternatively can seem to stand still. It may not be a key feature of flow for musicians, since keeping a sense of rhythm and time is inbuilt in the preparation and performance of music. However, some musicians have described a sense of time altering,

> *"and it passes so quickly that you don't even know how you did it, you just did", "the next thing I knew I was finished".*

Autotelic experience

An autotelic experience is what occurs when we engage in an activity purely for the enjoyment of that activity. The autotelic experience in flow is an end in itself and there are no thoughts of external or extrinsic reward, i.e., rewards that might be about financial gain, winning, recognition, status, or applause. Csikszentmihalyi said that autotelic experiences can "lift the course of life to a different level".[9]

People have described how during and following flow they have experienced intensely positive emotions and feelings of euphoria. There is a sense of total fulfilment and satisfaction, and no concern for extrinsic reward. Athletes have used words such as "buzz" and "rush". Musicians have used words such as "exhilaration", "amazing", "powerful", "intense".

They said,

> *"I had to hold back the tears the first time it happened to me", "I felt moved towards the end", "you're captivated yourself by what is going on", "I found it a very moving experience … that was to do with the music, the sheer depth of emotion within the work", "I felt really intense artistic feelings".*

Overall,

> *"It's really powerful", "really exciting", "the best drug", "an amazingly powerful experience".*

Flow as a unity

It is actually quite difficult and probably unfitting to separate the individual aspects of flow from each other, as they have been described above.

In descriptions of concentration there is the effortlessness of merging of action and awareness in the focus that occurs, and a loss of inhibition that is associated with a loss of self-consciousness. In the merging of action and awareness there is the ability to express and create that comes easily but is also executed by the performer with a sense of control. In loss of self-consciousness there is the focus of heightened concentration, and there is a freedom from inhibitions that is associated with the freedom of complete control and the merging of action and awareness. There is the lack of concern that comes with the loss of self-consciousness dimension that is also a feature of heightened concentration. In unambiguous feedback there is the adaptability and responsiveness that comes with the merging of action and awareness. In the sense of control there is the ability to take risks that may also stem from the freedom of inhibitions and loss of self-consciousness; and also the merging of action and awareness which allows risks and new creative interpretations to be carried out successfully, in the confidence and knowledge that unambiguous feedback will aid successful adaption to the risk taken, whether successful or unsuccessful.

This is the nature of flow. One dimension compels another into action and they act on, react to, and respond to each other resulting in an often paradoxical and powerful experience.

The descriptions of flow in this chapter illustrate flow as an immensely positive experience, one that is personally satisfying and that often increases the desire to experience flow again and again. This also results in a desire to continue to engage in the activity that brought about the experience of flow. This makes flow an extremely motivating force, one that can carry students and experts through years of practice and training.

During practice

The descriptions of musicians so far have all focused in on what it feels like to experience flow during performance. That does not mean that flow is only experienced during performance and only to very highly intense levels.

Musicians have also said that they experience flow during practice sessions sometimes.[10] It comes about differently, perhaps through repetition and focus and does not involve the high level or arousal of emotion that is experienced prior to flow during performance. It is less intense, less moving, less exhilarating, but the outcome is a similarly powerful feeling of body and mind working together, sense of control, loss of self-consciousness, focus, time transformation, clear goals and feedback, and autotelic experience.

Who wouldn't want to continue in an activity and persist in long hours of practice if this was one of the occasional benefits?

If you would like to find out more about your propensity to experience flow in music performance, fill out the following short questionnaire.

To do: take the flow questionnaire

Fill out the Flow Questionnaire below

For each of the statements, circle the number which describes your experience:

0 = never, 1 = not often, 2 = sometimes, 3= frequently, 4 = always

When I play music …

1.	I am totally immersed in it	0	1	2	3	4
2.	I feel like things just click into place	0	1	2	3	4
3.	I am 'in the zone'	0	1	2	3	4
4.	I feel in control	0	1	2	3	4
5.	I don't notice time passing	0	1	2	3	4

6.	I'm playing/singing better than usual	0	1	2	3	4
7.	I'm able to do things that I usually find difficult	0	1	2	3	4
8.	I know exactly what I want to do	0	1	2	3	4
9.	My body does what I want it to	0	1	2	3	4
10.	It feels really good	0	1	2	3	4
11.	I am not worried about what others may think of my playing / singing	0	1	2	3	4
12.	I experience these qualities when I perform	0	1	2	3	4
13.	I experience these qualities when I practise	0	1	2	3	4

Add up your scores for statements 1–11.

If you scored over 23 on statements 1–11, you have the potential to experience flow frequently and perhaps you have been. If you scored between 11 and 22 on statements 1–11, you may be experiencing flow sometimes. Whilst a questionnaire can be helpful in analysing experiences, you most likely don't need a questionnaire to tell you if you have had this experience. It's the kind of experience that once you've had it, you know you've had it.

Where the questionnaire might be most helpful is that statements 12 and 13 highlight to you when you experience flow, or in what kind of performance or practice situations you tend to experience flow. Also, it should highlight to you, which aspects of flow-like qualities you score lower on. Knowing this, you can now start to work on those aspects. At least being aware of them will highlight what aspects of flow you could try to experience more often.

3   How musicians prepare for peak performance

Ten steps to flow

Many musicians have found and *accept* that there are feelings they need to feel, thoughts they need to think, and things they need to do in order to experience the best possible performances. All the best musicians actively prepare psychologically and physically for performance and many musicians have actively sought out strategies and techniques to help themselves arrive at an optimal performance state prior to performances.

Performance can be extremely challenging, even for the best of musicians. Some musicians come to performance careers having loved to play music as a young student, and others come to performance having loved to perform. For some, of course, there is a mixture of both. But for all, there are times in life when performance can be challenging.

Musicians are not performing music in a perfect vacuum away from the trials of life. In a lifetime, many people experience other challenges which impact their performances and can add pressure and stress. There are times when musical and performance life can be a beautiful escape, but there are times when it is hard to disconnect from internal stresses when standing in front of an audience.

The good news is there are ways to cope, and strategies to use. These can be learnt and used by all musicians and performers, whatever the level of expertise, student or professional, novice or expert. Expert professional musicians have tools they use in order to help them perform at their best, deal with performance anxiety, cope with other life pressures and internal stresses.

Ten steps to peak performance

There are ten steps taken by and engaged in by expert musicians before achieving peak performance experiences such as flow. These ten steps affect three key areas of our psychology of performance: cognitions, emotions, and behaviours, i.e., thoughts, feelings, and activities (see Figure 3.1).

The steps that are cognitive aspects of performance are: first, having a challenge or being challenged by the performance and facing up to that challenge; second, the use of mental skills and strategies; third, automatising skills and/or memorising music; and fourth, concentration or focus.[1]

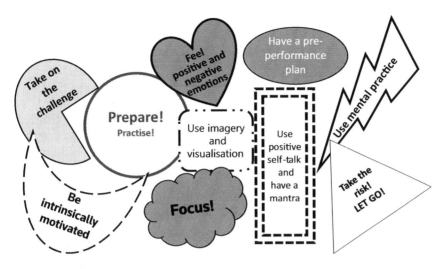

Figure 3.1 The ten steps to peak performance and flow

The steps that are primarily geared to the emotional aspects of performance include: first, feeling and accepting that there are feelings of intense or strong emotions that are both positive *and* negative; second, there is intrinsic motivation and love of the music being played; and third, there is a feeling of taking a risk and having to let go.

That both positive and negative emotions are often experienced before great performances is especially interesting – even great and renowned musicians experience negative feelings (i.e., anxiety, nervousness, fear, anger) sometimes (or even often) and in fact the research suggests that it is actually necessary to experience a range of emotions both positive and negative in order to perform well.

The behavioural steps to peak performance refer to routines and rituals, and carrying out activities that are beneficial to the player prior to performance.

1. Take on the challenge

When peak performance experiences occur during performance, the nature of the performance is usually one that is *perceived* by the performer to be a high level of challenge. It might be a performance that is significant to the player for some reason.

There are many things that make a performance significant for the performer. It could be that there will be a large audience, or a very intimate audience setting. Perhaps somebody important to the performer will be there, or maybe some colleagues or peers will be there. It could be that it is the first time of performing something new – new to the performer or a new song or piece of music – a premier of the music. It could be a competition or an examination, or it could be that the music has special significance for the player.

Musicians described the feeling of the challenge they faced when they experienced flow:

> "*It was new, it was exciting, the kind of thing that makes you feel 'I'm stretching myself here' and that's a good thing*", "*the bigger the challenge, the bigger the high*", "*it was a big challenge*", "*I was scared … but I relish being scared*".

All of the research on flow experiences has found that this high level of challenge is necessary for flow to occur. Flow doesn't happen when there is no challenge, or the level of challenge is low, or if the performer is bored with the music and the performances. For some, every performance is challenging, but there is a difficult point for professional performers when the challenge of performing may start to wane, and even become mundane. This can happen when touring and performing the same music, night after night. When this happens, the challenge of someone special coming to the performance, a critic attending, or a composer or songwriter, or a manager or record company, or the challenge of a change of co-performers, even a technical hitch, or a surprise venue change can actually be a welcome problem to deal with.

Pre-performance preparation – automatisation, mental practice, imagery, positive self-talk

In order to feel able to face the high level of challenge they perceived, musicians described needing to feel completely secure in their skill or ability in order to perform, and to carry out the challenge successfully.

Musicians have said:

> "*What allows you to have these sorts of experiences [flow] is that you have left no stone unturned in the preparation*", "*anything that was in my control I had covered and did to the best of my ability*", "*preparation is everything; I've got to know it very well so I can totally go into the music when I go out to play*", "*you must feel that you are totally secure, and then you can be free to let go, to create*", "*once you have done that, then the piece is really yours*".

Musicians described what psychologists call 'automatisation' of skill[2] – becoming so well acquainted with the music to be played that it was automatic; they describe carrying out exercises of mental practice and visualisation, they do explicit memorisation of parts – their own part and the parts of co-performers. They use mantras and positive self-talk in order to achieve a 'positive mental attitude' or to defeat the negative self-talk and the negative commentary that often go hand in hand, not just with performance anxiety but, with high expectations and desires to do the best you can, the desire to perform to one's best ability and the need to meet the expectations of audiences, mentors, managers, record labels, and all those involved commercially, by performing at consistently high standards.

The psychological exercises and techniques musicians use in order to prepare as best they can are all strategies used in elite sport and documented in the research of peak performance psychologists. The names given to such practice strategies are automatisation, mental practice, imagery and visualisation, positive self-talk, mantras, rituals and they make up part or all of the pre-performance preparation carried out by expert musicians. Each performer has discovered strategies for themselves, has tried and tested what works best for them and shapes what are well known strategies in the world of sport performance into their own individual tools, moulding them to suit their own needs.

Carrying out extensive preparation in the face of great challenge leads musicians to be able to say,

> *"I was very, very nervous but I knew it could be brilliant", "I was nervous, but I was feeling confident", "I was as stressed as it's possible to be … but I knew I could play it".*

2. *Automatisation of skill and memorisation*

For these high challenge performances, musicians describe carrying out high levels of preparation beforehand.

In these instances, "preparation is everything", "preparation is key" and pre-performance preparation is carried out to the point where musicians say they could have done it (played the music) in their sleep. "No stone is left unturned" and anything that is controllable is covered to the best of their ability.

Automatisation of skill occurs through physical practice and rote repetition, and also through use of cognitive strategies such as mental practice and visualisation. Part of the process of automatisation is the act of memorising. Memorisation is a key feature of classical music performance, and is also often utilised by jazz, traditional, and pop/rock performers.

Although we tend to think of memorisation in terms of learning a script, whether musical or verbal, 'off by heart' or from memory, memorisation has more functions that just this in music performance.

Memorisation involves the retention of *any* information for short term or long term use – whether this is muscular movements, cognitive planning, physical co-ordination, structure of music, layout of a performance, as well as learning notes, fingers, chords, switches, words from memory. (See Chapter 8 on mental practice, for more on memory and memorisation.)

There are occasions when classical, traditional, jazz performers perform with hard copies of the score of music in front of them. However, when musicians speak about their experiences of flow, they describe performances when they played without any music score in front of them, or performances where they had the score there but never needed to refer to it.

3. *Use mental practice*

Musicians described engaging in a lot of mental practice, and as time comes closer to a significant performance, they perhaps carry out more mental practice than physical practice. This is because it is such an effective way to practise. Also, they do it because doing mental practice eliminates the possibility of physical fatigue that might occur with too much practice and the 'over-playing' of music that can become mentally or emotionally draining, leaving nothing for the performance.

Mental practice for memorising

Playing complex music that has been composed prior to the performance, from memory – whether classical or jazz or traditional – can be a daunting experience but musicians say they feel most confident when they know the music from memory.

Therefore, musicians get to know the music so well that it is in the process of becoming automatised. Some musicians said that they specifically and intentionally memorise – in their heads – the names of every note, and/or the fingerings for every note, and/or finger patterns for chord sequences.

> *"I have to be able to name every note, every key change, finger pattern, I might even have names for certain chords", "I would have been able to sing all the parts, name all the notes … I knew it inside out", "I memorised all the written parts … not to have to look at the music is very liberating".*

This kind of knowledge and 'explicit' learning of notes is not unusual, with many musicians going to these ends in order to feel secure in their knowledge of the music to be played. Being able to go through from the beginning of a piece of music to the end, without their instrument, explicitly naming every note, fingering, finger pattern, chord progression in your head – this is mental practice. All this work is done away from the instrument, as part of the mental practice involved in memorising and automatising.

This is not easy work even for experts, although it does get easier with practice. One musician who said that they can name every finger for every note, also said that when they begin this process of learning "it might take several hours to do it, but by the time of the concert, I've done it so often in my head that I can do it very quickly".

Mental practice for technical difficulties

Musicians have spoken about practising specific passages that may have difficulty for them, away from the instrument, through mental practice. Mental practice can really highlight what is not known well enough so that it won't disappear or deteriorate in performance conditions – the notes, the fingers, the breathing, the bowing. By taking out the physical component, mental practice and visualisation of playing the difficult or challenging parts can be an immensely effective part of the learning process.

Mental practice can actually clear up difficulties faster than the physical practice. It may be mental practice that differentiates experts from students and amateur players. Young students are not keen to engage in mental practice, it seems like hard work when you're not even physically practising – they may feel like "what's the point of this?!".

Mental practice is also used by musicians to visualise movements they have to make to play certain notes or chords, mentally playing out not just the feeling of the physical movement, but also the look of it. A pianist said they mentally play out the action of "chords that are sudden, you visualise the actual sight of your hand going to the chord". A violinist said, "I practise the feeling of how far my hand has to leap along the fingerboard, and I also see it in my mind".

Mental practice for musical expression

Through mental practice, musicians can work out and practise musical expression. Musicians describe how they mentally hear how they would like the music to sound, the phrasing, and dynamics. They mentally practise different variations or ideas they might have about how to express the music.

> *"You're thinking of the emotion of the tune ... the words of the song", "I would go through the map of the piece in my head", "I have a mental image of how it should sound".*

Musicians talked about the importance of having well-developed musical ideas. It's important to understand what the music means, "each tune has a distinct character and you fall in love with them ... I'm always searching for a particular sound". Musicians described being consumed with the music in their heads prior to performances, constantly hearing it, how they want to express it, what the meaning is and how to communicate that.

> *"I sing it in my head constantly", "I make sure that I have an opinion of every single note of the piece so I know what I want to do with every single note", "I become immersed totally coming up to the performance".*

This type of absorption and mental practice is what builds the intense focus experienced prior to flow.

4. Use of imagery and visualisation techniques

Using imagery and visualisation is similar to mental practice, in that it is carried out and practised away from or without the musical instrument. But the difference between the two is *what* is practised. Mental practice is used to practise very specific aspects of notes, expression, fingers, breathing, and other details.

Musicians use imagery and visualisation though, to experience or imagine the venue, the stage, the audience, the instrument, the setting, and the feeling of what it will be like to perform. They imagine or visualise the feeling of being in a venue, being surrounded by particular people, the image of the audience, 'imaging' the feeling of the emotions they experience prior to and during performances.

The reason imagery and visualisation of the venue and the performance is used by musicians and athletes is as an aid to coping with performance emotions. It is one of the psychological strategies they use to manage their emotions and thoughts.

People describe how they would imagine being backstage, summoning all the emotions that they might experience at that point, then walking out onto the stage and how that would feel – the audience, even seeing specific people in the audience, maybe a friend, colleague or loved one, then the co-performers, and then the performance.

Musicians said things like,

> *"I visualise the venue", "I imagine what it will be like to be up there", "I go through everything, the preparing beforehand [backstage], the actual steps [to the stage area], you can mentally put yourself through it", "I try to recreate the situation beforehand", "I practise walking out, just to freak myself out, get the nervous feeling … then I'd start the piece".*

So, musicians describe how they evoke all the emotions they might feel just before a performance. They make themselves feel the apprehension, the excitement, the nerves, the concerns, the thoughts they might have.

Then, crucial to the practice experience, they either *mentally* perform through the music – having evoked all those emotions they mentally check that the music is stored accurately in their minds and they can play through it in their heads without the instrument, when feeling nervous/excited/psyched up/scared – or they actually turn to their instrument and *physically* play through the music, visualising themselves in concert, imagining the actual performance, and really putting themselves through the performance and the emotions, as close to reality as possible. This is the kind of 'simulation' strategy that is used also by athletes.

This is an excellent way of practising how to deal with anxiety or nerves or excitement, or anger or sadness, or even apathy – whatever the emotions that might be experienced are. It's one of the most effective tools that can be employed to cope with performance anxiety.

It's also an effective way of checking what you know or don't know well enough in the music when feeling those pre-performance emotions.

Mental practice and imagery techniques have been shown in sport psychology and peak performance research to be highly effective and almost equivalent to engaging in the actual physical act of the performance (see Chapter 8 for more on how to use mental practice and imagery).

5. Engage in positive self-talk and have a mantra

When preparing for a musical performance, it is important for musicians to be able to see their strengths and talents but it is also part of the performance process to be critical. In order to progress and develop, musicians need to be able to hear and assess what can be improved, they need to use critical thinking, be self-critical, and analytical. To improve, it is necessary to know what areas of their technique or expression can be improved. They have to face teachers and mentors constantly telling them how to be better and even the opinions of peers are important. Critical thinking and listening to the critiques of others, is part of the process of being a good musician.

Finding a good balance between the negative and positive is crucial. Having a healthy approach to what may sometimes seem to be negative appraisals of something very personal to the musician, is crucial. Critiques can become internalised, we can start to believe the criticism, it can become very personal and we tend to believe negative thoughts very easily. We seem to be hard-wired to believe negative thoughts more readily than we believe positive thoughts, although of course this may depend on the individual and the context.

Even the best of performers can feel apprehensive or have self-doubt coming up to an important performance. It is very easy for negative thinking to take over and it is really important that this does not happen. Negative thinking can snowball, and we can even 'catastrophise' a situation – only seeing the possible negative outcomes, without being able to believe in any good outcome.

It may be hard to believe that brilliant musicians have negative thoughts, but they very often do, and like anyone else, they have times in their lives when they have a greater need for psychological tools than at other times.

The kinds of negative thoughts that experts might have:

> *"Why did I take this gig? Part of you saying 'I wish I wasn't here' ", "why am I doing this? Am I able to do it? It's not good enough", "I knew it might happen to me that I would have a memory slip", "I suddenly realised there were tricky things I hadn't practised that day".*

Use of positive self-talk and positive 'mantras' are tools that expert musicians and athletes use to deal with the negative thoughts.

> *"I go for a walk and I have a little chat with myself", "I'm here and what's happened is too late, you can't do anything about it", "I have put everything into this, I have nothing to lose", "I really want to do this", "I just accept that this is a natural part of being human", "I try to have faith", "I accept", "I just risk it".*

Musicians have described having a 'cut-off' for negative thinking, a time prior to performance when they no longer allow themselves to think negatively. "I have a peak time for nervousness beforehand … and then I say 'ok, that's it', no more worrying. It's just about getting some control".

Instead they fill their minds with the music, with mental practice, with imagery and visualisation, and with positive self-talk, with imagining the "good vibes of the audience", anticipating "positive events rather than negative", making themselves think of "as many positive things as possible".

Many musicians have one or two mantras that they find useful. They repeat these mantras in their heads constantly prior to performances. For some, this is on the day of the performance, for others it may start days before a performance. How musicians came to use these mantras varies – some came up with them naturally themselves, others looked for help in self-help books, psychology texts, or by talking to other musicians.

Mantras are short, positive, motivating phrases that are easy to repeat over and over. Examples of mantras used by expert musicians include:

> *"You can do it! You can do it!", "I know the work, I know my stuff", "I really want to do this and I can do it!", "I'll feel ok once the music starts", "it's not about me! It's not about me!", "just go for it; don't be afraid to fail".*

These are real mantras, used repeatedly by real expert musicians prior to performing.

6. Purposeful focus and absorption

"Absorption" is a term used frequently by musicians when they talk about how they feel prior to performances where they experienced flow.

Immersion in the music evolves naturally as the music that is being practised every day floods the brain. But this immersion and absorption is also deliberately encouraged by musicians, through using mental practice and imagery techniques.

It is deliberately encouraged because this feeling of absorption can be enjoyable, and it is an important aid to freeing the mind of negative thoughts and images, from negative feelings, and from performance anxiety.

Quotes illustrating how musicians engage in mental practice and imagery (above) already show how musicians become immersed in the music they are to perform.

Musicians have described their focus as:

> *"I was 100% focused", "hearing the sound of every note", "being totally immersed in the music beforehand", "the music is constantly in my head", "deliberately absorbing myself in the music", "hearing my very first note and how I wanted it to sound".*

A crucial point illustrating how musicians deliberately absorb themselves in the music before a performance in order to decrease the likelihood of pervasive unhelpful thoughts,

> *"Involve yourself in the music and it takes you out of your self-conscious state".*

7. Have a pre-performance routine

In the field of sport psychology, 'pre-performance plans' are common practice and research has found this to be an effective tool when preparing for performance and for managing emotions – whether calming down or 'psyching up' for performance.

Pre-performance routines are extremely varied and each individual finds their own routine that is useful and beneficial for them. Often musicians find a few things that work for them, and these become rituals. Although varied, routines tend to incorporate eating, sleeping, relaxation, exercise, alone time, practising, rehearsing, and getting dressed.

Routines have a purpose. They work by structuring the day or the hours prior to performance and musicians can manage emotions by associating emotions that are relevant and hopefully effective with each part of the routine, working up to, or calming down to, their preferred emotional state by the time of the performance.

So, when relaxing, musicians are managing emotions and associating a feeling of calming or resting of the body and mind – "I do everything slowly, I'm very slow and measured about everything", "I take my time, trying to keep my body calm".

Sleep and naps are important for brain functioning and for physical rest. Research has shown that while we sleep the brain is working hard to process and synthesise information that we have learnt and practised during awake time. Preparing for performance is hard work and there is a lot of learning and brain processing involved. Sleep is crucial – "I have always had a performance routine that involves a sleep in or rest", "the most important thing for me is to have a nap in the afternoon", "I stay in bed late in the morning".

During exercise musicians can release surplus excess energy, letting go of tension, and thereby many musicians set aside time for this – "I do a little bit of exercising ... trying to get myself flexible", "I go for a walk on my own", "I like to do some yoga".

Some people are careful about their diet and how their stomach feels during and prior to performance, and so the type of food and the time of eating is important prior to a performance – "I just sit there with a coffee and a yellow snack", "I cannot eat", "I eat early and then have something light ... maybe a banana".

Alone time allows musicians to manage their thoughts and feelings – "I shut myself off and prepare", "I'm not very social on the day", "I avoid any confrontation", "I prefer to be in the dark", "silence is important", "I would distance myself beforehand".

With each activity in the routine, musicians attach specific emotions and thoughts to that activity, being very aware of how they *do* feel and how they *want* to feel.

> "Putting on make-up is an important time for focusing", "I find dressing really nerve racking", "I do a great deal of polishing of shoes and ritualistic laying out of clothes ... I do everything slowly", "you have to psych yourself up, get yourself enthusiastic", "the habit of the routine just sort of settles you", "my face and jaw have to feel right, I spend a lot of time working on that ... that is why I have the routine I have".

Many musicians set aside time just for breathing, particularly singers, and wind and brass players. String and keyboard players could learn a lot from them about this – "I do yoga breathing exercises", "I have my breathing routine", "I do a breathing exercise ... it slows the heart down".

The detail to which routines are carried out is very varied depending on the individual. For one person, a routine might be finely worked out from the moment of waking on the day of a gig to the moment of walking on stage, for another their routine might involve just one ritual that must be carried out.

Varying is the degree to which a performer depends on their routine. For some, they have a loosely planned routine that is flexible and they can cope if it doesn't all go according to plan, for another, they may feel if the one thing they rely on doesn't happen then they have great difficulty coping, having attached superstitions to the importance of that one ritual.

As with positive and negative thinking, a balance is important. Finding the right pre-performance routine that suits you is a highly useful and effective emotion-management strategy. But if this routine becomes too fixed or too heavily relied upon to an almost obsessive degree, then it is no longer healthy or functioning positively.

Of course, there are times when expert musicians find themselves in a position where it is not possible to carry out their routine, whether the reason be an unexpected performance, a delayed flight, a tour bus stuck in traffic, technical difficulties at a venue, venue difficulties, co-performers creating some obstacle, or just simply the day not going according to plan.

Whilst this might be a little upsetting, experts have to carry on and perform and entertain to the standard that is expected of them by their audience and co-performers. With practice, and out of necessity, experts become adept at adapting their routine to each situation, squeezing in the rituals that they find absolutely necessary. Or as this musician says,

> *"When you have to come up to a level and you don't have the luxury of being able to do it the way you would like to do it, it's amazing how you just live with it".*

8. Feel positive and negative emotions

Strong emotions are frequently experienced by all performers prior to performance. This is a natural occurrence – it happens when we care about something and it is the brain's way of getting us ready for an event.

Expert musicians are not immune to this and have described experiencing strong emotions. What is really interesting is that expert musicians describe feeling a *combination* of both perceived positive and negative emotions.

The experience of emotion is *perceived* and *interpreted* by us. These are two important stages involved in how we experience emotion and the thoughts and behaviours that result from the emotions we feel.

There are many theories of how and why we experience emotion, but one of the most well supported theories suggests that our *perception* of an event and the related emotions impact on our cognitive interpretation of that emotion. This in turn dictates the subsequent thoughts that we have, the physiological reaction in the body, and the behaviours that we engage in.

If we perceive an event as negative, as a threat to us in some way, the emotions attached to it are likely to be negative, as are the thoughts that we have, and the outcome will most likely be to engage in negative behaviours.

If a performance is perceived to be scary or intimidating we will have feelings of fear and nervousness, and our thoughts will be negative and fear-based; this will lead to a physiological reaction in the body whereby the body and brain instinctively prepare for danger by muscles tensing, adrenalin flowing, eyes dilating, evacuation of bodily fluids – i.e., sweating and diarrhoea, sometimes even vomiting. This is known as the fight or flight response. How we deal with this is the crux of solving the performance puzzle. Later, in Chapters 4 and 5, we'll look at this in more detail. But we can see already in this chapter that the way experts deal with this is through careful and detailed preparation, and by using thought and emotion management techniques such as mental practice, imagery, visualisation, positive self-talk, mantras, and by having a pre-performance plan in place.

Expert musicians described feeling a combination of emotions – both positive and negative. They have described sometimes experiencing very strong negative emotions, even feelings of terror and panic, but importantly they have described at the same time feeling positive emotions and having positive thoughts,

> *"I was hoping for the best but fearing the worst", "I was very, very nervous, but good nervous", "I was as stressed as it is possible to be", "I was under incredible pressure … really juggling", "I was very very nervous but I knew it could be brilliant", "I was nervous but I was feeling confident", "I was terrified … but I knew I knew my stuff", "you're always aware that there's a danger there", "I was feeling very positive within myself at the time".*

Expert musicians admit to feeling nervous, they accept this feeling as part of the performance process, possibly even enjoying the feeling, and they recognise other feelings of enjoyment, positivity, and confidence.

It is notable how expert musicians are aware of feeling a combination of emotions, a combination that includes nervousness and confidence. There may be an immense challenge ahead of them that makes them feel very apprehensive, but having prepared for the work physically, emotionally, and cognitively, having years of work and practice behind them, they can balance the nerves and the fear with the feelings of confidence that they have.

They remind themselves through use of positive self-talk and mantras of the confidence or the knowledge that they know they can do it, even in the face of fear. So descriptions like,

> *"You are constantly facing your innermost fears", "when you walk out it is very very scary, that's the scary moment, in theory anything could happen", "you are laying yourself bare", "you feel exposed", "It's like the walk to the gallows", "you feel the fear and face it", "it feels like riding a bike at top speed, if you fall off how do you get back on?"*

are balanced with thoughts such as,

> *"I knew it could be brilliant", "I did in general feel confident",*
> *"I was very positive in general", "I was excited … really looking forward to it",*
> *"I was scared … but I relish being scared", "I was nervous, but good nervous",*
> *"you are always a bit excited", "I was looking forward to it", "at the time I was*
> *feeling very positive", "I was feeling very positive within myself at that time",*
> *"I had absolute confidence".*

In these descriptions we can see that there are nerves or anxiety, but these feelings are recognised and accepted by each of the musicians as a necessary part of the process and even as a positive thing.

This recognition of emotions and acceptance of how you feel is really important. For many people, including experts, nervousness is part of the emotional package of performing. There is good reason for that – nerves, adrenalin, being "hyped up" or "psyched up" is actually necessary for performing at one's best. It is these feelings that give us heightened focus, heightened awareness, all our senses become aroused and heightened, there is attention to detail, a sense of something important or special happening or about to happen, and this helps us to perform at our best.

Experts say that "it is difficult without it [nerves] – it is 'flat' without nerves", the nerves "are going to come, and if they don't come then there's something wrong", "I wasn't overly nervous but there is this feeling of vertigo – that 'now is the moment', and you all of a sudden get scared".

Performance is special and if there is no sense of something special about to happen, then performances can sound flat or even boring. Not only does this sense of importance impact emotionally on the performer but an audience can also sense that tension and an atmosphere can be created that is unique and specific to live performance.

Expert musicians describe various levels of nervousness and not only does this vary from person to person, it also varies depending on the particular performance or a particular time in an individual's life.

Along with what might range from a mild feeling of apprehension to a major attack of nerves and panic, there will be other emotions involved – some people need to also feel calm and happy, or some need to feel invigorated and energetic, others may need to feel angry and aggressive, along with the feeling of anticipation or nervousness. Everyone has a unique blend of emotions that they require prior to great performances.

There can be a sense of fun "I wanted to have a bit of fun", or a lack of concern "I had no negative nerves", "the nerves gone and only excitement left", "I was just so relaxed and felt good", or acceptance, "you have to accept that this is a natural part of being human", "I had done a lot of positive work before going out there", and a feeling of happiness to be challenged, "I was very glad of the challenge".

Several emotions can be experienced at one time or prior to one performance.[3] In Chapter 4, you will read more on emotions before and during performance, how to manage them and how to become aware of the unique blend of emotions that you require in order to perform at your best.

9. Be intrinsically motivated – love what you're doing

We are intrinsically motivated when we are doing something we love to do, something that feels good, just for the sake of doing that thing, and for no other reason; when financial gain or critical acclaim, or audience applause or peer approval is of no consequence or at least it is of secondary benefit.

Of course, all professional musicians have to earn a living and make money and therefore the financial side is always a very present reality. In order to make money, concerts must be scheduled, audiences must want to hear their music, and whilst musicians want people to love their music, the absolute requirement for a performer to have an audience can also become a pressure or stress.

Many musicians have lots of other people around them who are in employment because the musician has an audience and makes money – agents, PR people, tour managers, co-performers, recording companies, assistants, and even make-up and wardrobe artists. Just like all student and amateur musicians, experts also have peers, family, colleagues, critics who they want to play for and even impress sometimes.

Like student musicians, professional musicians sometimes have performances where they are playing music that they may not particularly like, or feel a special affinity for. All these factors can lead to musicians being more 'extrinsically motivated' – more motivated by external factors, not something from within.

The more extrinsically motivated we feel, the more focused we are on anything but the music, the less likely it is that really good experiences such as flow are going to happen. You can read more about motivation and how to harness intrinsic motivation in Chapter 6.

Mostly musicians love what they do, even if they may have times when they are under pressure, tired, or just plain bored, and they feel they need a reminder of the 'love'. But there are always performances of music that they particularly love, have a special affinity to, or have co-performers that they love to play with, or a venue that they have particularly fond memories of.

On the occasions that expert musicians experienced flow, they described how much they loved the music they were playing at that time.

> *"I loved the songs we were playing and wanted everyone to love them",*
> *"I wanted the audience to love the music like I do", "I love this music more*
> *than anything", "I totally loved this music".*

Flow and peak performance experiences tend only to occur when that intrinsic motivation, that inner joy, or love of the music and the occasion is present, "I can only have this experience when I'm totally into the music".

10. Take a risk and let go

This final step of accepting the risk and letting go occurs before flow experiences, usually in the moments, or for some the hours, just before walking onto the stage, into the recital room, or into the exam room.

There is a feeling that after all the preparation and work has been done, the emotion management, having dealt with the nerves or sense of occasion, having "psyched up" or having calmed down, feeling totally absorbed, now what is left is a very real and clear sense of the challenge ahead.

There is challenge, excitement, anticipation, a mixture of fear and confidence. There is a sense of risk, for some even a sense of danger, and there is 'letting go'.

The sense of risk and of 'letting go' go together hand in hand. Musicians have described how this feels.

> *"I just have to go for it, it might be brilliant or I might fail", "it was do or die, I just had to let go and go for it", "there is nothing to fall back on, you are totally putting yourself out there", "it's either sink or swim kind of a feeling, and you just have to take the risk … and it felt like a huge one", "in theory, anything could happen", "I just decided I'm going to go for it, if it doesn't work out 'there we go'", "I just thought 'risk it, go for it'", "just do it, don't be careful, don't hold back", "you have to let go of all attachments", "don't be afraid to fail".*

This is an amazing experience – feeling the dread, the immense challenge ahead, feeling the sense of risk and letting it all go. It is a risk to walk into that performance spotlight and it is a risk to let go of attachments, of concerns, of fears and worries about making mistakes, about forgetting something, about falling, about dropping the instrument, about nobody liking the music, about letting people down, about not pleasing your peers, about not making money, about failing an exam, losing the next gig or even your entire career.

This sense of risk can happen whether you're playing to 20,000 people, or performing in an intimate recital room of 100 people, or walking into your grade 1 exam, performing at a school concert, or performing at a fun gig for friends.

As some experts said, "you are totally putting yourself out there", "it is a very naked experience", "you feel very exposed" and therefore you are risking things that really matter to you. But when the risk is felt and you have that feeling that you are going to let go or that you have to let go, great experiences can happen. This can only be done when all the work has been carried out and you feel complete confidence in your ability to meet the challenge.

In taking the risk and letting go, we reach out of our comfort zone, the safe zone, and we rise to the challenge. The reward is peak experience, flow – perhaps the best feeling in the world, the best experience of performance, a natural high, a natural altered state of consciousness. This is really what drives us for more, to carry on practising, to play more music, to perform again.

The ten steps discussed above are the processes of preparation for performances resulting in flow that were most talked about in my interviews with expert musicians.

Just as all musicians have their own individual emotional state, they also have personal strategies that differ from others, rituals or 'foibles' that are useful to them when preparing for performance. Just to give a little flavour of those things:

> *"I pray to a spiritually higher power", "If I have a good laugh before I go on stage, it just breaks the ice", "I love talking to the audience, a little bit of conversation, feedback from the audience … if I can have that it makes it easier for me to perform my best", "knowing that there's something bigger than yourself out there takes the pressure off", "I had a smoke", "I took a beta blocker", "as soon as I start to play, I know I'm back where I should be", "I had a sense of trust".*

It is important to be aware that flow does not happen all the time. It doesn't have to and it's not supposed to. Having prepared well, people perform at exceptionally high standards when not in flow. For some people flow happens very rarely, some musicians say half the time, others say it happens in one out of every three performances. The musicians who experience it regularly have tried and tested various strategies and routines, they have found out how they need to feel, what they need to think, and how they need to behave prior to performances. They really have it sorted in their heads and in their preparation.

But flow is elusive. Musicians acknowledged that although they may be able to set up all the conditions for flow to occur, it still might not happen. There are other factors that can happen, that cannot be controlled, that disrupt the experience of flow. However, great experiences and great performances will still happen.

Experiencing flow is not the be all and end all, it is not a necessity in order to be able to perform well. Musicians perform to very high standards all the time. But to be able to have glimpses of such special performances and such an amazing experience as flow is definitely a bonus to have sometimes, to say the least.

It pulls us out of our comfort zone, we get insights into how great we can be, we have moments of brilliance, ease, fluidity, and control, we see things differently in those experiences, it feels great, it gives us hope, it motivates us and gives us new standards to reach for in our everyday reliable sustainable great performances. It's there for the taking, why not have it!

4 Managing your emotions

"I cope with nerves by trying to accept them. They're going to come, and if they don't come then there's something wrong", "being able to use the adrenalin in a positive way ... it can be very touch and go, if you don't get it right, get focused, you're just concerned with your somatic responses".

Experiences of flow are quite literally awesome experiences. People describe feeling quite awe-struck about intense flow experiences; they describe feeling wonderful, feeling in control, feeling alert, focused and fulfilled, and playing at their best.

Descriptions of flow in Chapter 2 tell the story of how it feels to perform at one extreme end of the emotional and musical performance spectrum of experience. At the other end of the spectrum there are experiences of horrible performance anxiety – anxiety that can range from mild and controllable to anxiety that feels out of control – resulting in mistakes, memory slips, physical sickness, and feeling severely incapacitated.

Ironically, many expert musicians have described that the times they felt the most anxious is when their emotions and experience seemed to suddenly 'flip' into the best performance experiences of their lives. Most times, however, for most people, performance experiences probably lie somewhere in between these two extreme experiences.

Music performance anxiety (MPA)

For the most part, musicians play and perform music because of their love of music. But performance and sharing music with others is not easy for many people. As we can see from what expert musicians say about performance in Chapter 3, feeling nervous is part of the performance process. Awareness and acceptance of that is part of the process of learning to deal with the anxiety. Varying levels of anxiety are experienced by different people and in different situations. What is easy for one performer may be a nightmare for others. Some performers love huge audiences, but are terrified in small intimate venues; for others it's the other way round – they prefer small audiences to large audiences. Sometimes just one person in an audience can change how a performer feels. Many expert musicians describe feeling fine until suddenly spotting just one significant person – a family member, a peer, a colleague, or critic – in the midst of a crowd. This can completely change how they feel – either putting them under more pressure, or calming them down with their reassuring presence.

What is it?

Performance anxiety has been explored by psychologists in many contexts, including sport performance, public speaking, test-taking, and the performing arts, to name a few. Most people would rather do almost anything other than get up on a stage to perform. There have been surveys carried out asking people about their greatest fears and the number one fear tends to be public speaking, with fear of actual death coming in at number 2.[1] The comedian Jerry Seinfeld comically observed that this means that, "for the average person, if you have to be at a funeral, you would rather be *in* the casket than giving the eulogy"[2]. It seems like people really don't like to get up and perform in front of other people. So, if you experience performance anxiety, you are definitely not alone.

Performance anxiety has commonly been referred to as 'stage fright'[3] but this term does not adequately label the complexity of performance anxiety or the often multi-faceted consequences of it.[4] Anxiety occurs when we experience some kind of threat and in performance anxiety it is the performance that is viewed as the threat. But the performance context itself is not the only significant factor. Performance anxiety involves a sequence of interactions that goes back and forth, round and round between the performance environment, and our thoughts, our emotions, and our physiological arousal.

So, in relation to managing or changing your experience of performance anxiety, the answer doesn't just lie in changing or eliminating the performance context: the answer to managing it lies in changing the thoughts, emotions, and physiological arousal. Just as performance anxiety itself is multi-faceted, the solution to performance anxiety is multi-faceted. This means that in order to manage our experience of performance anxiety, we can use a variety of strategies and solutions – some that target thoughts, some that target the emotions and some that target the physiological arousal. Even a small change to any one of these can have a powerful impact on the whole process of anxiety.

Why does it happen?

"Why am I doing this ... why did I take this job?"

The main reason for anxiety in general is that it is part of the system that prepares us for threat.[5] The body and brain get prepared to act when faced with any adverse condition, challenge, or dangerous situation.

We experience performance anxiety when we judge a situation to be of great importance to us, and the importance of the situation is generally heightened by the presence of other people. Why is performance viewed by us as a threat when we're not in any physical danger? The roots of this are believed to be in our evolutionary psychological make-up. In order to keep safe, it was crucial that we were socially accepted and part of a pack. Any threat to our membership of the group was a threat to our survival. So, when we feel that we are going to be judged by our peers or colleagues in relation to our ability or our reputation, we perceive performance to be a threat.

Most musicians have times when they think, "Why do I feel like this? Why am I doing this? Why don't I just do a 'regular' job?" Even in sport, these are common thoughts of the elite and the expert. Johnny Sexton, world rugby player of the year (2018) and one of the highest points scorers in rugby union history, said recently,

"You get nervous, you get butterflies, you think 'why do I do this'?".[6]

There are many reasons why we feel anxiety before performing, and it's not just in music or sport – even those doing 'regular' jobs have times when they have to do something like present their work, or perform in some way in front of others, and experience performance anxiety. Those doing 'regular' jobs often think it would be great to be a musician, to 'play music that I love all the time as my job'.

The *perception* of stress or danger in music performance is experienced for different reasons by different people. Being the centre of attention can be difficult for some. There is 'exposure' of the self or vulnerability, and there is judgement from others. There is the potential for social gain or loss – you could be great, but not everybody will think you are, and some people might love you or your music, but not everybody will. Perhaps the most important people to you might judge you or criticise you. You might be performing something very difficult or playing at something very special, singing or playing music that has special importance to other people and you don't want to let them down. There is self-expectation and achievement, having worked hard we want to see the results happen in the performance; a lot rests on that one particular moment in time, where there are no second chances. Then there is the fear of the unknown, uncertainty, and factors that are completely outside of our control.

The perceived importance of the situation is influenced by any one or more than one of the above factors. How we view or *perceive* the performance situation – what we think about, how much we think about it, how negatively or positively we perceive the situation – has an automatic effect on how we feel emotionally, and the extent of arousal our body responds with. Basically, the level of threat we view the situation to be, affects how we feel and the level of physiological arousal we experience.

Fight or flight: responses to danger

"I was terrified … I was about as stressed as it's possible to be."

Once in the 'fight or flight' process, our whole body responds in order give us the ability to fight the threat or flee the threat. The physiological reaction allows the body to respond and adapt to the stressors or pressures in our environment. The higher the level of danger we perceive, the higher the level of arousal we feel. If we perceive the performance situation as highly dangerous or stressful, our body reacts accordingly. This is natural, this is how we cope with and adapt to all situations in life (see Chapter 9 for more on the fight or flight process).

But, an unhelpful cycle of negative thoughts and feelings can easily come about. What happens is we perceive stress or danger; that stress is interpreted cognitively and emotionally by the brain based on our previous experiences of that particular kind of stress, how we dealt with it on previous occasions and the subsequent outcomes we experienced. Being the source of emotion including fear, the amygdala is the key activator of the body response and what happens next in the body all depends on the amygdala and the type of thoughts you are having about the situation. Then the body reacts, there is a surge of hormones and the neurochemicals in the brain change. Levels of the neurochemicals – adrenalin, dopamine, serotonin, norepinephrine, cortisol – alter in order to make us ready to act, to make us more alert and ready to fight or flee a threatening situation.[7] We become alert to the changes in our body, and if we interpret this negatively then, in turn, our thoughts become more negative, our feelings become more negatively perceived, our body reacts again, our thoughts and feelings become again more negative, and so on.

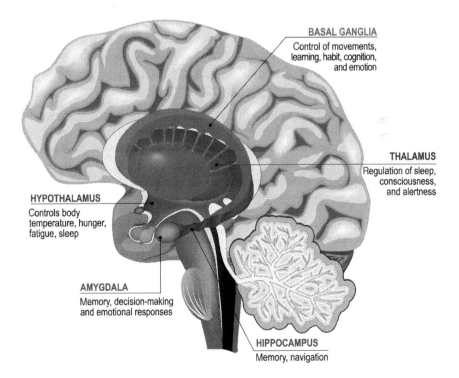

Figure 4.1 Where fear is located in the brain: the amygdala

Emotions-thoughts-behaviours loop

So as we can see from the fight or flight process of getting the body and mind ready to act, our thoughts, emotions, and physiological responses are intricately linked and they influence our subsequent behaviours – how we behave in this situation, how we deal with it.[8] The thoughts we have about ourselves, about a situation we are facing, and about others around us, affects the emotions we feel, how our body reacts and then the behaviours we engage in. Likewise, the emotions we experience affect our thoughts and our behaviours; how we feel in our body affects our emotions and our thoughts. Then the behaviours we engage in, in turn, affect the thoughts we have and how we feel emotionally.

How we *perceive* the situation we are in, the challenge ahead, impacts on our thoughts, our emotions, our behaviour, and the outcome. The initial *perception* of the performance is the very beginning of finding the remedy for performance anxiety. How dangerous, stressful, or pressurised we perceive the situation to be affects how we think and feel, and how our body will respond.

> *"When you walk out, it's scary … that's the scary moment … anything could happen in theory".*

When performing, there are many factors that we have little or no control over. These factors will vary depending on the performance situation and your level of

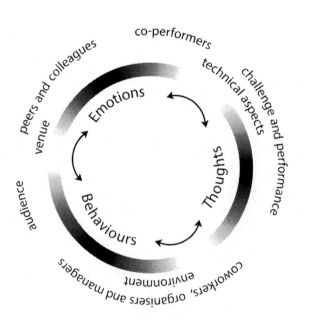

Figure 4.2 The emotions, thoughts, behaviours loop, and impacting performance factors

involvement in the organisation of it. But they tend to be for example, the venue itself – the size of it, the temperature, the feel of it, the set-up, the size of the audience, who will be in the audience, technical aspects of the performance – sound, acoustics, level of lighting, co-performers – their mood or attitude – and even organisers or other people involved in making it happen.

Situated in the midst of all this, is you the performer. What you do have is control over how you appraise, perceive, or interpret the situation. You have control over how you think about it, and you can choose to use strategies to help you manage your thoughts, feelings, and physiological response. (Chapter 5 will show you tips and strategies for dealing with and managing your thoughts and perceptions. Chapter 9 offers ways to calm the physiological response of the body.)

When we experience performance anxiety, when we are faced with a performance that scares us, negative thoughts and feelings can snowball and gather strength. If not prevented or stopped in its course, this cycle of thoughts, feelings, and physiological reaction, can turn into full blown panic. We start to 'catastrophise', meaning that a process has been set in action where we can only see negative outcomes or even total catastrophe; the result of this is that the body and mind go into hyper-arousal. This is very difficult to come back from in a performance situation.

What we want to do is stop that cycle in its tracks or prevent it from even starting, and we do this by knowing how to target the types of symptoms of performance anxiety and by having strategies to do that.

Negative effects of performance anxiety

"It's a nasty feeling."

The symptoms of performance anxiety fall into four types – physiological, cognitive, emotional, and behavioural and each of these types of symptoms impacts on the others.

1. **Physiological symptoms** include sweating, tension, shaking, dry mouth, tight throat, pounding heart, butterflies in the stomach, nausea, diarrhoea, shortness of breath, less fluent and even awkward co-ordination between the senses and between muscle groups, more constrained movement.[9]

2. **Cognitive symptoms** include loss of focus, distraction, worry, negative thoughts – the 'inner critic' takes over, heightened focus on the negative symptoms, heightened negative awareness of other people, deterioration of memory, breakdown of memory, catastrophisation, less efficient decision-making, delayed responses, skills usually carried out unconsciously become conscious – 'de-automatisation', increase in likelihood of similar thinking in future.

3. **Emotional symptoms** include nervousness, fear, panic, loss of self-esteem, inadequacy, sensitivity, sadness, anger, worry, guilt, shame, and many other emotions that are related to these emotions or are versions of these core emotions.

4. **Behavioural symptoms** include loss of motor control, less efficient co-ordination, making mistakes, mistakes snowballing or one mistake leading to another and another, carrying out ineffective responses – being late, making excuses, avoiding, over-reacting, putting in more effort to try to control some aspect of performance which takes concentration and mental resources away from other aspects, the main goal or the key task involved, leaving/cancelling performances/dropping out.

That's a lot of possible symptoms! You won't experience all of these, of course. But if you are experiencing performance anxiety, you will be affected by symptoms in each of the categories or types of symptoms.

The performance task involved may be highly sensitive to the negative effects of physiological over-arousal; like all motor tasks, the physical playing of a musical instrument can be highly sensitive to such negative effects, for example playing music is greatly affected by shaking fingers, sweaty hands, muscle tension, shallow breathing, dry mouth, tight throat. Singing is greatly influenced by muscle tension, dry throat, tight throat, tense diaphragm, shaking.

Since the symptoms of performance anxiety are inter-related, each impacting on the others, a complex chain of events can be initiated that can become a vicious cycle. When you become aware of sweaty hands, shallow breathing, dry mouth, or shaking, this awareness can increase the negative thinking: "oh no, my fingers

Table 4.1 Symptoms of performance anxiety

Cognitive	Physiological	Emotional	Behavioural
Distraction	Sweating	Fear	Loss of motor control
Negative thoughts	Muscle tension	Panic	Awkward co-ordination
Worry	Shaking	Loss of self-esteem	Mistakes
Catastrophisation	Dry mouth	Feelings of inadequacy	Mistakes snowballing
Heightened awareness	Tight throat	Sensitivity	Ineffective responses
Memory breakdown	Pounding heart	Sadness	Blaming others
Delayed reponses	Butterflies	Anger	Awkward movements
Inner critic takes over	Nausea	Guilt	Focus on negative symptoms
Focus on negative symptoms	Diarrhoea	Shame	
De-automatisation of skill	Shortness of breath	Nervousness	
	Awkward co-ordination	Loss of confidence	

won't stop shaking, I won't be able to control it … I'll make mistakes", or "oh no I feel sick. I'm going to have to go to the toilet … it's going to happen right when I'm on stage". These negative thoughts lead to further arousal and increased negative thinking and feelings of nervousness: "this always happens to me … my lips are too dry … I feel sick now … I can't sing that bit … I didn't practise that other bit enough … I'm going to drop the instrument … so and so is here to hear me … I always make mistakes there … I'm going to forget the words … my throat feels too tight … my mouth is dry … my hands are shaking so much I won't hit the right notes". The 'inner critic' goes on and on, one self-criticism leading to another, until catastrophisation sets in. You can no longer believe or entertain the idea that anything positive can happen.

"You're constantly facing your innermost fears."

Thoughts occur such as 'I'm going to make a complete fool of myself', 'I'm going to fail', 'why am I doing this?', 'I'm useless, no good'. There are all sorts of thoughts that we can have, and they can cover every possible angle of the performance.

Each instrumentalist has their own particular physical aspect of playing that can become the focus of their thoughts – the tension or dryness or shakiness. Or it could be other – people oriented – who is in the audience, a critic, a peer who judges, a best friend, or family member; or self-oriented – "I always mess up … I always say something stupid"; or achievement oriented – you've worked hard, you want to do well, but "I can't remember this bit … I didn't practise enough … I'm not good enough…". When experiencing performance anxiety the number of things that self-doubt can cover seems endless, and they all make you feel even worse physically. Your inner critic is willing to take you down in any way possible and your body seems totally committed to helping with the take-down.

In these moments the inter-relation between symptoms, between body and mind, seems like a horrifying thing and a system that just doesn't really work for us.

But it is possible for you to take back control. It can be managed and prevented from taking control of you. When we start to manage even *one* of the symptoms, the other symptoms are impacted too, and this time for our positive benefit. Taking one step at a time, by changing even one thought, one behaviour, we can start to change and manage our experience of anxiety. We can decrease our arousal level, we can decrease our level and intensity of negative thoughts, we can manage our emotions. Just as one negative thought can lead to another, one positive thought can upset the balance of negativity and can lead to another positive thought and a more positive level of arousal in the body. The feeling of nervousness and anxiety can be 'flipped', turned around for your benefit, and not only have you feeling like you can manage your anxiety but even have you experiencing flow. That body-mind connection is an amazing system that you'll welcome whole-heartedly.

You know if you experience or suffer performance anxiety to the extent that it negatively impacts your performances; however, the following questionnaire is a short, reliable music performance anxiety inventory that is used in research and diagnosis of performance anxiety in musicians and music students. Try filling it out!

To do: take this music performance anxiety (MPA) questionnaire

	None of the time		About half of the time			All of the time	
1. Before I perform I get butterflies in my stomach	0	1	2	3	4	5	6
2. I often worry about my ability to perform	0	1	2	3	4	5	6
3. I would rather play on my own, than in front of other people	0	1	2	3	4	5	6
4. Before I perform I tremble or shake	0	1	2	3	4	5	6
5. When I perform in front of an audience, I am afraid of making mistakes	0	1	2	3	4	5	6
6. When I perform in front of an audience, my heart beats very fast	0	1	2	3	4	5	6
7. When I perform in front of an audience, I find it very hard to concentrate	0	1	2	3	4	5	6
8. If I make a mistake in front of an audience I usually panic	0	1	2	3	4	5	6
9. When I perform in front of an audience I get sweaty hands	0	1	2	3	4	5	6
10. When I finish performing, I usually feel unhappy with my performance	0	1	2	3	4	5	6
11. I try to avoid playing on my own at a (school) concert	0	1	2	3	4	5	6
12. Just before I perform I feel nervous	0	1	2	3	4	5	6
13. I worry that my parents or teacher might not like my performance	0	1	2	3	4	5	6
14. I would rather play in a group or ensemble than on my own	0	1	2	3	4	5	6
15. My muscles feel tense when I perform	0	1	2	3	4	5	6

Source: Music Performance Anxiety Inventory (MPAI-A; Kenny & Osborne, 2006)[10]

Questionnaire key

Add up your scores

Find your total MPA score simply by adding up **all** the numbers you circled.

If you scored over 75  Red alert

- you experience a very high level of music performance anxiety (the highest possible score is 90). You feel like you can't manage the feelings of anxiety, that they are out of your control, and the anxiety takes over. But it is possible to manage these feelings and thoughts – you just need to take action now. Start trying out strategies from each chapter and incorporate them into your daily routine.

If you scored between 60 and 75 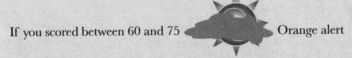 Orange alert

- you experience quite high levels but you have been managing MPA quite well, perhaps sometimes better than other times. You should take action to help yourself on every occasion by trying out strategies from each of the chapters. Find what might suit you best and start to incorporate into your daily routine.

If you scored between 30 and 60 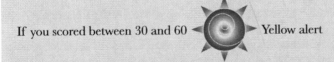 Yellow alert

- you experience mild to average levels of MPA. Perhaps you have learnt how to manage MPA well, and in a way that really works for you – in which case, well done, and keep doing what you are doing! Or perhaps you aren't sure what you're doing or why you sometimes feel more nervous than at other times. Either way, try out the strategies from each chapter. Find out if there are some strategies that you can implement to benefit your performance so you have more positive experiences more often.

If you scored between 0 and 30  Ice blue alert

- you experience little or no MPA. I've given you an ice blue alert – you may actually wish to consider changing some aspect of your performance preparation or performance situations in order to feel a little more performance 'ready' and a little more challenged. Feeling challenged and more apprehensive than usual prior to performance will actually benefit your performance, making you are more alert, more focused, giving you energy and therefore enabling you to rise to the occasion. Perhaps by adding some strategies from these chapters you can add to your performance experience so that you can have more positive experiences of performance.

Level of physiological effects

Add up your scores

Add up statements 1, 4, 6, 9, 15

If you scored over 25  Red alert

- you experience adverse physical symptoms quite severely and find it very hard to manage them. You find that they have a very negative impact on your level of performance. This is manageable though. You simply need to take action in order to be prepared for future performances.

If you scored over 16 Orange alert

- you experience quite a lot of adverse physical symptoms of MPA, and sometimes they are making it difficult for you to perform at the level you want to perform at. Perhaps sometimes you are able to manage the symptoms better than other times. By using mental skills strategies you will be able to manage the symptoms more consistently.

The thoughts you experience and the physical symptoms of MPA go hand in hand. Compare your scores for these two types of symptoms. Are you in the same colour 'alert' category for each, or is one score higher than the other, putting you in a different category of MPA 'alert'; compare to see if you are more impacted by worrisome thoughts or by the physical symptoms.

Negative thoughts score

Add up your scores for 2, 5, 7, 8, 12

If you scored over 25: Red alert

- you experience worrisome and negative thoughts quite severely. They often snowball, and you find it very hard to control them. Your thoughts have a very negative impact on your level of performance. This is manageable though. You simply need to take action in order to be mentally prepared for future performances.

If you scored over 16: Orange alert

- you experience quite a lot of negative thinking about performance, and sometimes your thoughts are making it difficult for you to perform at the level you want to perform at. Sometimes you are able to control the thoughts better than other times. By using mental skills strategies you will be able to manage the symptoms more consistently.

How many experience MPA?

The number of musicians who experience performance anxiety is hard to say, but a conservative estimate from various research studies would suggest that well over half of all musicians have experienced anxiety at some stage. Talented, hardworking, brilliant, expert, professional musicians are challenged with performance anxiety to varying levels at times. They use strategies to combat their anxiety.

Some musicians experience performance anxiety before every performance, some experience it only before very important or stressful performances, and others experience it to different levels depending on the performance. Performance anxiety is not one-dimensional; it changes, it fluctuates – increasing and decreasing depending on the situation, the person, and what's going in their life. Research reporting the numbers of musicians who experience performance anxiety varies. One study showed that of 155 professional classical musicians, 59% experienced debilitating performance anxiety. Another study that asked musicians in 56 orchestras about their performance anxiety, found that 70% believed that performance anxiety was having a negative effect on their performance ability. Another study of orchestral musicians found that 96% were experiencing health problems that were related to performance anxiety. Three studies that investigated third level college students' experiences of anxiety found 83%, 84%, and 21%

were experiencing debilitating performance anxiety – a very large variation in findings there.[11] Little is known about the performance anxiety experiences of pop, rock, jazz, traditional, or folk musicians, but one study that explored the experiences of 'popular' musicians said these musicians indeed experience anxiety significantly more than the general population, i.e. non-musicians.[12]

The reason for the variation in numbers of people experiencing performance anxiety is mostly because the research studies vary in how they are carried out, who is asked, what questions are asked, how the questions are asked, and how performance anxiety is measured. Depending on these factors, people occasionally over-estimate their feelings, but mostly people under-estimate or under-report their feelings of performance anxiety, i.e., they don't want to be completely open and honest about experiencing performance anxiety to a researcher, and even perhaps to themselves.

There are a number of reasons for this. It may be that they just don't want anyone to know, but mostly it's for more complicated reasons than this. For example, it may feel to them as though saying something about how they feel out loud, or to someone else, will make their feelings suddenly very real and hard to ignore, maybe the anxiety will worsen, maybe they are hoping it will just go away on its own if they don't really look at it or talk about it. It seems that, just as in non-musical life, there is perhaps a stigma surrounding psychological issues, so there is also a stigma concerning performance anxiety. This means that sometimes we find it hard to admit to ourselves and/or to others that we experience it. This stigma also extends to gender, where studies tend to show that more girls than boys report experiencing performance anxiety.[13] Perhaps more girls do indeed experience performance anxiety, or perhaps more girls admit experiencing performance anxiety. However, as we're going to see in the following sections, the heightened emotions and heightened physiological arousal relating to performance and challenge are actually beneficial to performance. Perhaps if we were more aware and more accepting of this, it would be easier for us to confront and combat performance anxiety.

Is it here to stay forever?

> *"Although I was nervous, I was in general feeling good about myself and I had done quite a bit of work on myself."*

Experiencing performance anxiety is not a personality trait. Emotions fluctuate, we change, life events impact on us, and so a state of anxiety is not forever – it comes and goes, it fluctuates in the level to which it is felt, it changes depending on the context or situation – therefore it is only natural that sometimes we don't want to deal with it, in the hope that it will just go away or get better on its own.

It can be a very real concern for some musicians that those who employ them or co-performers who play with them will hear about their anxiety and not be so keen on booking them or wanting to perform with them. In the music world, competition for work can be immense. People have to perform even when very ill, having to hide their illness for fear that someone else can easily step in and replace them, forever.

Actually, likewise, musicians don't often talk about their peak experiences or good experiences. Apart from often being very humble people, and very busy people who don't have time to stop and analyse their personal performance experiences, musicians sometimes fear that if they speak about their great performance experiences out loud, they will go away, or somehow disappear. Psychological preparedness can be quite vulnerable and so it is indeed worrisome to talk about it or analyse it with full confidence, in case, by so doing, it might just disappear or evaporate. Nobody wants to jinx it when they have it good!

Psychologists don't believe that talking about your experience can make it go away, of course. If that was the case, simply talking about anxiety would be the only remedy needed. However, psychologists aren't the ones who have to get up and perform at consistently high standards in front of an audience. But then again, psychologists see the very positive results that can come from talking and analysing performance experiences. Awareness, acceptance, discussion, talking, listening to others, all aid the performer in finding solutions for anxiety, lack of focus, memory difficulties, or indeed for any performance issue.

Whilst the circular impact of emotions, thoughts, and behaviours is constantly in motion, our environment also shapes us; as do the people around us and the events that occur in our lives, things that we don't have any control over. But within our own control is our reaction to those people and events. Although we may not always feel like we have much control, our emotions, thoughts, and behaviours are ours and we can shape, manage, and harness them to make our experience more negative or more positive.

So, although the experience of anxiety or stress associated with performance varies depending on the individual, MPA is very common. A certain level of it is completely normal and is actually beneficial to performance. However, when it increases to a point where you are feeling huge discomfort, fear, and stress every time you perform and you feel your performances are being severely negatively impacted by the anxiety more often than not, this can have a general detrimental effect on self-esteem and confidence. MPA is classified in the diagnostic manual used by psychologists and psychiatrists (the DSM-V)[14] under social anxiety disorders, which may be diagnosed as a disorder if occurrences and characteristics are pervasive for more than six months.[15] MPA has more to do with social anxiety and social phobia than it has to do with having a personality trait of anxiety. Social anxiety and social phobia are treatable and controllable, with the correct strategies and therapy.

Whilst performance anxiety itself is not a personality trait, and therefore can be managed and harnessed, perfectionism is sometimes considered to be a personality trait, and perfectionism is known to impact on performance anxiety.

"Some days you're just fighting with yourself; it's a battle in your head."

If you have thoughts that seem to be overly concerned with flawlessness, with making mistakes or rather not making mistakes, thoughts that are highly self-critical, if you have almost impossibly high standards for yourself and your achievements, if you lack compassion for yourself and your efforts, you may be a perfectionist or certainly tending to lean towards perfectionism.[16] Whilst all good performers are able to critique their skills, being overly critical and being perfectionistic can have quite debilitating effects on a performer, on performance anxiety and on self-esteem. Musicians who have exceptionally high standards for their own performance and who are overly reliant on what other people think of their playing, have more debilitating performance anxiety than musicians who may well have high standards, but are more realistic and focus on their own sense of fulfilment rather than the fulfilment, opinions, and expectations of others.[17]

That might sound all very well and easy to say, "hey don't be too perfectionistic", but if you are a perfectionist, how do you deal with this and how do you combat it? Compassion towards yourself is crucial, as are having realistic goals and expectations. Also important is seeing the big picture and the journey of learning you are on. Chapter 5 shows you how to challenge your thoughts and how to think more positively about yourself and Chapter 6 will help you with goal setting and how to put more emphasis on yourself and your own fulfilment in music and music performance.

Importance of nerves for good performance

"I always get nervous; I don't think you should be doing it if you don't."

When you took the MPA questionnaire above you will have found yourself in one of the 'storm alert' categories. If you found you were category orange or category red, don't panic!

This does not mean that you're not cut out for performing, and it does not mean that you can't get this under control. Many performers feel nervous before performance. I've said this already. All good performers feel nervous. Some of the best performances happen to people when they are most scared.

What the weather alert category (of the MPAI questionnaire key) is really telling you is to what extent you need to prepare psychologically and how soon you need to start preparing. The chapter on focus is going to tell you that you can't expect focus to just happen of its own accord, you have to decide to focus. It's the same with performing anxiety.

You can't just expect to be able to perform well under these conditions, you have to decide to, and you have to decide to do something about it. You actually need performance anxiety to perform well. But you need to be able to manage it, and you need to start training well in advance of performances, by using the strategies in each of these chapters.

Performance anxiety, or 'stage fright', is a common human experience. Faced with adversity or challenge, the body has to move into a higher gear in order to adapt to the situation and we have a nervous system that does that for us, whether we like it or not. The 'fight or flight' response prepares us for immediate action, and as I said above, the level of arousal in the body depends on the level of perceived adversity. There are performance theories that explain how the emotions we experience prior to performance impact on our performance ability.

Making emotions work to your advantage

A number of psychologists have explained why and how emotions work to our advantage to make positive performance experiences. Coming up is a brief outline of three key and really useful explanations.

Yerkes–Dodson model

A well-known law of performance which has been quoted, tried, and tested frequently throughout the years is the Yerkes–Dodson theory (1908)[18]. Otherwise known as the inverted-U hypothesis, it says that our quality of performance actually

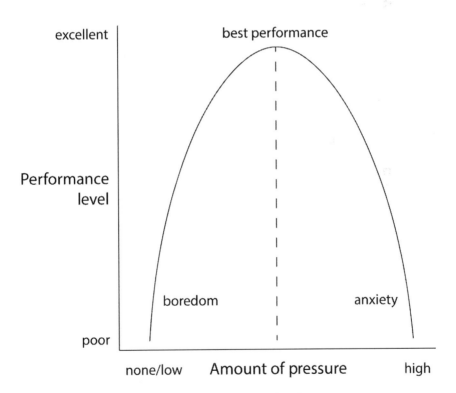

Figure 4.3 The inverted-U relationship of pressure and performance

improves as our arousal level increases from low to moderate. Performance is at its best when our body's level of arousal is around the moderate level. However, the theory also says that if arousal continues to increase above moderate, it leads to maladaptive anxiety and a decrease in performance quality. If you've experienced performance anxiety, you know this already.

However, in one way, this is very reassuring – 'arousal' or nerves or anxiety is required for good performance. Performance is actually aided by the nervousness and arousal that occurs in the body. Although this sounds simple, it's not that easy to control your levels of anxiety, and each person, situation and task even, has their own unique optimal level. Furthermore, what is a moderate level for one person might be too little for another and yet too much for someone else. Each of us has our own individual levels of optimal arousal, so don't worry if it takes some experimentation to find out what yours is.

Flow theory

Flow theory[19] suggests that there is a point somewhere between boredom and over-arousal when peak performance and peak experience can occur. This explanation acknowledges a range of possible performance emotions that exist on a spectrum, with boredom at one extreme and hyper- or over-arousal at the other extreme. At the same time, it emphasises the importance of the level of challenge and skill perceived by the individual. Somewhere in the middle of the spectrum for each individual is a point where flow and peak performance can occur. This point is dictated by your own appraisal of your skill level and by the level of challenge.

Experts on flow suggest that in order to have peak experiences there must be a challenge (i.e., the performance) and there must be a 'challenge–skill balance'.[20] The challenge–skill balance (as explained in Chapter 1) occurs when the individual *perceives* themselves to have the skills to meet the challenge. So it's not necessarily your actual level of skill that counts – but your *belief* that you have the level of skill to take on the challenge. If this seems unlikely to you – read more about self-efficacy and mindset in Chapter 6.

It has been found in research on flow that it is when the challenge is perceived to be just outside the reach of the level of perceived skill, that peak experiences occur. It is this slight gap between perceived skill and perceived challenge that, feeling confident they have the skill, forces the performer to reach out of their comfort zone a little in order to rise to the challenge, and ultimately create 'flow'.

You can see in Figure 4.4, that flow can occur even when skill level is perceived to be low, as long as the challenge is perceived to be one that meets the level of skill. That's why flow can happen for anyone at any level of skill.

When skill level is high, the level of challenge perceived needs to be high in order for flow to occur. If the challenge is not great enough, there is boredom, apathy, dissatisfaction. If the challenge is too great, then the result is anxiety, unhappiness, stress. Achieving the right level of challenge and skill can be managed by your

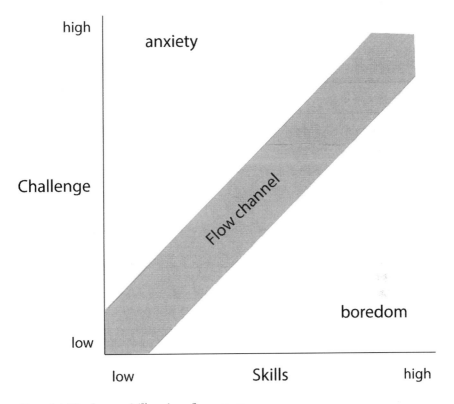

Figure 4.4 The flow model[21] – where flow occurs

perception and *appraisal* of the challenge and your skill level, and by managing your thoughts and emotions in relation to those.

It's all about perception of the challenge and perception of your skills. As has been shown by musicians' experiences of flow, if you perceive that you face a challenge and also believe that you have the skills to meet that challenge, then peak performance can occur.

The Zone of Optimal Functioning

There is no correct or perfect way to feel. There are no specific emotions that the best performers experience. It is important for each person to find which emotions are *helpful* for them, and which emotions are *unhelpful*.

The third and very prominent explanation of how even perceived negative emotions can work to our advantage is one that is widely used in sport psychology. The Individual Zone of Optimal Functioning (IZOF),[22] is really relevant and highly useful to you in understanding your experience of emotions prior to performance and managing those emotions.

The Zone of Optimal Functioning recognises the importance of your individual experience of emotions and the involvement of more than one emotion prior to performance. It has shown that each person has their own individual combination of optimal emotions, a particular blend that they require in order to perform at their best.[23]

For example, one performer might have an optimal blend that includes anger, aggression, enthusiasm, determination, being 'geared up'. Another person might need to feel excited, happy, apprehensive, nervous, and confident. Someone else might find they perform at their best when their emotions include feeling chilled out, calm, sombre, sad, resilient. Another might find that feeling terrified, anxious, confident, prepared, and excited are the emotions they require to perform at their peak.

Our perception of an event, a performance, or of how we feel, can be positive or negative. As we've seen from the testimonies of expert musicians in Chapter 3, our perception can be – is most beneficial to performance when it is – a mixture of both positive and negative emotion. This is especially true of the emotions we feel prior to performance. Feeling both *perceived* negative emotions and *perceived* positive emotions is actually the most beneficial to your performance.

Why do I call them 'perceived' negative emotions and 'perceived' positive emotions? Because, although there are indeed general positive and negative emotions such as happy or sad, when it comes to performance, we might perceive an emotion as a positive one, but in reality it does not positively impact our performance. We might perceive an emotion as negative but in reality that emotion is actually particularly beneficial to our performance. Therefore, it is perceived to be negative but actually it might be *positive* for you.

For one person, anger might be perceived to be negative but for another it might be perceived as positive. It all depends on the individual, the context, the reason for the emotion and the purpose of the emotion. We all experience emotions differently, in different situations and with different purpose. Emotions exist on a spectrum and are nuanced in ways that are special to each individual.

Most people feel many emotions prior to performance and these emotions are on a spectrum of positive and negative, as well as high and low in the strength or level of arousal of each feeling.

The following exercise is essential for you to carry out – it will help you to explore which emotions and level of arousal of each emotion is optimal for you. By doing this exercise you will find your zone of optimal functioning (page 59). It will help you to become more aware of how you feel, help you accept that these emotions are actually an important part of your process and you will then be able to set about harnessing those emotions in order to experience more enjoyable, satisfying performances that fulfil your potential.

To do: find your zone of optimal functioning

Finding your zone of optimal functioning – this is a version for musicians, adapted from Hanin's (2000) IZOF: theory for performance in sport.[24]

There is no one way or no right way to feel before performing. We all have our own combination of emotions that works for us. Here's how to find you own unique optimal blend of emotions:

Part 1 of finding your IZOF

1. Look back on past performances. Choose your **most recent favourite** or **best** performance.

    What was it: _____

    Taking a few minutes, try to remember it as vividly as possible, remember how you felt during it and how you played. Relive it in your mind.

    Now try to **reflect** on *before* the performance, again taking a few minutes to remember and relive what you did and how you felt on the day of the performance.

    Make notes of any important details you remember about this performance, any factors that stand out in your mind about the performance, or the hours/days/weeks prior to the performance.

    _____
    _____
    _____
    _____
    _____

2. How did you **feel**? What emotions can you remember feeling before the performance, in the minutes before, in the hours before, even maybe the days before.

    Try to recapture as vividly as you can *how you felt on the day* of that performance.

3. Make a list of those emotions (see the list of emotions in Table 4.2 on p. 63).

    Try to choose four positive and four negative emotions (you may even find you have more than five of each; that's ok).

    Write P+ for 'positive' beside the positive emotions and N+ for 'negative' for those emotions you perceive to be negative.

Helpful positive emotions: | **Helpful negative** emotions:

_____
_____
_____
_____
_____
_____

(The point of the + is that these were positive and negative emotions that you felt prior to your *best and favourite performance*, therefore both the positive and negative are **helpful** emotions for you to experience prior to performance.)

Already, you will be starting to be more aware of the presence and range of important positive and negative emotions prior to a performance that you enjoyed and in which you felt you performed well.

4. Think about the *intensity* to which you experienced each of these emotions and rate them on a scale between 1 and 10, where

1 = not very much   5= moderately   10 = very much.

For example, a list might look like this:

Absorbed P+10   Impatient N+9

Excited P+9   Scared N+8

Enthusiastic P+9   Wary N+7

Confident P+9   Aggressive N+6

What you will find is that there are a number of emotions you experienced prior to your recent favourite and best performance. These emotions varied in intensity and they included positive and negative emotions. You might find that you even experienced emotions that seem to contradict each other, for example excited but also calm, terrified but also confident, purposeful but also regretful. It is possible to experience a number of emotions; you just might not experience them all to the same level of intensity.

Part 2 of finding your IZOF

This part works through similar steps, but this time try to remember a recent 'not so good' performance or *worst* performance.

1. Look back on past performances. Choose your **most recent 'not so good'** or **worst** performance.

   What was it: _____

   Taking a few minutes, try to remember it as vividly as possible, remember how you felt during it and how you played. Relive it in your mind.

   Now try to **reflect** on BEFORE the performance, again taking a few minutes to remember and relive what you did and how you felt on the day of the performance.

   Make notes of any important details you remember about this performance, any factors that stand out in your mind about the performance, or the hours/days/weeks prior to the performance.

   _____
   _____
   _____
   _____
   _____
   _____

2. How did you **feel**? What emotions can you remember feeling before the performance, in the minutes before, in the hours before, even maybe the days before.

   Try to recapture as vividly as you can *how you felt on the day* of that performance.

3. Make a list of those emotions (see the list of emotions in Table 4.2).

   Try to choose four positive and four negative emotions (you may even find you have more than five of each; and again, that's ok).

   Write P– for 'positive' beside the positive emotions and N– for 'negative' for those emotions you perceive to be negative.

   Harmful negative emotions: **Harmful positive** emotions:

   _____   _____
   _____   _____
   _____   _____
   _____   _____
   _____   _____

   (The point of the – is that these were positive and negative emotions that you felt prior to your *worst performance*, therefore both the positive and negative are **unhelpful, even harmful** emotions for you to experience prior to performance.)

Already, you will be starting to be more aware of the presence and range of important positive and negative emotions prior to a performance when you did not perform well.

4.   Think about the *intensity* to which you experienced each of these emotions and rate them on a scale between 1 and 10, where

1 = not very much   5= moderately   10 = very much.

For example, a list might look like this:

Quiet P-9	Fearful N-
Confident P-8	Sluggish N- 5
Pleasant P-7	Tense N-5
Relaxed P-7	Distracted N-6

Or another list might look like this:

Quiet P-8	Panicky N-8
Alert P-6	Fearful N-7
Immersed P-5	Distressed N-5
Distracted N-4	

IZOF: put parts 1 and 2 together and compare

Putting parts 1 and 2 of the IZOF together

Compare the **best** performance and the **worst** performance.

Compare the helpful positive and negative emotions you experienced before your best performance with the harmful positive and negative emotions you experienced before your worst performance.

Consider how the lists differ (you can even put them on a graph – see Figure 4.5).

Put your four lists of emotions in order of intensity

N- increasing in intensity
N+ increasing in intensity
P+ decreasing in intensity
P- decreasing in intensity

Write them in on the graph (Figure 4.5 on p. 64)

Table 4.2 List of perceived positive and negative emotions

Generally perceived **positive** emotions

Alert	Active	Dynamic	Energetic
Delighted	Relaxed	Comfortable	Settled
Content	Daring	Overjoyed	Taking risk
Vigorous	Exhilarated	Glad	Determined
Pleased	Set	Satisfied	Easy
Motivated	Slow	Inspired	Calm
Resolute	Motivated	Peaceful	Excited
Stimulated	Unhurried	Thrilled	Light-hearted
Quiet	Fierce	Carefree	Cheerful
Focused	Nice	Merry	Absorbed
Pleasant	Happy	Single-minded	Agreeable
Confident	Immersed	Friendly	Quick
Certain	Brave	Fast	Sure
Bold	Courageous		

Generally perceived **negative** emotions

Afraid	Discouraged	Fierce	Fearful
Dispirited	Jittery	Scared	Depressed
Nervous	Panicky	Distracted	Uneasy
Angry	Inattentive	Restless	Aggressive
Detached	Sorry	Down	Furious
Scatty	Unhappy	Violent	Doubtful
Regretful	Annoyed	Uncertain	Sad
Irritated	Indecisive	Cheerless	Distressed
Irresolute	Tense	Anxious	Helpless
Strained	Apprehensive	Unsafe	Tight
Worried	Insecure	Rigid	Concerned
Inactive	Tired	Alarmed	Sluggish
Weary	Disturbed	Lazy	Exhausted
Dissatisfied	Intense	Worn-out	Apathetic

You can graph it

When I work with musicians, I put all the emotions that they have on their lists onto a graph. You can do this too – see the sample student musician graphs below. You can use the sample provided or you can make your own on the computer. But you can even just do it with pen and paper. Figure 4.6 and 4.7 are two sample IZOF graphs.

Your lists of helpful emotions and harmful emotions may be two strikingly different lists, or they may include some of the *same* emotions. But even so, you will probably find that the level of intensity to which you experienced the emotions is quite different, and the blend of emotions is different.

For you to do this analysis of the emotions you experienced is important in order for you to become really aware of and to accept your own unique experience of performance, and in order for you to be able to manage and harness your emotions more beneficially in future performances.

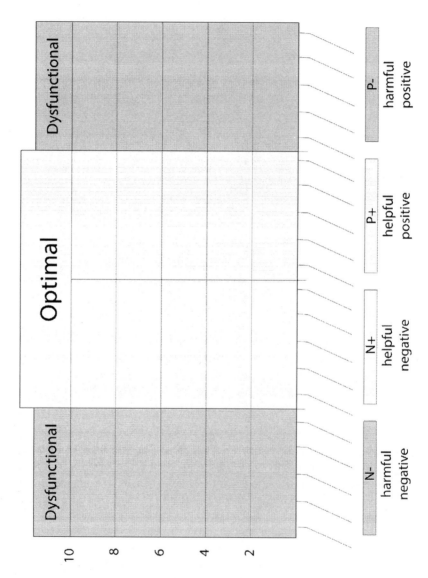

Figure 4.5 Graph your emotions for your IZOF

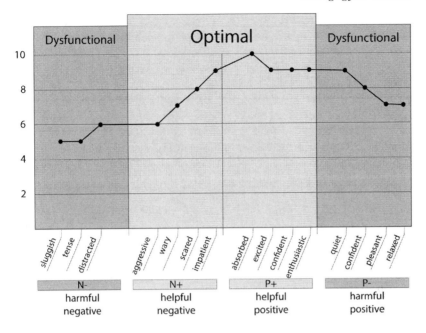

Figure 4.6 Sample IZOF of student musician 1

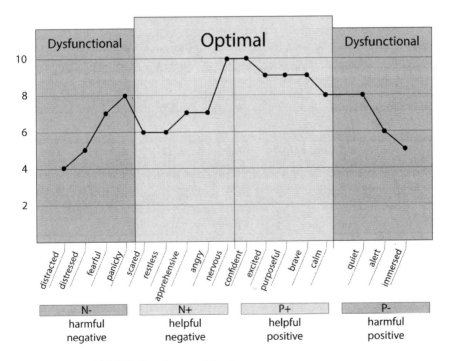

Figure 4.7 Sample IZOF of student musician 2

I recommend that having made this initial assessment of your experiences of emotion, you now assess more past performances and go through the same steps for other good and not-so-good performances. Look at the emotions you experienced, compare and contrast them, and come to be more familiar with your experiences of emotions prior to performances.

You may have experienced positively perceived emotions that for you are actually harmful to your performances. Perhaps the time you felt casual, calm, collected, and satisfied, was actually accompanied by feeling a low level of focus, preparedness, alertness. Or perhaps you have felt too excited and aggressive. Or too confident. On the other hand, negative emotions too intensely felt may have led to one of your less enjoyed and not-so-good performances. Perhaps you felt too anxious and worried, or too angry, or too apathetic.

You might notice that there is a crossover of emotions between good and not-so-good performances, and similar emotions experienced, but it is the *level* of arousal or the intensity to which you felt them and the blend of the emotions that made the difference. It might be the combination of other emotions that differs between the performances. Look closely at your lists, and think about the differences in the combination of emotions that you experienced.

Now that you have found your own unique blend of optimal emotions, continue to keep a diary of your emotions prior to future performances. Keep note of the emotions and the intensity to which you felt them.

Remember, there is not one 'right' way to feel prior to performance: there is only 'your' way. Find your unique blend of emotions for optimal functioning. Then find the way to manage and harness those emotions that are helpful for your performance, using the strategies that other musicians, expert musicians use.

Because emotions, thoughts, and behaviours are all connected and each impacts on the others, emotion management requires that you carry out thought management (Chapter 5), mental practice (Chapter 8), visualisation (Chapter 8), and physiological activation management (Chapter 9).

Managing your emotions

> *"I was scared … but I relish being scared."*

In this book and particularly this chapter, you might have noticed that when talking about the challenges faced in performance, I use the words 'perceive', and 'interpret' or 'view' and 'appraise' quite a lot. For example, I use phrases like 'how you *perceive* the performance' or 'how you *view* the performance', or 'the *perceived* negative emotions you feel', or 'how you *interpret* your emotions'. This is because it is your *perception* of a performance situation, or your *perception* and *interpretation* of how you think and feel that impacts on how you think and feel and how you respond.[25]

> *"I don't like the feeling [of nerves]. What I do is I imagine I'm in a very boring job and been there for years and suddenly you've got this chance to feel these butterflies. Take the chance and enjoy it!"*

Our perception of a situation or an event is not a factual reality. It is merely our perception of events at one moment in time. And this can vary for different people. Each individual perceives and interprets and responds in their own way. And how we perceive the performance context can even vary in our own minds depending on the day, or on our mood, or on the people around us that we are spending time with, or on a particular phase of our life.

Changing your perception of a performance, your perception of how much of a threat it is, can be a useful start to dealing with your emotions in relation to it. But for those experiencing severe levels of performance anxiety it is not always totally helpful, or even possible, to immediately or instantly change how threatening you perceive or view the performance to be. Instead (or as well as), it is important to deal with the reality of how you feel about it.

So, be realistic about your perception of the event, because pretending you feel fine, or trying to play down the importance of the situation, or pretending that there's no stress, does not usually work. Most people who perform have experienced feeling totally fine about an event, and then standing in the moment and having the horrible realisation that they are suddenly terrified and that they are not prepared for feeling like that. People describe their body suddenly shaking, or their mind going totally blank. When we feel very scared about a performance, it's more beneficial in the long run to be aware of how you really feel, and accept how you feel – *before* the performance.

Yes, be realistic, be aware of how you feel and admit it to yourself. Only then can you start to prepare psychologically and musically for the performance. If you feel scared, if you feel this upcoming performance to be a performance equivalent of a highly dangerous situation, then the great thing is that you have the option to prepare for that, you can deal with it. You can use all the strategies in advance, you can prepare musically, emotionally, cognitively, physically and you can go into the situation fully armed, totally confident that you are ready to cope with the situation.

Coping with stressful situations

> *"I'm very confident, at the same time I would always be feeling 'am I going to be able to do it, am I going to make that note, is it good enough?!'"*

In life in general, not just performing, we all have stressful situations that we have to cope with. We tend to have our own personal ways of coping with stress. These are 'coping mechanisms' that somewhere along the way we have learnt to use. Sometimes these are beneficial to us but sometimes we get into a pattern of using the same old coping mechanisms that just don't work for us anymore, and maybe even never did.

Sometimes we use the same coping mechanism in very different situations, or perhaps we hit on a way of coping years ago and have been relying on that ever since but find it no longer works for us. One type of coping mechanism can be useful to us in one situation but possibly it just doesn't work in another situation. Often we can find something that works for us and we just stick to it over time, no matter what the context is. However, over time, we change and develop, and we need different or new ways of coping. It may be that we need to think differently about how we cope with stress depending on the situation or the level of stress we are coping with.

What is 'coping'?

The most widely used psychological approach to coping defines 'coping' as "constantly changing cognitive and behavioural efforts to manage specific external and/or internal demands"[26]. Basically, our coping mechanisms should change, and they can be and should be tailored to our individual, specific needs depending on the situation.

There are two key types of coping that we can use – one is known as problem-focused coping and the other is referred to as emotion-focused coping. Problem-focused coping looks to the *cause* of a problem or issue, the situation or the challenge in order to change it or adapt it in order to cope. Emotion-focused coping addresses the internal response to a problem, issue or situation in order to cope with the feelings and emotions that arise as a result of the situation.

In performance situations, we can focus on emotion-focused coping to learn to deal with and manage the feelings that arise in relation to performance. Problem-focused coping is not quite so useful since in general we can't change the fact of the performance or the challenge we are facing.

There are two other types of coping – appraisal-focused and avoidance-focused coping. Appraisal-focused coping is very useful to performers as this type of coping mechanism addresses the way we think about the problem, and aims to change how we 'appraise' or perceive the problem in the first place. Earlier we saw how the way we interpret or 'appraise' situations can affect our physical response to it, so when we interpret a performance as threatening our body responds to 'threat'.

So with this type of coping, we cannot change the problem itself, but we can change how we view the problem. In order to make use of this type of coping, we have to challenge our perceptions of performance, the importance of the situation, the negative thoughts we have about the performance and about ourselves as a performer. By doing so, we can change a situation that was perceived to be threatening into one that is more manageable; it might still be stress-inducing but, at the very least, it will be non-threatening, and has potential to even be enjoyable.

Avoidance coping is thought to be the least effective style of coping. It is probably fairly obvious that this style of coping involves avoiding the issue, the feelings, and the thoughts altogether. This coping strategy can work if the stress or the worries and concerns are fleeting, possibly last-minute thoughts that, if we are distracted from, will go away once we start to play or engage in the performance.[27] However, more persistent stress and anxiety cannot be dealt with by avoiding it and is best managed by strategies and coping mechanisms well in advance of the challenge ahead.

Which coping strategy to use

The effectiveness of coping mechanisms is really based on choosing the right strategies for you. Coping strategies that work for one person may not be ideal for someone else, and so trial and error may need to be used, particularly if working on this on your own.

Emotion-focused strategies and appraisal-focused strategies are the two categories of strategies that you should use most; but it is also important to know when to use avoidance coping. If you find that you over-focus on the negative, particularly at the last minute, and if you have done a lot of work using the strategies in this book, then you may need to introduce some avoidance into your thought management.

> *"About a week before a big one or the start of something, I would have all the panic, the dreams, classic panic attacks, go through all the possibilities of what could go wrong, jittery for a day, but I do all the things ... the practise, the mental stuff, visualising, thinking, running through everything in my head, then become completely calm and totally in control."*

The solution to performance anxiety isn't to change or eliminate the performance. The solution is to use strategies that target each of the types of symptoms that you experience – emotional, cognitive, and physiological. Throughout the book there are strategies for helping you to deal with emotions, thoughts, and physiological responses, as well as strategies for focusing and for effective practice, such as mental practice and visualisation.

Due to the multi-faceted nature of performance anxiety, and because all the symptoms are inter-connected with each other, implementing even one strategy starts to change the pattern of anxiety that you have been feeling prior to performances.

The really amazing thing that we know about flow experiences is that fear, terror, anxiety, although not always very pleasant feelings, can actually 'flip' into an extremely positive feeling and a powerful performance experience.

You can use the thought management techniques in Chapter 5 to help with appraisal focused coping. You will need to use techniques such as, rationalising your thinking and challenging your thoughts to help you manage how you appraise the performance situation. Turning negative thoughts into positive thoughts, using a mantra and putting together a pre-performance thought management plan will help you manage your thoughts and emotions.

Since your thoughts impact on your emotions, and your emotions generate thoughts, managing your thoughts falls under emotion-focused style of coping also. Understanding how emotions impact on your performance and using the IZOF, in this chapter, will aid both emotion and thought management.

See all the strategies in your coping toolkit in the box below.

To do: your toolkit of strategies

Table 4.3 Strategies toolkit

Tick off the strategies you have tried and found useful:

	Emotion focused coping	Appraisal focused coping
IZOF (Chapter 4)	*	
Diary of thoughts/emotions (see Chapter 5)	*	*
Rationalise your thoughts (Chapter 5)	*	*
Challenge your thoughts (Chapter 5)	*	*
Stop! and replace (Chapter 5)	*	*
Dispute your thoughts (Chapter 5)	*	*
Use a Mantra (Chapter 5)	*	
Motivational orientation (Chapter 6)	*	*
Awareness/knowledge (all chapters)	*	
Mental practice (Chapter 8)	*	
Visualisation (Chapter 8)	*	
Pre-performance routine (Chapter 10)	*	
Mindfulness meditation (Chapter 9)	*	
Relaxation exercise (Chapter 9)	*	
Breathing exercise (Chapter 9)	*	
Exercise (running, yoga, walking, etc.) (Chapters 9, 10)	*	

* Strategies should be incorporated into your daily practice and way of being. Using once is not enough and will not work to your advantage.

Key tips from this chapter

- Become aware of how you feel before performance – all the range of emotions you feel and thoughts you have.
- Accept how you feel.
- Be informed about what happens in the body and mind when under pressure, why it happens, and the impact.
- There is not one 'right' way to feel prior to performance. There is only 'your' way. Find your unique blend of emotions for optimal functioning.
- You can stop a cycle of perceived negative emotions in its tracks or prevent it from even starting by knowing how to target the types of symptoms of performance anxiety and by using strategies to do that.

5 Managing your thoughts

"I try to anticipate a positive event rather than a negative event ... I try to think as many positive things as possible", "I imagine the good vibes of the audience, then you feel more positive about the whole experience", "I talk to myself a lot!", "to have the skill to empty your brain of the clutter and thoughts takes practice".

Our thoughts and perceptions about ourselves and our world are what make up our reality. How we think about ourselves and the world around us impacts on how we feel and how we behave, and likewise, how we feel and the behaviours we engage in, impacts on our thoughts. The emotions-thoughts-behaviour loop is very much a cycle of interconnecting and interdependent experiences, as we saw in the previous chapter (Chapter 4).[1]

The thoughts we have affect the neural activity in our brain. They affect the release and activity of neurochemicals such as dopamine, serotonin, adrenalin. They affect the inhibition and re-uptake of neurochemicals from and into cells in our brain. This means that the thoughts we have affect the level and kind of neurochemicals that are floating around in our brain, neurochemicals that might make us feel more likely to be happy, satisfied, alert, motivated, or rewarded. This in turn affects how we feel and the subsequent thoughts we have.[2]

Positive thoughts, in a variety of ways, stimulate the activity of neurochemicals dopamine, serotonin, oxytocin, adrenalin, and even GABA, a neurochemical with such an impressively long name it's got a nickname! Each of these neurochemicals makes us feel good in its own way. Their increased activity, in turn, stimulates more positive thoughts and emotions, as well as energy, motivation, relaxation, reward, connectedness and subsequently, behaviours and positive outcomes. It's a cycle that keeps going. However, negative thoughts will lead to the decrease in activity of these neurochemicals – less dopamine, less serotonin, less GABA 'floating around' our brain for our benefit. This in turn leads to us feeling more negative, having more negative thoughts. Again, there's a loop of activity that leads to negative emotions, behaviours, and outcomes.[3]

Many of our thoughts and beliefs about ourselves are quite consistent and remain much the same over periods of time, but they are actually changeable through both conscious and unconsciousness means. Also, our thoughts about ourselves can differ quite substantially depending on the context we are in or depending on the people who are around us, influencing whether we feel good or bad about ourselves.

Is it the situation? Or is it your personality?

You might have noticed that sometimes in life, in some social settings or school or work settings, you feel confident or positive whilst there are other times when you are highly self-critical and low in self-esteem. Sometimes, we aren't aware of why we feel different or even *that* we feel different.

For example, someone who feels their social skills aren't great might feel more at ease and more confident in a small group of people, but feel out of their depth and low in self-confidence at a large party. Or, a teenager might feel quite confident about their music abilities and feel able to perform with ease when in their school setting, but less sure of their abilities when playing in a band with those selected specifically for their musical talent.

For some people, their thoughts about themselves might tend to be quite negative in general, whilst others' thoughts are more positive in general. This can make it seem as though being confident or being anxious is a personality trait. But very often it is the *situations* in which we find ourselves and how we interpret those situations, that make the difference in how we feel – whether we feel confident or whether we feel vulnerable.

Also, we have certain periods of our life that affect how we think, how we feel, and how we behave because of the experiences we have had. For example, the presence or absence of someone special to us in our lives can have a significant impact on our self-esteem, motivation and even belief in our own ability, either positively or negatively.

Have you ever done a quiz in a magazine or paper and when it asked a question about how you feel or behave, you thought, 'well it depends on the situation' but in a quiz you aren't given that choice. Take for example, the question 'when standing in a queue, do you …? a) chat to the person next to you, or b) keep your eyes on your phone?' For most of us, it probably depends on the situation – what you're queuing for, or how long it takes, or what the other people around you in the queue are like, or how you feel that day. There are many possible reasons why you might chat or why you might not want to, that don't rest solely on whether being chatty or not is a personality trait. It's as if we feel the same all the time in all situations and interpret those situations the same every time. But we don't.

And so, is it the performance situation? Or is it me?

There are some performance situations that you might feel quite confident in, and others that make you feel more nervous. Some people feel more comfortable with a large audience, others feel more at home with a small audience. There are times in life when we feel quite nervous about performing, and we have other times when we feel confident.

We have the ability to change how we think, to challenge ourselves and our thoughts. We can turn our thoughts around, from negative to positive and even from positive to negative. How difficult this is to do can depend on your recent experiences of performance, how attached you are to those thoughts, the level of habit involved, and how much, or how little, you want to change and feel you are able to change. Once you realise and believe that you have control over this and that it is actually possible for you to change your thoughts, then you need to allow for the possibility of letting that happen, allowing yourself to do it. You can take control but it helps if you believe that it's possible.

Many of the strategies in this chapter and the book stem from cognitive behavioural therapy (CBT). The emotions-thoughts-behaviour loop – that our thoughts impact our emotions and our behaviour – is one of the main concepts of CBT.[4] By rationalising our thoughts and by using mental skills, we can manage how we think, and that will impact on how we feel, which will impact on how we behave.

Become aware of your thoughts

The first step is to become more aware, more conscious of how you think about yourself and the things you say to yourself. It is important to identify your thoughts, your negative thoughts, and your positive thoughts.

Start to become more aware of the kinds of thoughts that you are having on a daily basis and in relation to particular events, activities, or people. Perhaps you are generally quite confident or positive about yourself, and can't quite work out why you are experiencing such anxiety in relation to music performance. Or perhaps you feel anxious or worried in most settings in your life. If so, this is something to think about and to ask why. It would be unfair to expect yourself to think that it is possible to enjoy performing without anxiety and self-criticism, if you are generally very hard on yourself, or feeling low in self-esteem.

However, starting to become aware of your thoughts in relation to life in general and in relation to performing in particular, is a really important first step to take in managing your thoughts. You might find that you have formed a habit of patterns of thinking that may not be helpful to you. Knowing that your thoughts, emotions, and behaviours are intricately linked, one impacting on the other, will help you to see how all of these play a part in your performance experience.[5]

Become aware of your negative thinking

"Why am I doing this? Am I able to do it? Is it good enough?"

To do: keep a diary of emotions and thoughts

Start to keep a diary of emotions and thoughts that you have in relation to performance, to your playing or singing, your practising, your rehearsing.

This does not have to be detailed or take a lot of time. You could just keep a small notebook with you or use your mobile phone notebook or calendar to keep note of the thoughts you have about yourself. Keep track of dates and times, what's on that day, the challenges you face, the people around you. Be brief but write or type out in full the thoughts that you have.

Look over your thoughts at the end of each day and then as the days progress look for any pattern of negative thoughts and positive thoughts. You might find you have quite a good balance of positive and critical thoughts. You might find you have a lot of confident, positive thoughts. Or you might find that in general your thoughts are largely negative and critical.

Do you notice a pattern of thinking about yourself or about performance that may not be helpful? You might be quite shocked at the number of negative, or positive, thoughts that you are having about yourself. Too much of either is not conducive to optimal performance.

It might sound surprising because having a positive mental attitude is very important to optimal performance, but being too positive in the face of a challenge that needs to be faced up to realistically, and even critically, is not likely to lead to optimal performance conditions. Likewise, too much focus on negative thoughts about yourself is not likely to lead to optimal performance conditions.

After extensive research and statistical analysis, Barbra Fredrikson[6] showed that in order to feel positive in life in general, there is an ideal ratio of positive to negative thoughts that we should have. She found that for every negative thought we have, we need to have *three* positive thoughts. This is because for many of us, our negative thoughts seem to be so much 'louder' than our positive thoughts. The negative thoughts seem to have more impact on us, we seem to take them much more seriously; we are more likely to believe the negative thoughts than we are to believe the positive ones.

Whether your thoughts are an accurate assessment of your performance or of your playing/practising is not really relevant. They're most likely not an accurate assessment. But the point is that if your thoughts are tending to be negative and critical without any focus on positive thoughts about yourself, you will believe these negative thoughts wholeheartedly. This will directly impact on how you feel about yourself and ultimately impact on how you play, sing, or perform. People don't perform really well solely because they are great musicians; nor do they perform really badly solely because they are really not good enough. Our standard of performance is directly impacted, not just by our level of preparation, and some might say talent, but by the thoughts and feelings that we have about ourselves.

The good news is that these thoughts are changeable and adaptable. The bad news is that we tend to believe negative thoughts more easily than we believe positive thoughts. But knowing this means we can fix it.

To do: rationalise your thinking

Think about an upcoming performance or rehearsal, some challenge that you are aiming towards. Perhaps you want to manage your thoughts and feelings about it so they can best aid your performance. If you are feeling apprehensive or even fearful about it, you probably have many thoughts about how things can and might go wrong. Where have your thoughts come from? Have you experienced it before? Or heard someone else talking about it? Ask yourself, what is the worst that can happen? How intolerable would it be and how would you cope? Also, ask yourself how likely is it that the worst will come to happen?

If you have been experiencing a great deal of performance anxiety, or even feeling terror and panic, these questions are ones you know well. You have probably already tried to rationalise your thinking many times, and perhaps not found it helpful. Rationalising your thinking is only one step in the management of emotions or of performance anxiety.[7] It is not the whole answer. Sometimes we know quite well that we are over-thinking something or that we are only seeing the negative outcomes, but knowing this doesn't necessarily help us feel any better.

Cognitive distortions

It is important to keep a check on our thinking and question ourselves and our thinking. Psychologists have found that there are a number of flaws in our reasoning, particularly when we are thinking about ourselves. These are referred to by psychologists as cognitive distortions, because they are flaws in our thinking that everyone falls prey to. Common cognitive distortions include overgeneralisation, black and white thinking, catastrophising, confirmation bias, internalised thoughts, 'should' statements.[8] Let's take a look at each of these.

Overgeneralisation

We tend to generalise one scenario or experience to all experiences. If something awful happened once, then we believe it is quite likely to happen again. Of course, we do this particularly in relation to negative experiences. We have a mental filter that tends to dwell on the negative rather than on the positive. Everyone at some point does this. We believe the negative about ourselves more readily than the positive. If we already tend to let our negative thoughts run riot, then we will remember the negative aspects to all our performances, or to one or two, and generalise this feeling or experience to all future performances, without thinking about any of the positive aspects or the positive experiences.

Black and white thinking

This happens when we think in 'all or nothing' terms, 'it's going to be brilliant!', or 'it's going to be awful', 'I'm going to be terrified', 'I'm going to mess it up', thinking in absolutes without letting ourselves be aware of more realistic outcomes. These thoughts can take hold more easily than the more moderate thoughts, such as, 'I might make a few mistakes ... but mostly I will play all the notes', 'I might be tense for a while ... but I will be able to relax into the music', 'I might shake at the beginning ... but I will become less focused on my body as the music begins', 'I might lose focus for a few bars ... but for the most part I will be fully absorbed'. All or nothing thinking can take hold, and can easily spiral into catastrophing.

Catastrophising

The negative thoughts can start to run riot, and you may feel like you have no control over them. The chatter inside your head can be all-consuming. One negative thought leads to another, and it snowballs, until you think there is nothing you can do right. When this happens *during* a performance, it's very hard to get control of it and it becomes absolutely impossible to focus on the music, your expression of the music or execution of the skills you need in order to play the music. As we see in the chapter on mental practice, it is only possible for us to hold one image at a time in our minds. So if that image is negative, then it is impossible to have a positive image at the same time. The negative thinking, negative imagery, and negative forecasting of what you are going to do wrong next, becomes very real and the outcome can be very debilitating to the self, to your self-confidence, to the present outcome and to future possibilities of positive experiences during performance.

Confirmation bias

We look for evidence that confirms our beliefs. This is a common bias in every aspect of our lives. When we believe something, or want to believe something, we tend to see only the things that confirm our beliefs. We even seek out events, experiences that confirm our beliefs. For example, if we hear something about someone, we think 'oh yes I remember the other day I saw that person do whatever', something that basically confirms what we just heard.

In terms of performance, we tend to look for evidence that confirms our beliefs about ourselves and about performing. When we believe that we are going to make a mistake, we think of all the times it happened. When we believe that we are going to forget the music, we easily remember all the times that actually happened. When we believe that we have little control over our nerves, we think of all the times that it happened to us and we lost control. We even think about the evidence in great detail, imagining every moment or reliving every moment of how it felt at the time, how it went wrong, and how it felt afterwards. This confirms our beliefs even more. Over and over we look for evidence to prove that we are right.

When we believe something to be true, we are less likely to seek out evidence of our being wrong, evidence that disproves our thoughts and assumptions about ourselves. We are less likely to look for examples of times when what we presume to be true is actually not true, times when that awful thing we fear did not actually happen, when we didn't forget the music, or make mistakes, or get a dry mouth, or shakey hands. Furthermore, even if we do think of such an occasion when mostly things went well for us, we tend not to imagine these occasions in such great detail or with such vivid imagery as we do the negative evidence. We dismiss the occasions that prove us wrong in our beliefs and assumptions.

So it is really important that we rationalise our thinking. It is vital to question yourself and your reasoning. Think about times when what you believe is going to happen did not actually happen before. Think of occasions when you played well, when things went well for you. Relive those times with as rich an imagery and memory as possible, and as many times as you can. Perhaps you have times when you overcame a difficult moment, mistakes, shakes, dryness, lack of focus, tension, or negative chatter in your head. Remember those times, those positive experiences, and count them; focus on them and relive them. It may be important for you to make this one of the strategies that you use, set aside time to actually relive your previous positive experiences.

Thoughts become internalised

It can be easy to discount the positive occurrences and achievements. We tend to account for a positive experience as 'luck' or attribute it to someone else's role in how things went, or that we were having an unusual and rare 'good day' that time. Our thinking can go from 'I **feel** untalented' to 'I **am** untalented', 'I **made** mistakes' to 'I **am** useless at this', '**that performance** wasn't good' to '**I'm** not good', and so we label ourselves, and these labels can become internalised. When we internalise a thought or a label, it becomes a belief that we have about ourselves, and the beliefs become self-fulfilling.

'Should' statements

We criticise ourselves (and others) using a lot of *should* statements – 'I should have done more practise', 'I should not have said I'd do this', 'I should have played a different song', 'I should not have got distracted', and so on. We even blame ourselves for things that are not our fault or our responsibility, or we blame factors that are not the cause of the issue. This makes fixing the issue much more difficult.

So there are a number of cognitive distortions that can hamper our practice and performance, and the outcomes. Being aware of these natural human cognitive distortions, accepting and being honest with ourselves about our thoughts and feelings is the first step, as it is with all the strategies in managing our thoughts and emotions in performance.

To do: challenge your thoughts

Something to think about

Ask yourself: Am I engaging in black or white thinking?
   Am I constantly and consistently confirming my negative beliefs?
   Look for evidence to the contrary.

Start to make consistent efforts to check this.

When you find yourself thinking about all the times that it went wrong – you forgot the music, or you were distracted, or you made errors of some kind.

Stop yourself, be aware of the negative thought, and make concerted efforts to focus on times when it did not go wrong, when you did not do that thing you were certain you would do.

Are your negative thoughts running riot in your head?

The rest of this chapter provides some strategies for dealing with these negative thought processes.

To do: stop! and replace

STOP! Negative thinking and REPLACE with positive thought

If you've been keeping a notebook of your thoughts or have jotted down your thoughts in your phone, then you will already have become more aware of how you think about yourself and your performance.

The 'stop! and replace' technique involves becoming aware that you are thinking negatively, stopping your thoughts, stopping yourself from catastrophising, and from letting one negative thought lead to another, and then replacing the negative thought with a positive thought.[9]

The three important steps here are

1. Become AWARE of your negative thoughts.
2. STOP the flow of negative thoughts.
3. REPLACE the negative thought with a positive thought.

On becoming conscious of the negative thought(s), shout silently inside your head 'stop!' and immediately replace the negative thought with a positive thought. It is common practice to clap hands or stamp a foot at the moment of saying 'stop!'. The idea is to startle yourself out of the thought process so that you are able to think afresh with a new positive thought.

This might require some pre-planning of positive thoughts, especially if you've become so used to thinking negatively about your performance and/or playing that you find it hard to think of a positive thought. You might be able to think of other positive aspects about yourself, or your performing, or how you can cope, or about the upcoming challenge. Think about what you *can* do, what you have managed to do well in the past, times when you have overcome nerves or played well despite feeling nervous.

The ABC model

Albert Ellis was the forerunner to Cognitive Behavioural Therapy (CBT) and his theory is the foundation of CBT. He saw that knowing *why* we feel something isn't always ultimately helpful and he was more interested in the effect our thoughts have on how we feel. He was possibly the first person in western psychology to look at the impact of our 'self-talk', and positive self-talk now forms one of the key mental skills of sport and performance psychology, as well as CBT.[10]

Ellis believed that our emotions are caused by how we think, that we have some control over them and that we have choices, that we have free will over how we think and feel, and that we need to take responsibility for our choices and our thoughts.

In the ABC model, A stands for 'activating event', B stands for 'beliefs' and C stands for 'consequences'.[11] We have an event that activates our thoughts and feelings somehow – for example, a performance. We have beliefs about how that should go or how we should be in that performance. Then there are emotional and behavioural consequences.

Typically, we think that it is the activating event that causes the emotional and behavioural consequences or A → C. But according to Ellis, it is our beliefs about

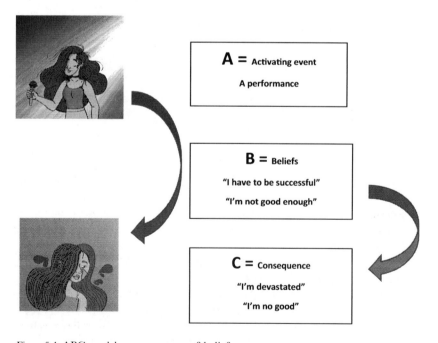

Figure 5.1 ABC model: consequences of beliefs

the event and our part in it that cause the emotional and behavioural consequences. i.e., B → C. This means that if we change our beliefs about the performance, we can change the emotional and behavioural consequences.

Our emotions and how we behave are a result of what we tell ourselves at B. If we tell ourselves that we must be successful, or that we aren't good enough, we aren't ready, or that we always make mistakes, this will impact how we feel before the performance, during the performance and after the performance.

We can change what we say to ourselves. Instead of saying, "I have to be successful", or "this performance must go well", you could say, "I want to be successful, but I don't have to be this time", or "I would like this performance to go really well but it's the first time I'm performing this music and if it doesn't go really well I'll learn from that". We can figure out things to say to ourselves that might change our feelings from extreme nervousness or pressure to perform well, to feeling manageably nervous. So our beliefs and how we talk to ourselves have a huge impact; we can change our 'self-talk', the things we say to ourselves.

The ABC model became the ABCDE model, with D standing for 'disputation' and E standing for 'education'. In terms of performance, education means learning about all the factors involved in performance and all the strategies you can use, then using them and learning what works for you and how to use them most effectively for you.

Disputation means disputing your beliefs, disputing the things you say to yourself. So if you have a pattern of negative thoughts and negative self-talk when you are faced with performing, then you need to dispute the self-talk you engage in, turn the thoughts around from negative to positive. At the very least turn the self-talk into more accepting and compassionate self-talk. Yes, be compassionate to yourself.

Disputing negative thoughts and beliefs

A really effective way to prevent the negative thoughts from gaining strength is to explore the evidence *for* the negative thought, and the evidence *against* the negative thought. So, you take the complete opposite view of the negative thought, and provide evidence for the opposite.

Ask yourself if what you are saying about yourself is actually true. Is that negative thought really accurate? Think of at least three reasons why it *is* accurate and true. Find three pieces of 'evidence' for its accuracy.

Then think of at least three reasons why it is *not* true. Find three pieces of evidence for how your negative thought is *not* true.

This can be difficult at first, for those who really believe the negative things they say about themselves. When you really believe something negative to be true, it is hard to find reasons for why it is not true. Look for evidence of the opposite of what you believe to be true.

To do: disputing your negative thoughts[12]

Two methods of doing this – one simple, one more complex

Method 1

- Write down the negative thoughts you have.
- Try to make them into short statements. Give clarity to the negative thought – simple and concise. It can seem quite harsh when you see it on paper.

The evidence

- Write down at least three reasons why it is true.
- Write down at least three reasons why it is *not* true.

Example: I always have a memory slip

- Think of three times you forgot the music.
- Think of three times when you did *not* forget the music. Relive these examples as vividly as possible and try to keep them in your mind. Refer back to them any time you have this thought.

Example: I'm so nervous for this and I know I will play badly

True because:

- I always play badly when I get this nervous.
- I have got this nervous before and I know what happens.
- I can't see any other outcome.

The opposite is true because:

- I have been nervous before and didn't play badly – think of three times.
- Yes, I'm nervous but I can manage it – think of examples of times you managed.
- Nerves can make me play better – think of examples.
- I need the nerves in order for it to be good – think of examples.
- I can play this music – think of examples.
- I have practised, I have done the work – think of examples.
- I will do my best. All I can do is give it my best shot – examples of having done this before.
- I will take the risk.
- I'm actually not as nervous as I have been other times.
- I have more experience with nerves now.

- I have more experience with performing now.
- I have been nervous before and played well.

Method 2[13]

- Write down one negative thought.
- In a clear simple statement (or use one you already wrote above).
- Example: I always have a memory slip.
- Change this statement to an opposite *in as many ways* as you can:
  - I do *not* always have a memory slip – think of three times you didn't have a slip.
  - I always *remember* the music – think of three times you remembered the music.
  - Other people have memory slips – think of three times you've heard others have memory slips. Did it matter? What happened? Do they still perform?

This technique forces us to immediately refute what we are thinking, and forces us to back up the opposite of what we were thinking with hard evidence. It is a very effective, simple way to immediately turn negative thinking into positive, especially if you are finding it hard to think of a positive thought about a particular aspect of your performance and playing, a positive thought that you can believe.

It's also a realistic way to think positively about your strengths and weaknesses, particularly beneficial for those who are sceptical not only about their own strengths, but also about the effectiveness of positive thinking. It forces you to be aware of your strengths, whilst at the same time not ignoring your weaknesses.

Using a mantra

"I've done the work … I know the stuff", "I can do it, I can do it",
"you're singing really well, you're singing really well, the voice is going
and it's there".

Even when we try to think positively, even when we put in all the effort to see the evidence for how well we have done in the past, how well we have performed on previous occasions, still the negative thoughts might persist, filling up your head with more meaning and value than a thousand positive thoughts. If you have difficulty thinking positively, or if you find that the negative thoughts pervade your thinking even when you try to stop them, then using a mantra can be really effective.[14]

A mantra is a short statement with key, positive words that are important or meaningful for you. A mantra can shift negative thinking to positive, and change how we feel. You can make up your own, or you can use someone else's. There are some examples of expert musicians' mantras above, and another list of experts' mantras on page 85.

When using a mantra at first, it's not even important that you believe the words. Repeat the mantra over and over, use it every day, every hour. Without having to do anything else, and without even believing the words at first, the positive thoughts change your brain activity by altering neurochemical activity, even when you don't believe the words wholeheartedly.

It is not possible to have more than one image in your mind at any one time, so if you flood your brain with positive images and positive thoughts about yourself, then the negative thoughts get flushed out. This changes how you feel about yourself and how you think about yourself.

You might be thinking right now that there is little point in thinking positively if you're really not good enough at some aspect of your music playing or perform-ance. But that's not entirely the case. Yes, all musicians need to work on the weaker aspects of their musicianship, whether it's some facet of their technique, expres-sion, knowledge, or performance. You do too and most likely you are working hard at it. So, of course it is important to carry out good practice preparation, but as you do that, you can also work on your cognitive and emotional approach to performance.

When we think more positively about ourselves we do better, we perform better, we play better. It's unfair to yourself to expect to perform well whilst thinking very critical thoughts about yourself at the same time. It is actually impossible to per-form well, no matter how much preparation and practising you have put in, when thinking critically and negatively about yourself and your playing.

Sometimes, without realising it, we can become quite reliant on or attached to our negative thoughts about ourselves. We get into a *habit* of thinking about our-selves negatively or about a specific aspect of ourselves, and that habit can be very hard to break free from. When we have a negative idea about ourselves, when we repeat this thought often enough, it becomes internalised. It becomes a part of who we think we are. It can be hard even to imagine what it would be like to think positively about some aspect of ourselves or our performance.

The negative perception you might have of yourself is not actually realistic or factual. Your perception is just your *perception* of how things are at that moment in time; your thoughts are just *thoughts*. None of it is fact. You can have different thoughts that will change how you feel, and ultimately change how you play or perform.

Just as negative thoughts can easily become internalised, positive thoughts can also be internalised and become part of who we think we are, how we see our-selves. So, even if you are using a mantra that at first you don't believe, repeat it often enough and in time you will internalise it.

The positive thoughts are assimilated into our thinking – our brain makes room for them in our thought processes. If you are in the habit of thinking negatively and find it difficult to break out of that habit, then you may find it consoling to know that there is room for both. For the moment. You can keep some of your negative thoughts, and some of them are indeed important in order to keep you practising and improving. But you want to add some positive thoughts to the mix. Add a mantra.

Sometimes performers can even be a little superstitious about negative thinking, feeling that maybe a certain quota of negative thinking must be carried out in order for a performance to go well. In this case, it might be helpful to put a limit or time deadline on the negative thoughts.

Many musicians do not allow themselves to think negatively once they reach a certain point prior to a performance. Often this is a conscious decision with a definitive moment in time before a performance where they say 'that's it, no more negative thinking'; for others it's a habit they have become used to employing.

To do: get a mantra

Use one of the examples below or make your own short concise statement of positive affirmations

It can be really effective to say your positive affirmation in the third-person – so using your full name instead of using "I".

Try both, and see how you feel.

Choose a mantra or a couple of mantras, that you can use, with ease, without having to think much about it – you may already have one. Repeat it over and over – at times when you feel bad, or when you notice you are being very critical of yourself, when you become aware that you are thinking negatively, and also just use it randomly, remembering to say it to yourself. But especially use your mantra repeatedly on the day of your performance and the days coming up to the performance.

The following list is the mantras that expert musicians use themselves, mantras that are specifically used by expert musicians in the days or hours before a challenging performance.

To do: take one or more of these mantras and use as your own

- 'You can do it! You can do it!'
- 'I really want to do this and I can do it!'
- 'I've done the work! I know the stuff!'
- 'It's not about me, it's not about me'
- 'I'll feel good once the music starts'
- 'Put everything into it! I've nothing to lose'
- 'Go for it! Don't be afraid to fail'
- 'I can do this'
- 'Risk it! Go for it!'

Examples of mantras for general positive thinking

- I am strong and powerful. I can do this!
- I have people who love and care about me
- I am improving everyday
- Today I choose to be confident
- If I fall I will get back up
- I accept who I am and where I am right now

To do: pre-performance thought management plan

Put together your pre-performance thought management plan.

Decide which of these techniques you are going to use, if not all of them.

Put the techniques into use every day, and in good time before a performance.

Effective use of strategies and techniques will not happen instantly. There is no magic wand. Thought management must be *practised* and used daily. You wouldn't expect to be able to learn and to skilfully play a new piece of music on the day of a performance. Likewise you cannot learn and skilfully use a new way of thinking or being on the day of a performance. The techniques must become part of your daily practice, part of your daily routine.

Techniques to incorporate into your daily routine

- Challenge your thoughts.
- Use the stop! and replace negative thoughts.
- Dispute negative thoughts: turn negative thoughts into positive thoughts.
- Choose your mantra.
- Select a cut off time for negative thinking prior to a performance. Be realistic about when you can cut off your negative thinking habit or quota.
- Beat the negative thoughts with positive thoughts. Because for some reason, as humans, we tend to believe the negative thoughts more easily than we do positive thoughts, this means that the negative thoughts have greater impact on you. So you need to make yourself think more positive thoughts than negative thoughts – beat the number of negative thoughts with a greater number of positive thoughts. Remember the positivity ratio of 3:1.

- Start to incorporate mental practice and visualisation exercises into your practice every day and increase the time you spend mentally practising as you approach a performance (see Chapter 8 and how musicians use mental practice). Use available time when you have nothing else to do – travelling, waiting – to carry out mental practice and visualisation.

Use the Toolkit tickbox below to tick off which strategies you are going to use or have tried already.

To do: your toolkit of strategies

Table 5.1 Strategies toolkit

Tick off the strategies you have tried and found useful

	Tried it	Helpful
IZOF (Chapter 4)		
Diary of thoughts/emotions (see Chapter 5)		
Rationalise your thoughts (Chapter 5)		
Challenge your thoughts (Chapter 5)		
Stop! and replace (Chapter 5)		
Dispute negative thoughts (Chapter 5)		
Mantra (Chapter 5)		
Motivational orientation (Chapter 6)		
Awareness/knowledge (all chapters)		
Mental practice (Chapter 8)		
Visualisation (Chapter 8)		
Pre-performance routine (Chapter 10)		
Mindfulness meditation (Chapter 9)		
Relaxation exercise (Chapter 9)		
Breathing exercise (Chapter 9)		
Exercise (running, yoga, walking, etc.) (Chapters 9, 10)		

Strategies should be incorporated into your daily practice and way of being. Using a strategy once is not enough and will not work effectively or to your advantage.

Key tips from this chapter

- You can manage your thoughts, train, and change your thoughts.
- By changing your thoughts, you impact a loop of emotions-thoughts-behaviours that can alter your experience of performance.
- We tend to believe negative thoughts more readily than we believe positive thoughts about ourselves.
- For everyday positivity and confidence, there is a positivity ratio of 3:1 that we should adhere to. Three positive thoughts for each one that is negative.
- There are strategies you can use that can help you manage your thoughts – being really aware of your thoughts, challenging your thoughts, turning negative to positive, replacing negative thoughts, positive self-talk, using mantras.
- It's not magic unfortunately – you have to practise and make the exercises part of your everyday routine.

6 Motivation

"I loved the songs I was singing and I wanted everyone to love
them", "I love entertaining people, I love getting praise and I love being
the centre of attention, but you're not going to get in the zone if you're
only there for the praise … you have to love it for what it is and have
a love for doing it".

Motivational orientation: what motivates you?

People engage in activities such as music for all sorts of reasons, and the more
complex the skill level and the more years of playing music, the more complex the
motivational reasons for playing are.

Where music is concerned, it is possible to be motivated for more than one
reason. People may play for fun, because of their love of music, for social reasons,
because they love performing, because they love being challenged, for social gain,
for financial reward, to please others, to entertain, to express themselves, to feel
emotion, to experience meaning, to escape, because they love being alone with
music, because they love to play music with others, for sensory stimulation, for
aesthetic stimulation, because they love to create, to achieve, to pass exams, to win,
and so on; there are multiple possible reasons to play music.

Our 'motivational orientation' is a concept used to describe the reasons we
carry out or engage in any activity. There are two key types of motivational orientation, two main ways in which we can be motivated to do something. One is
called intrinsic motivation and the other is called extrinsic motivation. Research
on flow has shown, and indeed we can see from expert musicians' descriptions in
Chapter 2, that we are more likely to experience flow when we are intrinsically
motivated, rather than extrinsically motivated.

So, what is intrinsic motivation and what is extrinsic motivation?

We are intrinsically motivated when we engage in an activity purely for the enjoyment it brings when we are doing that activity, because we love doing or experiencing that pursuit. When our motivational orientation for a particular activity is
intrinsic, when we are doing something we love to do, we seem to automatically

enjoy being challenged by that activity, we enjoy exploring and learning new things when engaged in whatever the activity is.

Extrinsic motivation can be described as the kind of motivation we have when we do something for the external rewards we might receive, rewards that are different from the pure enjoyment we might feel when engaging in an activity. We are extrinsically motivated when we are motivated by external gains or external rewards such as praise, applause, recognition, prestige, reputation, prizes, or financial reward.

Flow itself has been described as an 'autotelic' experience (see Chapter 2) – a really positive experience that occurs when engaging in an activity for the pure enjoyment of that activity. People play music for all sorts of reasons, and music provides many opportunities for both types of motivation – intrinsic and extrinsic – and because music can do so much for us, because there are so many intrinsic reasons to play or perform music (expressing ourselves, escapism, challenge, fun, stimulation, creativity), it provides great opportunities for the possibility of experiencing flow.

Motivation and self-determination

Research over a number of decades has explored *why* people engage in activities such as sport, leisure, work, education, music, extreme sports. Psychologists have been interested in trying to work out why we choose the activities we choose. Why do some people choose extreme sports, others choose music, for some it's reading, and for others its gardening?

If it's music, why music? What is it that drives people to want to play a musical instrument, to perform, to practise for hours and years, and why do some people not continue? Why are some not compelled to practise, or to practise but not perform? Psychologists are interested in finding the explanations for why some people practise more than others, why some perform more than others, why some people reach higher levels of achievement than others, why some people disengage or dropout. Coming to an understanding about motivation and motivational orientation has been essential to finding the answers to these questions.

A number of theories have been put forward by psychologists to explain the reasons why we take part in the activities we choose. The most influential theory has been the theory of self-determination.[1] This theory proposes that there are actually a number of types of intrinsic motivation and a number of types of extrinsic motivation that explain our reasons for engaging in an activity.

> *"It [the music] was new, it was exciting, the kind of thing that makes you feel 'I'm stretching myself here' and that's a good thing".*

The theory of self-determination says that we can be intrinsically motivated to learn – for the pleasure of learning something new or developing; and we can be intrinsically motivated to *achieve* – for the pleasure experienced when attempting to accomplish something; and thirdly, we can be intrinsically motivated to *experience*

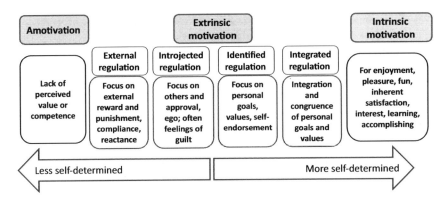

Figure 6.1 The continuum of motivation (adapted from SDT theory, Ryan & Deci, 2000)

stimulation – that is to engage in something in order to experience the stimulating sensations it provides, whether sensory or aesthetic or exhilaratory.

> *"The ego becomes very dangerous", "if you're playing to the audience, you're not going to have flow".*

On the other end of the motivation continuum, is extrinsic motivation (see Figure 6.1). We can be extrinsically motivated for various reasons and this theory says that there are four types of extrinsic motivation. We can be motivated by external reward – for example, praise or money (it's called external motivation). We can be motivated by some kind of guilt or internal pressure to do something (called introjected motivation) – for example, "I have to do this because if I don't I'll feel bad" or, "if I don't do this, I'll be letting someone down". We can be motivated to do something because we see it as important to our overall, general personal goals (called identified motivation) – for example, "I'm going to do this exam because I want to have certain qualifications which will aid my career", or, "I'm going to do this gig because it's an important stepping stone in my career". Finally, we can be motivated to do something for external reasons that have become so integrated into our selves that they are very similar to being intrinsically motivated (integrated motivation), for example, "I don't always enjoy practising for hours a day but I do it because I love to perform music with others and if I don't practise I won't get to perform", or "I don't love the idea of doing an exam, but if I do it, it will benefit my career, and I am more likely to get to do what I love for my job".

Good cop, bad cop – sometimes you need both!

So, intrinsic motivation brings all the feel-good factors. Intrinsic motivation is great. When we are intrinsically motivated, we love doing the activity, we enjoy it, it is easy to engage in it because of that love and enjoyment, we become absorbed in it when we do it, it makes us feel good, we learn, we grow, we develop, we achieve, we are fulfilled and happy.

On the other hand, extrinsic motivation starts to look like the 'baddy' of motivational orientation by comparison. With extrinsic motivation, we have feelings that we are doing the thing because it makes us money, or people like us more when we do it, or we feel bad when we don't do it.

In reality, we need to be extrinsically motivated by some things some times. We tend to be motivated to do something for more than one reason. Even when we're fulfilled and happy engaging in something we love, sometimes we still like, and even need, to have other people's regard, and we still need to have goals that involve money, security and other people's support in order to live and survive. So when a musician decides to engage in music for their livelihood, for their 'job', intrinsic motivation may have been what started them out in music or the thing that kept them going and persisting through the years of hard work, but extrinsic motivation becomes an important part of the mix of reasons *why* they do it. When a young music student loves playing music, they are still likely to be motivated by friends, parents, exams, competitions, by praise, or social gain, as well as by many other factors.

The interplay between intrinsic motivation and extrinsic motivation can become complex, and various factors, internal and external, can impact on our orientation towards intrinsic or extrinsic motivation.[2] We can experience both intrinsic and extrinsic motivation at the same time for the one activity – for music – but ideally, it's better to be more intrinsically motivated than extrinsically motivated. It is important to keep an eye on having a balance between the two types of orientation. Whilst it's natural to enjoy performing, to enjoy applause and praise, to want to gain the positive regard of others, or to need to receive payment or a salary, it's crucial for ultimate enjoyment and satisfaction that intrinsic motivation (love and enjoyment) is the chief reason for playing music.

Why is intrinsic motivation better for you?

> *"We played to 3,000 people and we'd bring the house down, standing ovations, but it's nonsense … if you have to gauge everybody's opinion of it, then there'd be nothing left for yourself".*

You might ask, why is it better to be intrinsically motivated than extrinsically motivated? Praise, applause, reward, money all sound good! But you'll see more reasons for the benefits of intrinsic motivation as you read on.

The main point is that intrinsic motivation leads to better experiences, happier experiences, more fulfilment, to growth, development, enjoyment, and achievement. These are things that not only impact on our musical experience, but impact on us in life in general and in our whole feeling of self-worth. In music, intrinsic motivation leads to more satisfying experiences, more flow, more peak performance, and more peak experience.

Extrinsic motivation tends to lead to us feeling more self-conscious, more aware of and more reliant on other people's opinions of us, which increases performance anxiety and decreases our own feelings of self-worth. We become increasingly more reliant on those opinions for our self-esteem and sense of self. When we become more self-conscious we tend to become more self-critical and do a lot more self-scrutinising. Relying on the opinions of others, even when the feedback is positive, leads to an undermining of the self and self-esteem.

To do: enhancing intrinsic motivation

- If you find yourself becoming increasingly extrinsically motivated, it might help to remind yourself why you are doing this in the first place. Find opportunities to more often play the music you love, even if in practice only.
- Perhaps it is possible to, at times, be more selective about the gigs, the music you are playing, and to be more selective about who you are playing with. Make sure that sometimes you are putting yourself first and what you want.
- It can help to reassess goals and priorities, and to ensure that you are playing music that you love, not playing music that you dislike too often, and that you are open to a range of music opportunities.
- Encourage and develop a growth mindset, connections with others, a sense of autonomy, and consider your immediate and long-term goals (read the coming pages and 'to dos').

There is one other type of motivation – called 'amotivation'. We experience amotivation when we cannot see that our efforts are having any effect on the outcome. So, a student who is practising but can't see any improvement in their progress may come to feel amotivated. Amotivation is most commonly linked with dropout from any activity, whether that is music, sport, or school. The roots of amotivation or the reasons that might lead someone to not be able to see any link between their efforts and their results, may stem from a number of factors that could be altered with support, before the final 'dropout'.

Three basic human needs – what drives our intrinsic motivation?

So if you want to feel more intrinsically motivated, experience more intrinsic enjoyment, or remind yourself of the joy you used to feel, there are three basic human needs that drive your inherent joy of learning to play music, or the inherent 'feel-good' factor when you play music, or engage in any activity.[3]

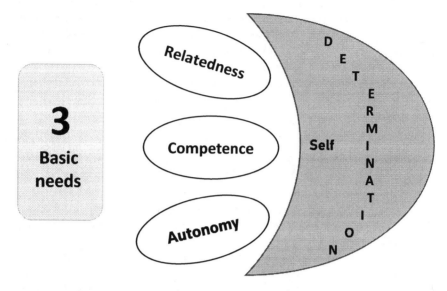

Figure 6.2 Three basic human needs

These three 'needs' are:

- *competence* – feeling able, effective, competent, or good at something;
- *relatedness* – feeling a bond with and connected to others; and
- *autonomy* – feeling you have some control and choice.

Feeling competent

> "For me, the sense of achievement is important. Otherwise I wouldn't want to practise! It's like positive reinforcement", "the challenges were delightful".

We have an inherent, built-in drive or need to feel competent, to feel we can do something, to feel that there is something that we are good at, to feel that we are good, getting better, achieving, effective, able to do the thing we enjoy doing. In music learning and playing, how you feel about your ability has a hugely important impact. Interestingly, all the research (in many areas, as well as in music) shows that how you think about ability, how you 'perceive' your ability, has more impact on your development and achievement than *any* other factor in learning and achieving, including actual ability level.[1]

How you think about your 'ability' affects achievement: what is your mindset?

What is significantly important here for students of music to know is that *how* you think about 'ability' in general and how you think about your own ability has massive implications for your level of enjoyment, intrinsic motivation and your ultimate, even long-term, achievement in music. Whether you believe that ability is fixed and unchangeable or whether you believe that ability can be worked on, is malleable or changeable, has a very important and key impact on your learning, enjoyment, and actual achievement.

As I said in the preface, there is ongoing debate in many areas of research, including in psychology and in education, on the subject of 'nature versus nurture' – whether our levels of achievement are defined by innate talents or by our life and learning experiences. A huge amount of research would suggest that no matter what talents or abilities you believe you were born with or not born with, it is the life experiences of learning, engagement, resources, support, practice, strategies, mindset, motivation that impact significantly on our level of ability, our level of achievement and the outcome of our endeavours, whether that is in music, sport, maths, languages, poetry, or whatever the activity.

Research has shown that if you believe that ability is fixed and unchangeable, you are less likely to deal effectively with 'failure', you are less likely to view not playing well or not playing at a high enough standard as something you can change, something you can do something about, something within your control. You are less likely to take on challenges and difficult tasks.[5] You are less likely to use specific and effective practice strategies. You are less likely to use effective psychological strategies. You are less likely to be persistent in learning. You are less likely to have a 'growth' mindset.[6] And you are *more* likely to blame (and shame) yourself in the face of failure – rather than attributing failure to effort or practice strategies or resources, which are most likely the actual reason. In doing so, you risk your whole sense of identity as a musician. All this, *if* you believe in fixed ability, 'talent', 'giftedness', if you believe that you are born with innate, unchangeable ability and that *you* cannot have an impact on your level of ability.

When you *believe* that ability can be improved and developed, then you believe that effort is important and you are more likely to use effective practice strategies. You are more likely to pursue learning and practice, you are more likely to attribute failures to the amount of practice you did, the type of effort you put in, to specific practice strategies you used, or more likely – didn't use. You are more likely to persist through challenges and difficulties. You are more able to protect your sense of self as a developing musician. Ultimately you are more likely to achieve higher levels of accomplishment and more likely to feel good about yourself, even in the face of difficulty or failure.[7]

To do: encourage a growth mindset

- It's important that you emphasise the effort you put in rather than the level you have reached.
- Praise yourself or your student musician for *effort* put in, for time spent and particularly for the practice strategies you use.
- Look for a range of practice strategies; try a variety of strategies. Students who use more varied learning and practice strategies reach

higher levels of achievement. Experiment and find what works best for you and be flexible enough to be able to use different strategies for different challenges, different genres, technique and expression.

- Try not to be perfectionistic about standard of playing. As a musician, you may have to be able to be critical in order to improve, but there's a balance, and too much perfectionism can have negative consequences (*maladaptive*).
- Don't compare yourself to others too much.
- Keep focused on your own goals, what's important to you, your own development and your own accomplishments.
- Try to develop a 'growth' mindset – rather than a fixed mindset. Actively discourage any thoughts you have about 'talent' and 'gifted-ness'. When you believe you can grow and develop, you will grow and develop. When you believe that you can achieve higher standards of playing, you will achieve higher standards.

Neuroscientific research in recent years has shown us the malleability of the brain. There is a field of study on brain plasticity that has shown that the brain has the ability to change and is constantly changing, through learning and the experiences we have over our entire lifetime.[8] Connections of neurons – neuronal networks – develop and strengthen through experience and practice. New connections are constantly being made and old, unused connections decay and disintegrate. How the brain gets rid of unused connections is called 'pruning'.[9] You might imagine a tree with branches growing off each other, new buds, new growth on the branches that are looked after, whereas the old decaying branches are pruned by us.

The brain does something similar. There is interconnectivity between vast networks of cells. Those that are used and looked after grow, strengthen in their connection and form more connections. Those that aren't used, decay.

This means that when you practise you make new connections between brain cells; when you practise more and when you use varied strategies you strengthen the connections in a network of cells.

It also means that when you don't practise enough the new connections you make are not being strengthened by consistent practising. When you do sporadic practice, those new connections constantly have to be made and re-made in each new practice session. It's not very efficient; it takes so much longer to learn some-thing new, and it leads to boredom.

The research from neuroscience provides important evidence for the argument that we can change, develop, and accomplish through learning and practice.

Feeling related and connected to others

"We just melded together, really connecting, really communicating and responding to each other".

We have an inherent need to feel a bond with other people, to feel like we belong, are connected to others and accepted by others.[10] Learning and playing music is quite dependent on other people and relationships with other people a lot of the time. There are teachers, friends, parents, other players, and groups of co-players – band, orchestra, choir, chamber music, and people who make up audiences – family members, friends, peers, teachers, and strangers. All these relationships have the potential to impact your motivation, positively or negatively.

To do: developing connectedness[11]

- Joining in activities that bring about interactions with other student musicians, with other like-minded people, will impact positively on motivation to play music and to practise. Teenage music students may feel the benefits of engaging in musical activities that are more social than solitary. If music practice becomes too isolating, this may have negative consequences. It's important to join music groups, a band, an ensemble, orchestra, choir, in order to hang out and engage with other people who have similar interests.
- Of course, for the student for whom there is plenty of musical social outlet, they need to keep in mind the importance of maintaining their love of music by doing their individual practising.
- Parents of student musicians should try to understand the importance of developing social bonds and social music playing as well as carrying out individual practice.
- A warm, respectful relationship with significant teachers or leaders, will help satisfy needs for relatedness. A relationship that goes both directions, works for both people is healthy and 'needs'-supporting.
- Teenagers like to feel respect for, as well as warmth from, a teacher or mentor; younger children respond better to warmth, fun and enjoyment.

Research shows that strictness, coldness, ignoring the moods or feelings, and the friendship-needs of the student musician will only negatively impact on the student's motivation. Respect, qualifications, and stature of a teacher are important to teenage students, whereas warm, affable, and fun qualities are important to the young student.

Students who have the highest levels of achievement have good positive parental support and involvement.

Feeling autonomous

> *"When a lot of other people are involved, managers and promoters, and you're on the road night after night … you can start to lose sense of yourself".*

The third of the three basic needs is 'autonomy'. We need to feel we have some 'autonomy' – control and choice in our lives and within the activities and social settings in which we participate. We need to feel that we are the cause of our own actions, that we have some freedom, choice, and control in the things we do and how we do them. Music training can be quite structured and rigid even, particularly in classical music training. To feel autonomy, choice, control does not mean there should not be structure within the learning context. You can feel like you have choice and control within the structure of music training, but it may need some consideration about how to do that, if you are not feeling like you have some control and choice in what you are doing.[12]

There is standard repertoire that has to be learnt when studying any genre of music, and whilst studying a wide range of repertoire and songs is important, it is also important to feel like there is some element of choice.

To do: developing a sense of autonomy

- You, as a music student will feel more autonomous when you are involved in decisions about what to learn, and the goals for the next stage of development or training.
- It is helpful if you understand and take part in developing your own practice goals.
- Incorporate time in practice schedules for fun playing, or for developing other musical goals that are perhaps not primary to their instrumental studies but can provide outlets for creativity, expression, and feeling in control and autonomous.

"You're doing a job, and sometimes you're doing the same job every night … it completely negates the reason for playing music in the first place".

In music performance and training, there are ways to fulfil and support each of the three basic needs – competence, belonging, and autonomy. Some people may have more need to have one or two of the needs fulfilled, but all three are important. When these needs are not fulfilled the result can be a decline in enjoyment, happiness, confidence, ability, sense of identity as a musician, decline of intrinsic motivation. This can happen almost without you noticing but ultimately it can lead to loss of intrinsic motivation altogether and to giving up learning and playing music.

So, consider all of the ideas for developing competence, relatedness, and autonomy. If you are feeling low on intrinsic motivation, if your enjoyment levels are fading, it may be because even just one of these factors needs some attention. All you have to do, is think about which it might be, and take some of these ideas for developing that one aspect of your musical life.

Another way of thinking about motivation

Another influential theory of motivation (achievement goal theory) says that when we are intrinsically motivated we are 'task' oriented and when we are extrinsically motivated we are 'ego' oriented.[13]

We are 'ego' oriented when we are focused on demonstrating superior ability to others or gaining some sort of social status or recognition. We are 'task' oriented when we are intrinsically interested in learning, improving, and mastering a task, for the pure enjoyment of improving and mastery for its own sake.

What happens when we are motivated by 'task' orientation?

> *"Sometimes when I won a prize, my focus was not to win the prize, but to play as best I can. And then that is usually what won me the prize".*

All the research that has been carried out in sport settings has shown that good things happen, in relation to achievement, enjoyment, and satisfaction, when we are task oriented, whereas there can be more negative consequences when we are 'ego' oriented.[14]

Likewise, our motivational orientation influences the outcome of how we think, feel, and behave when we are taking part in music. It is believed that the kind of motivation we have for something determines the kinds of goals we have. Also, how we define success determines the kinds of goals we have, our achievement goals and our motivation orientation. If our definition of success is being the best we can be, or putting in effort and getting results from that, trying hard, learning, improving, mastering skill, and enjoying that, then we are more likely to have 'task' orientation. If we are motivated because we want to improve, we want to master a task, we want to challenge ourselves and develop our skills ('task' orientation) then we have goals to achieve for our own sake and for the sake of improving itself and the satisfaction that we gain from that. This is a really positive thing and has lots of other positive consequences.

The research in sport and in music has shown that people who are 'task' oriented are more satisfied, experience more positive emotions, practise and engage in the activity more, enjoy practising more, use better learning strategies and more varied learning strategies, have higher self-esteem, and have more stable self-esteem. This means that our self-esteem endures even in the face of setbacks, mistakes, failures, when we are motivated by 'task' rather than 'ego'. Also, when we are 'task' oriented we are much more likely to experience optimal experiences such as flow.

What happens when you are motivated by 'ego' goals?

> *"When I won competitions, it was because I loved the music", "I could never play my best when I was playing for a prize or for a grade … I always played my best if I played because I wanted to play or the audience had to be entertained".*

On the other hand, if we define success as being better than others, when we are entirely motivated to show that we are the best or better than others, for some external reward such as praise ('ego' orientation), then we will have goals that are concerned with winning, gaining marks or grades in exams, gaining praise, reward, applause. These are 'ego' achievement goals.

This doesn't seem like a bad thing – to win, gain praise, and reward – and it's not. But the research shows that 'ego' achievement goals work best for us when they are low level and when they are combined with having a high level of 'task' achievement goals. So, we can have both kinds of achievement goals, but it's best when those goals are primarily 'task' achievement goals.

One of the most notable revelations of research on achievement goals and performance, is that both musicians and sportsmen/women say that winning is *least* likely to occur when their priority is winning. How ironic is that! It seems that winning (be it a competition, or respect, or reward) is more likely to be gained as a sort of by-product of being engaged in the performance for more 'task' oriented and intrinsically motivated reasons. In the case of music, this might be taking part in a performance because you love the music you are playing, or taking part in an exam or competition but being focused on the music – the expression and communication of the music, rather than on the external outcome of having someone else's opinion of you as the performer.

The international concert pianist, Lang Lang has said, "Don't think about competition as a competition … Your biggest enemy is not anybody but you. Be nice to yourself. Be open and connected to the music. Just focus on the music".[15]

Being 'ego' oriented has been found to have some negative consequences. People who are more concerned with demonstrating superior competence compared to others usually have a more fragile sense of their own ability, and a more fragile and unstable self-esteem. When our personal definition of succeeding depends on the opinions of others, gaining praise and reward, rather than being founded on our own efforts and achievements, then our self-esteem is easily brought down or heightened momentarily. And in this case our perception of our own ability becomes dependent on others telling us if we are good or how good we are. This leads to a heightened awareness of others and a heightened self-consciousness. When we are overly concerned with validating ourselves and our performance through others, we become fearful about our own adequacy and are then more likely to question our adequacy and ability. Being fixated on displaying superiority can become maladaptive and it is ultimately quite debilitating.[16]

It is not good for your self esteem to evaluate yourself based on how you are getting on in music compared to others, or how you are performing compared to others. If you are experiencing performance anxiety it is particularly important to make conscious efforts to take your focus off comparing yourself to others and off the standards and opinions of others. Focus on yourself, your progress, small developments you make, and on the music you enjoy playing.

To do: developing task motivation

- Focus on yourself and on your own accomplishments.
- Keep a mental note or even a diary of small steps, progress, and developments you make each day or at the end of each week.

- Notice how you feel when you play well, or when you improve on something.
- Encourage your own sense of accomplishment without looking to others to confirm it.
- Although as a musician you have to be aware of others' standards and how you are doing in relation to other people, it is also crucial to be able to look to yourself in order to know how well you are doing or not doing and to be able to find satisfaction, happiness, and fulfilment from your own opinion and sense of self.
- It is important to find a balance between being aware of the standard of playing you need to achieve, and being able to block out the opinions of others in order to focus on your personal progress and achievements.

Flow is greatly affected by motivational orientation. It has always been linked to intrinsic motivation. The research shows that people who experience flow more often are those who are *primarily* or only 'task' oriented, motivated for intrinsic reasons, such as enjoying practising, loving to play, loving to perform particular pieces of music or songs; those whose perceptions of success are concerned with learning, improving, mastering skill, expressing musical emotion, enjoyment of the feeling – physical, emotional – of playing music.

Good cop, bad cop – again, you need both!

A blend of 'task' and 'ego' orientation has been found to be extremely beneficial in many cases of performance, as long as 'task' is the primary orientation, with a lesser level of 'ego' orientation.[17] Really this is more realistic. We can't always be experiencing high levels of task orientation. For professional and student musicians, each gig or concert is different and the likelihood of experiencing flow can depend very much on the music that you are playing. Of course there are times when professional musicians are performing music they don't 'love' or that they enjoy less than other music. Likewise, student musicians have to learn and perform the standard repertoire of their instrument which may not always be to their liking, and often times they are even examined on it. But on the occasions when the music is enjoyable for the performer, flow is much more likely to occur. So a musician, professional or student, may be 'task' oriented or intrinsically motivated most of the time but there will be performances when, for various reasons, this is not the case.

Why do some people practise more? Is it all about motivation?

Flow, motivational orientation, *perceived* ability, and time spent practising are inextricably linked, each impacting on the other. People who experience more flow have higher levels of intrinsic motivation or 'task' orientation, have high levels of *perceived* ability and spend more time practising.[18] The direction of the link between these factors is not known. It is not known yet which comes first – practising more, experiencing flow, being intrinsically motivated, or feeling competent. But we do know that they are all related.

Many psychologists and researchers are interested in finding out what it is that makes some people reach higher levels of achievement than others, what makes some people spend more time practising and engaging in their chosen activity, why some people persist in training and practising for long hours over many years, why some people persist through setbacks and failures. It's something we all want to know the answer to! It may be that it is the ability to become completely absorbed in an activity and the ability to experience flow in an activity, that is the underlying crucial factor that answers these questions.

You may have heard of the 10,000 hours rule or that ten years of work and practise can make an expert (read more in Chapter 1). There is a body of research to show that this is indeed the case. Interestingly, singer/songwriter Billie Eilish spent her hours with her brother creating music from a very young age in a room where her brother had written '10,000 hours' above his door frame.[19] They *knowingly* set about putting this theory into action doing something they loved to do.

But it may not, or cannot, simply be a matter of 'putting in the hours'. Who could put in those hours without gaining rewards of some kind along the way to sustain that level of persistence? Those rewards may be personal achievement, a sense of satisfaction, autonomy, a feeling of connectedness; the basic needs that are all related to the experience of flow. It's more possible to gain those rewards when we are doing something that we love, and something in which it is possible for us to become immersed in, absorbed in.

We become absorbed when we are doing something we love to do, i.e., when we are intrinsically motivated. When we become absorbed we spend more time in that activity, more time practising and training. When we become absorbed we feel more confident, more satisfied, more comfortable, and we are more willing to take risks, to reach out of our comfort zone and try new things. When we become absorbed and spend more time in our chosen activity, we progress and develop.

When we become absorbed we can experience flow, and when we experience flow, we reach new levels of skill, of involvement, and of development; we take risks with ease and confidence, with a sense of control and a lack of concern about others and what they think. We get to see what we can really do, we get to experience ourselves doing and feeling something different from our usual non-absorbed, easily distracted, very conscious, and even self-conscious, states of being.

As well as having a feeling of freedom from the usual drudgery of getting stuff done and 'working' or practising, it is also freedom from caring what others think, and it frees us from our own thoughts. Being absorbed, being in flow, is an escape from the banality of our usual, conscious state of being. We escape our conscious selves, we escape the opinions of others. In that escape we have the opportunity to see ourselves at our best. According to Csikszentmihalyi, the pioneer of flow research, the effect is not just felt during those moments while absorbed, and while in flow; actually, the impact has a long-lasting effect on our development and growth in music.[20]

Even when we don't experience flow, motivational orientation has important consequences for achievement, as well as enjoyment. Intrinsic motivation significantly affects the amount of practice people carry out and therefore it is a crucial factor affecting achievement.

To do: take a short questionnaire to determine your achievement goal orientation

Take the questionnaire (Perceptions of success questionnaire (POSQ), Roberts, Treasure, & Balague, 1998)[21]

When taking part in music, I feel most successful when ...	Strongly disagree	Disagree	Not sure	Agree	Strongly agree
1) I am the best	1	2	3	4	5
2) I do better than others	1	2	3	4	5
3) I show other people I am the best	1	2	3	4	5
4) I try hard	1	2	3	4	5
5) I really improve	1	2	3	4	5
6) I overcome difficulties	1	2	3	4	5
7) I beat other people	1	2	3	4	5
8) I succeed at something I could not do before	1	2	3	4	5
9) I perform to the best of my ability	1	2	3	4	5
10) I reach a target I set for myself	1	2	3	4	5
11) I am clearly better	1	2	3	4	5
12) I accomplish something others cannot do	1	2	3	4	5

- Add up your scores for statement numbers 4, 5, 6, 8, 9, 10: task orientation
- Add up your scores for statement numbers 1, 2, 3, 7, 11, 12: ego orientation

Total score for statements 4, 5, 6, 8, 9, 10 will tell you what you score on task oriented achievement goals.

Scoring higher than 19 tells you that you have high level of orientation toward task achievement goals. You have a good sense of your enjoyment of music and the internal benefits you gain from achieving something because you enjoy it or because you want to make progress for your own internal sources of enjoyment and reward.

Scoring between 13–18, means that you have a mid-range level of orientation toward task achievement goals. This means that you have some sense of your own internal enjoyment, achievement, and rewards gained from playing music. However, this could be developed further and you should compare your task score with your ego orientation score. Ideally, a lower ego orientation score together with this score or higher task goals score is more beneficial for you, your development, joy, reward, and self-esteem in music.

If you scored less than 12, you have a low level of orientation toward task achievement goals. You could benefit from developing internal feelings of joy, achievement, and reward when you play music. Look at your score on the ego statements, to see if you have a high score on this. If you have a high ego orientation, you would benefit from having a better balance between task and ego orientations.

Total score for statements 1, 2, 3, 7, 11, 12 will tell you what you score on ego oriented achievement goals.

Scoring over 19 on these ego orientation statements means that you have a high level of orientation toward playing music for external and extrinsic rewards. This is fine, great even, as long as you also have a high score on the task achievement goals; and this is possible – many performers score high on both. Some people are motivated to play for their own joy and sense of achievement, but also for external rewards. If you have a low score on the task goal statements, try to develop your love of music, sense of joy, and internal achievement when you play music.

If you scored between 13–18 on the ego goals statements, you have a medium level of ego orientation toward playing music for external and extrinsic rewards. You will probably have a high or medium score on the task goals also, as people often do. If so, this is a good combination. It is better for your sense of self, internal joy, and achievement to have a *higher* task score than ego score.

If you scored under 12, you have a low level of orientation towards ego achievement goals. Compare this score with your task goals score, which you will probably find is higher. This is an ideal combination of goal orientations. Many musicians have high task achievement goals combined with a low ego achievement goal orientation.

To do: setting goals and completing goals

Set your own standards and set goals that are important for you.

Become aware of your improvements and how you are developing, or not developing. When you are aware of your own standards and progression, you are in a better position for setting goals that are reasonable and attainable.

- Set reasonable, attainable goals for what you would like to achieve yourself and work towards those.
- Think about what you would like to achieve by next year. How do you go about doing that?

- What do you have to achieve each month in order to reach your goal at the end of the year?
- What do you need to achieve weekly in order to achieve your monthly goals?
- What do you need to achieve daily to achieve the weekly goals?
- This way you set small attainable goals, and keep to them. If you don't keep to them, re-assess your monthly and annual goals and set more attainable goals.

Are you setting attainable goals?

- If you are not reaching your goals, you need to re-evaluate.
- Or perhaps you have set goals that are too easy.

Are there other goals you can add? Other music?

- Are there other groups you could join? Other genres of music you would like to add to your repertoire of abilities? Could you listen to more music? Read about music? Are there other areas in which you can set goals, that would improve your own level of competence?
- Set small goals that are achievable and tick them off as you reach them.
- Be aware of small steps of progress, these are important for motivation and self-esteem.
- Reward yourself, congratulate yourself. Then if others also reward or congratulate you, that's an added bonus, but not something you are relying on.
  This can be difficult when you are attending weekly instrumental lessons, where someone you admire (hopefully!) is commenting and critiquing your practice and progress.
- Try to be involved and engaged with your teacher when setting goals for your development. Even if this is difficult, you can still set your own weekly and daily practice goals.
- Have a list on your phone or diary, and tick items off as you complete them. Acknowledging progress, even small steps of achievement, is a really important part of goal setting.

Locus of control: do you believe that what you achieve or don't achieve is within your control?

Some people tend to attribute success or failure to external factors or events, events outside of themselves, and some people tend to attribute their successes or failures to events related to themselves. The way in which we attribute our successes and our failures, our achievements and our setbacks has been found to have a huge impact on our self-esteem and confidence, on our motivational orientation, on our ability to cope and on our ability to continue engaging in music following these setbacks, failures or successes.[22]

For example, one person might attribute not winning a competition to the fact that the judge of the competition displayed a preference for a different style of musical interpretation, or that someone else just happened to play better on that day. These are *external* attributions and mean that this individual has an 'external locus of control', meaning that they blame their loss on factors other than themselves. Another person might attribute their loss to their own playing not being good enough, or that they had performed badly – these attributions illustrate someone with an *internal* locus of control. Which attribution results in the player maintaining their self-esteem? Which attribution results in the player feeling bad about themselves, and having the effect of lowering their self-esteem or confidence?

These examples of attribution might give the impression that having an *external* locus of control is more beneficial to you than having an internal locus of control. It would seem that attributing failure to the judge (external) and not to the self (internal) might lead to keeping your own sense of self-esteem and self-worth. But it is a little more complex than that.[23]

If you attribute success and failure to something about you that is *possible for you to change* or work on or improve, then it is always beneficial to you, whereas *external* attributions are actually linked to lower self-esteem, lower levels of confidence and lower levels of success in general.

To explain this further, the crux of 'locus of control' is whether we interpret what happens to us, and the outcome of what happens to us, as being in our control or not.[24] If we attribute an outcome to something that we *can* control or change, then this is more beneficial to us in the long run. So when we have a setback or a disappointing result, if we attribute this to something that we did that we can change, then that is beneficial. Likewise, when we win or perform well, attributing this to something that we did that is in our control is also beneficial to us in the long-term.

Locus of control is generally described in two parts. First, we attribute the outcome of what happens to us either internally or externally. *Internal* attributions might be that we are boring, stupid, clever, musical, unmusical. An *external* attribution would be that the other person (for example the judge or examiner in a competition) is stupid, unmusical, clever, or wise. Another example is attributing our success or failure to a situation, perhaps a particular venue (external attribution) or attributing the success or failure to how we behaved or performed in that situation or venue (an internal attribution).

The second part to attribution is that we can attribute the outcome of an event to something that we can *control*, to something we can work on or change. Or we can attribute the outcome to something that is not controllable (usually referred to as stable/unstable). For example, we can attribute a setback to the amount or type of effort we put in, which is something we can change. Or we can attribute the setback to some fixed level of ability that we might think we have, and that we have no control over – something we cannot change.

When we attribute an outcome to the amount of effort or more specifically the type of effort, the type of practice strategies we used, then this is something that is within our control, and that we can do something about for the next time. This kind of attribution doesn't affect our feelings about ourselves as a musician or as a person in a negative way. Instead of saying, "I wasn't good enough", we can say "I didn't practise enough" or "I didn't do the right kind of practice often enough"; and we can pinpoint specific practice strategies that we could have used, didn't use, but can use in future, in order to achieve a different outcome.[25]

Table 6.1 shows the kinds of factors that are internal or external and controllable or not controllable, and shows the kinds of things we say to ourselves based on internal/external and controllable/uncontrollable attributions.

Table 6.2 shows the kinds of things you might say, when attributing your success or failure to internal/external and stable/unstable factors.

The ideal attribution for maintaining or increasing self-esteem, confidence, self-worth, and intrinsic motivation is to attribute both successes and failures to factors that are internal and controllable (unstable), the attributions that are in bold in the shaded boxes (see Table 6.2).

After that, the next best is to attribute *success* to internal and stable factors and attribute *failure* to external and stable factors. External and unstable attributions are never really beneficial in any situation, for long-term achievement, self-esteem, or motivation.

Some people tend to be 'internals', some tend to be 'externals'. But it can depend on the situation and it is something you can change.

Table 6.1 Locus of control

	Internal	**External**
Stable and unchangeable	Level of ability *(when perceived as fixed)* Level of musicality Level of intelligence Personality trait e.g., a performer, an introvert, an extrovert, a communicator, expressive, etc.	Task difficulty Venue, judge, examiner, teachers, resources
Unstable and changeable	Effort Amount of practice Type of practice Practice strategies used Knowledge of/about music Engagement in other musical activities Motivation Mood Energy/fatigue	Luck Opportunity Chance

Table 6.2 Locus of control with sample self-statements

| | Internal | | External | |
	Failure attributions	**Success attributions**	**Failure attributions**	**Success attributions**
Stable and uncontrollable	You might say: "no matter what I do, I'm never good enough", "I'm just not a performer", "I don't like crowds", "I'm not a technical player", "I'm never expressive enough", "I'm not musical"	You might say: "I'm always good", "I'm a great performer", "I'm so musical", "I'm a great technical player", "I'm always an expressive player"	"the music doesn't suit my style of playing", "the examiner didn't know what they were talking about", "the judge doesn't like my style of playing", "my teacher didn't teach me that properly", "my instrument isn't good enough"	"the music shows me in my best light and hides my weaknesses", "the examiner just prefers the piece I played", "my teacher is great", "it's great I have such a good instrument"
	Failure attributions	**Success attributions**	**Failure attributions**	**Success attributions**
Unstable and controllable	"I didn't practice enough", "I didn't practice the hard parts enough", "the type of practice I did wasn't good", "I didn't put in enough effort", "I didn't get enough sleep", "I had a row with x beforehand and I let it upset me", "I didn't do any mental practice or breathing beforehand"	"I put in a lot of practice", "I did the right kind of practice", "I knew the music really well", "I have been doing a lot of playing in different groups recently", "I got lots of rest beforehand", "I did breathing exercises and lots of mental practice"	"I was unlucky with the examiner", "I was unlucky that the other competitors were so good", "I didn't get the chance to show how good I am at other things", "it was just one of those days"	"I was lucky with the examiner", "I was lucky that the others didn't play so well", "the right opportunity just came my way", "everything just happened to go my way"

To do: evaluating a setback

When you experience a disappointing *setback*, where you didn't perform well or where you didn't receive the reward you were hoping for (a win, an exam grade, or praise):

- Find factors that are *internal* and *controllable* to attribute your experience to, for example:

   "I didn't practise the technically difficult parts enough" and 'I can practise the hard parts more the next time';

   "I haven't been practising scales as much as I could have", "I will start putting more emphasis on scales in my future practise goals";

   "I didn't do any psychological preparation – mental practice, breathing exercise, visualisation", "I am going to start a routine of strategies that I will implement in my everyday routines";

   "I didn't check my memory of the music as much as I could have", "I will start to use mental practice to memorise the music";

- Don't use excuses or give reasons that are internal and uncontrollable. For example, that you just aren't good enough, you always make mistakes, you're not as good as other people, etc.

- Try not to use excuses or give reasons that are external and uncontrollable. For example, other people had some good luck that you didn't have, the examiner didn't like your style, etc. But in times of disappointment this one is better than the internal/uncontrollable reasons.

To do: evaluating a success

Likewise, when you experience a *success*, where you performed really well and perhaps even received a reward (a win, or exam grade, or great praise):

- Find factors that are *internal* and *controllable* to attribute your *success* to – for example, "I practised really well for this", "I put in the right kind of practice", "I covered everything that needed to be covered", "I was focused on what I needed to do", etc.

- Don't say it was due to luck, or your co-performers, or the venue, or your great instrument – all external/uncontrollable factors.

   Of course, you can acknowledge these factors as playing a part, but it's important to check your list of things you did that made this achievement possible, so that you can do the same for future performances.

- Try not to attribute your successful experience to internal and uncontrollable factors – e.g., "I'm very talented" or "I'm just a really good musician". This will not help future preparation for future accomplishments. It's important to recognise the work you did and specific criteria that enabled you to be successful on this occasion.

It's all related

Believing that you are in control – that there are things you can do, practice strategies that you can use – protects your self-worth, your self-esteem, and harnesses confidence that you can do better next time. This is linked with self-efficacy and beliefs about your ability (as you read earlier in the chapter).

Believing that there are factors that you can control is linked to your beliefs about your ability. When you have a fixed mindset about your ability, when you believe that your ability is fixed – i.e., that you are either musical or not musical, 'talented' or 'not talented', a good musician or not – you will attribute your failures and successes to factors that are internal but out of your control, you will believe that there is nothing that you can do that will change the outcome of your efforts. As you read earlier, fixed mindset about ability is linked to lower levels of achievement, and to dropping out of the activity.

Having a fixed mindset really impacts on our beliefs about whether we have control over the outcome of our efforts. This is what we call '**self-efficacy**'. And research has shown that self-efficacy – believing that we can do something – has quite an astounding impact on our levels of achievement. As I said earlier, when you believe you can grow and develop, you *will* grow and develop. When you believe that you can achieve higher standards of playing, you will achieve higher standards.[26]

In education and in sport, research has found that the factor that most often predicts achievement is self-efficacy.[27] This is not because believing in yourself is the key to everything or because the only thing that matters is confidence: it is because of its relationship with many other factors that affect achievement. Self-efficacy is linked to so many other positive components – it's linked to engagement and persistence, to growth mindset, motivation, achievement goals, growth and development, fulfilment, and satisfaction. So people who have high levels of self-efficacy, people who believe they can do it, also believe that they have the power and control to impact on their progress and development. They believe their ability is not set at some fixed point over which they have no control, rather they believe they can use strategies and practise to achieve what they want. They have growth mindsets, they tend to be intrinsically motivated, they are more easily absorbed and engaged in their activity, and they spend more time practising.

Key tips from this chapter

- Intrinsic motivation leads to more positive outcomes.
- Both *intrinsic* motivation and *extrinsic* motivation can be experienced at the same time.
- Flow is more likely to be experienced when motivation is primarily intrinsic.
- You are more likely to feel fulfilled and happy in your musical engagement when you are primarily intrinsically motivated.
- There are three basic needs – to feel competent, to feel connected to others, and to have autonomy. These should be encouraged and supported in your musical activities, by you and by those around you.
- Set goals for yourself.
- Focus on your own progress, development and effort you put in. De-emphasise the opinions and standards of others.
- A growth mindset is key to motivation, achievement, self-efficacy, and positive experiences.

7 Concentration and focus

"Immerse yourself in the music and it takes you out of that self-conscious state", "I deliberately absorb myself in the music, in order to block out the other stuff".

Everybody has times when they find it difficult to really focus on what they're doing when performing. What I mean by 'focus' is being able to concentrate on the most important thing you're doing at every moment, even though there may be many other distractions. By distractions I mean anything other than the main task – so for example, distractions could be the audience, your co-performer(s), your own thoughts, your own body, the bit you just played, the mistake you made, how brilliantly you just played that difficult passage, an upcoming passage or piece or song, or words.

Focus is when you are *doing* exactly what you are *thinking*.[1]

Sometimes we are aware that we are having difficulty focusing on what we should be focusing on, other times it is something that we take for granted. You are probably used to becoming easily absorbed in the music and concentrating effortlessly on the music you are playing during practise sessions or during rehearsals. Perhaps during practise sessions your mind wanders, but you are not aware of losing focus, because when you're not in front of an audience, it isn't a big deal and not something to worry about too much.

Our focus is extremely susceptible to being distracted by other factors; it's how our brain works. The brain has evolved to be aware of all imminent threats. Being easily distracted is particularly the case when we believe there to be a very real threat, such as a performance – if you interpret the performance as a threat, an experience in which you could get hurt in some way. We experience a hyper-awareness that comes about when we feel threatened, apprehensive, nervous, or anxious.

When you are hyper-aware you will tend to notice things you hadn't previously noticed. It could be passages of the music that aren't as technically tidy as you had thought, i.e., you haven't practised them as much as you could have; or perhaps there is phrasing that you had overlooked, i.e., you're winging it on the interpretation a bit; or in the venue it could be that it seems as though you are suddenly sounding very loud or very soft; or you become very aware of the possibility of making mistakes, or forgetting words, notes, or switches. You might simply become hyper-aware that you're not very focused and this itself can be distracting.

Alternatively, you might find that your attention is drawn inward – to how you feel in your body, perhaps a little more tense than you had expected to feel, or that your breathing is shallow, your lips are too dry, your legs too shaky, your tummy feeling sick, your thoughts shifting rapidly.[2] Your attention is drawn to aspects of your inner experience of feelings and thoughts or to your inner experience of how you are going to produce the music. Sometimes it can feel like your body isn't up to the job and you can't get it under control.

The mental spotlight

The thing about focus is that we are always focusing on something, it's just that sometimes we focus on the *wrong* thing. We don't *lose* concentration, or *lose* focus, we just happen to be focusing on something other than the thing we're supposed to be focused on[3] – like the very notes you're supposed to be playing right at that moment in the moment, or before a performance focusing in on the difficult parts or on the audience or on someone else, or focusing inwardly on to how you feel inside.

Psychological theory has likened concentration to a mental spotlight, a spotlight that we can shine on one aspect of our experience, and then move it to another, and another. Like having the zoom lens of a camera, we can 'zoom' in on something or someone or a feeling or thought, but then we can shift that spotlight or lens of the camera onto something else. We selectively attend to one thing or another. This mental spotlight thing is also known as selective attention.[4]

There are two key implications of this analogy to a spotlight. The first implication of the spotlight analogy is key to resolving your focusing problems before or during performance, and it is this – *you* can *shift* the direction of your mental spotlight. You can change the direction of its focus, the direction of your focus. You will have experienced times when you leap from one thought to another, one second you're imagining the delicious dinner or dessert you're going to have later, the next you're noticing a slight headache, the next you notice the notes you're playing, the next you're wondering did your friend get the text message you sent earlier. We can shift from one thing to another very quickly.

During performance, or prior to performance, as long as you become aware of what your spotlight is aimed at, what you have zoomed in on, what thought or feeling has become the focus of your spotlight, you can change it, you can move it onto some other aspect of the performance, another thought, another feeling. You can control that.

Selective attention

The second implication of the mental spotlight idea is that when we selectively attend to one thing, or whilst we shine our mental spotlight on one thing, it's not possible to shine it on something else at the same time. So while you are performing, or even prior to your performance, if your spotlight is focusing on the applause at the end of a performance, or on your shaky legs, or your shaky bow hand, or on the really difficult part that you wish you'd practised more, then it's impossible to also focus on the music you are playing, the sounds you are producing, the emotions you want to express.

One of the main reasons visualisation, positive imagery, and positive self-talk works (as you will also read about in Chapters 5 and 8) is because we can only have one image in mind at any one time, we can only have one thought at a time, one focus at a time, and so in the case of positive imagery if you have one positive image that you are focusing on, it's very difficult for the negative images to sneak in.

Unconscious attention

Now, as a musician, you know this isn't altogether completely true! You've probably found yourself many times playing notes, making sounds, expressing musical intentions – doing quite complex tasks, while you were completely fixated on some other part of the music that is coming up, or even playing whole pieces of music or singing a whole song while your mind was thinking about something else entirely and almost without noticing what you were doing.

You can do this because of a second type of attention, known as unconscious attention or divided attention.[5] This is our ability to do two tasks at the same time. But this only works because *one* of the tasks has been *highly practised*, and is something you can do automatically. So, when your mind wanders while you are practising, you'll find you can carry on playing if you have already played this music many times. However, if it's something new to you and your mind wanders, you'll most likely find that you get stuck, or have to stop playing, thereby often bringing your mind instantly back to the notes of the music you are trying to play or the words you are singing. When learning a musical instrument, over time you learnt new things, notes, techniques, that at first you really had to focus on but with repetition they become unconscious. This kind of knowledge is referred to as *implicit* knowledge and the physical know-how of *how* to play an instrument is known as *procedural* knowledge. You have come to know how to do many things that, now, you no longer have to think about in order to do it.

Likewise when you come to learn a new piece of music or a song at first you have to pay attention to what you are doing – at first maybe to the notes of the melody or harmony, the chords, sometimes you have to pay more attention to the rhythm, then phrasing and interpretation, and expression. The learning is *layered* and each aspect of producing the music becomes unconscious with repetition of playing and practising (you'll read more about this in Chapter 8 on memory and memorising).

The point being, with practice, aspects of the task of playing music and performing become unconscious and you find you are then able to focus on other things when you are playing. Sometimes you focus completely on what you are doing as you are doing it, other times you find you are directing your mental spotlight at something other than what you are doing in that moment – how you feel, or your thoughts about upcoming passages, or about your body, your nervousness, or someone in the audience.

Impact of anxiety on focus: 'choking under pressure'

"I went totally blank until the last song … I had no idea what I was doing. And yet we had played these songs a thousand times!".

This unconscious attention, and the ability to carry out skills and tasks that we have practised without even thinking about it, is a wonderful ability until we are in a situation where that doesn't seem to happen and we can't manage to carry out the skills we thought we had practised, or play the music we thought we knew so well. Sometimes in highly pressurised situations people experience not being able to do what they had practised doing or what they are normally able to do.

Sport psychologists have come up with a term for this feeling – 'choking under pressure' is specifically relevant to concentration and how anxiety affects concentration. What happens when we 'choke' is that skills we can normally do, fail when we are under pressure.[6]

This is a phenomenon experienced by all performers at some point and often takes us by complete surprise, because suddenly something we were able to do in our own home or in rehearsal, perhaps even something we took for granted as being easy, fails to work at all when we feel anxious. Of course, this is a scary experience. Anything could happen next, when we're unprepared for this experience.

This may seem like a skill-related problem or a memory problem, but in sport psychology, this is considered to be an *anxiety-based attention* problem. When we become anxious, we start to attend to the 'wrong' thing. Our concentration becomes focused on something that is not the immediate task we are carrying out. Due to anxiety, this 'something' is usually ourselves – our thoughts or feelings or how we feel physically. This is something that can happen to anyone, irrespective of their ability, under certain circumstances, or at a certain stage of their life or stage of musical development. It is not a personality trait, and therefore it is not here to stay with you forever.

Why does 'choking' under pressure happen?

One theory is that when we are nervous, we focus more on ourselves and the importance of the skill than we normally would.[7] We become very aware of what we are doing, how we are doing it and the importance of it *not* going wrong. Suddenly we become very conscious of doing something that we had previously done without even thinking about it. Every action is called into question to the point where you might even think you have no idea what the next note is or how to play it.

Another theory is based on more complex theories of how memory and knowledge processing work. But basically, it suggests that anxiety impairs how well and how fast the brain processes information and memory of information. Whilst anxiety makes us put more effort into our performance, that same effort can take away from the required processes, which leads to inefficient processing of information and skill, and the outcome is a decline in our ability to carry out the desired task.[8]

Whilst this may explain why it happens – what's important to know is that it can happen to anyone and there are strategies that performers use in order to prevent it from happening, or in order to deal with it when or if it does.

Key questions about focus, then, are how is the performer to focus on the task at hand – performing the music, the notes that should be played right now in the moment – when so much else has the potential of taking up our focus and concentration?

How can you focus on producing the music when all you can think about is the mistakes that could maybe, possibly, potentially be made, or the way your body feels like it wants to run away?

What exactly is it that the performer should focus on in order to be able to focus on performing the music? What part of the performance can you focus on that doesn't make you so focused on the fact that you feel sick to your stomach, or that you don't seem to be able to breathe, or that your limbs are shaking so much that you won't be able to hold the instrument, never mind play the music? Or even on the possibility that you are bored playing this music and your mind is wandering.

To answer these questions, this chapter suggests some strategies that musicians use and that sport psychologists have found highly effective. First, though – what is it that distracts musicians?

Typical distractions for musicians

It's a good idea to become aware of the things that typically distract you and the times or situations in which you are more easily distracted. This might seem obvious – because some of you know exactly when and what it is that you are focused on when you should be focused on your own playing. But sometimes and for some people, we're not always aware of what it is that distracts our focus from the music. It's not always nerves that affect our focus. It can also be that you're not that interested in the performance or the music you're playing, you may be bored by it, or not challenged by it, or perhaps you are tired. So, in these situations other factors can easily distract us.

Distractors can be fleeting thoughts or routine occurrences of everyday life, but the most challenging and serious distractors are those that concern the performance itself. Distractors can be external and internal. They can be things that are outside of our control and things that are within our control. Distractors can have a severe impact on our focus during a performance, but also, thinking about possible distractors *prior* to a performance can severely affect our focus in the hours and days before a performance, as well as during the performance (see Table 7.1).

Table 7.1 External and internal distractions

External distractions	Internal distractions
Audience – being there/noise/disruption Co-performers The commercial side of music Venue set up Technical aspects/acoustics Your instrument	Your own thoughts Thinking too far ahead Thinking back to mistakes Analysing/catastrophising Your physiological response 'Playing to the audience' – looking for applause

What distracts the experts?

The most common distractors for expert musicians are nerves, their co-performers, the commercial side of music, the audience, what musicians call 'playing to the audience' and the general pressures of performing.[9]

The audience

> *"The hardest audience is when your peers are there ... maybe even just a couple of them ... and if you know them well and you know who is competitive and who isn't, that is the hardest."*

In music performance, the audience has a huge impact on the level of the challenge perceived by the performer and it can become suddenly distracting. Sometimes the presence of just one significant person can change how we perceive the performance, either negatively or positively and this can affect the thoughts and feelings of even the most experienced performer. The audience member who distracts could be a friend, family, critical significant others, teachers, colleagues, or an examiner or judge.

> *"I did not lose awareness of the audience. It was bad", "When there's a separation between audience and performer ... you're up here and they're down there, there's a distance".*

Being too aware of the audience or a particular person in the audience can make even the experts feel self-conscious and it distracts them from the music. For some performers not feeling connected to the audience distracts them from the music, and at other times the audience can be too close.

> *"It was a very small, intimate venue ... they were right there beside me ... I felt very exposed."*

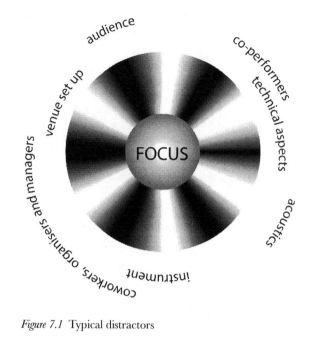

Figure 7.1 Typical distractors

'Playing to the audience'

> "*If you play to the audience then you're starting to get removed from this [flow] state*", "*I love being the centre of attention but you're not going to get in the zone if you're only there for the praise*".

Expert musicians often refer to a difference between playing *for* the audience and playing *to* the audience. The crux of the difference between these two states seems to be that when you want to communicate and express the music and play music *for* the audience there is a different, perhaps more intrinsic feeling for the musician, than when you play *to* the audience. Playing *to* the audience is about performing with the main purpose being to gain praise, to impress, for applause. In this case there may be something superficial or 'staged' about the performance. This would contribute to the difference between playing for intrinsic reasons and playing for extrinsic reasons. (There is more on the topic of motivation in Chapter 6.) Of course (as discussed in Chapter 6), there is always entertainment, maybe staging and drama in a performance, but the underlying reasons for the performance and the underlying focus for the show and the music can still be all about the music, rather than the applause.

> "*The ego becomes very dangerous.*"

Nerves

"You can get the jitters … And it can spread through the ranks."

Nerves are distracting for anyone, even for the experts who have come to know how to deal with how they feel before performing. Sometimes you can be caught off guard by something unexpected – someone in the audience, another player, or by making an unexpected mistake.

"It can be very hard to stomp on the fact that you've made an error … It can eat away at your confidence", "some days you're just fighting yourself".

For the most part, expert musicians welcome feeling nervous and accept it as part of the process of performing, with the knowledge that they perform better when they have some feeling of nervousness. They have become adept at dealing with their nerves, and many also have practised using strategies to manage their emotions prior to performance. But just like anyone else, experts can have days when they have other stuff going on that makes the nerves more difficult to deal with, or they have times when other factors got in the way of preparing for the performance, psychologically, technically or musically.

"You can get a kind of meta-nervousness – you get nervous about being nervous", "any time I haven't dealt with them in advance I've actually been overcome with nerves in the moment".

Co-performers

"If the group isn't playing well that can side-track you."

Other players can be distracting – some days things don't come together as well as other days, and there can be various reasons for this. But musicians find other players a distraction from the music when the attitude and approach of other players to the performance and to the music is different to their own. Just like students, expert musicians sometimes have to play with people who are not their, let's say, 'optimum choice' and it can be difficult to ensure that the music and the meaning of the music are the absolute focus of the performance when this happens.

"They have to love the music you're playing … They have to be the right people, but your duty is to make sure you never play with the wrong people."

Pressures of performing

"It's hard not to want to do well … and the more you want to do well the more self-conscious you become."

Our feelings about a performance differ and alter depending on the purpose of the performance, whether it's for enjoyment, for work, for examination, or competition. Performances that are judged or graded may be difficult to enjoy for the performer, since the primary purpose is not the enjoyment of the music for either the performer or the listener. In this case, the focus is on how well you play, the standard to which you execute the skills of music performance. It can be hard to get really focused on the music when you are distracted by the pressure of being judged.

"It's a strange lifestyle, on your own, in hotel rooms, going into orchestras, just you, on your own."

For expert, professional musicians, the constant performing, constant touring, constant preparing of repertoire for new performances, and often the constant combining of more than one job can be very draining. Experts have to, or should try to, do what they can to take care of their physical and mental health. However, it's not always possible to do this – they are not always performing in the best possible conditions and sometimes they are having to perform without the support of loved ones or without the support of the people who 'should' be supporting them and are even paid to do so, but perhaps have other priorities.

"A lot has to do with playing every night. You cannot deliver every single night."

Of course, when expert musicians say that it's hard to deliver every night, they *are* actually 'delivering' every single night. Because they are professional and hard-working and so good at their job, the audience never notices the fatigue that may have set in or that they are hearing anything less than the best possible performance. Really the only person that is not being 'delivered' to, the person on whom the toll is taken mentally and physically, is the musician themselves. The only person noticing and feeling the difference is the musician.

Being under pressure like this and performing night after night can lead to a feeling of apathy. This is not an optimal condition for focus or for positive experiences of performance.

"Apathy! It's hard to do anything about that. You don't feel like it, so you just kind of play and get through it", "you're playing the same stuff night after night … You'd pull the same trick out of the bag just so you'd get a clap. You know 'here's the high note' kind of thing", "with this boredom thing where you're playing every night the same music and you're improvising in the same places every night and you just get fed up listening to yourself … so in a fit of recklessness you'll do something that in your right mind you might never do … but you think f*** it, I'd rather get lost than listen to the same stuff I was playing last night".

So, it might involve a bit of risk, but sometimes there are solutions to apathy!

The commercial side of music

"Sometimes around venues and promoters there's a lot of tension, and you have to get that out somehow."

These pressures, the fatigue, and the feeling of apathy can come about as a result of the commercial side of music. It's the double-edged side of success and fame. As a musician, you might want to be heard, and want an audience to want to come and hear you play. But with respect, reputation, success, and fame, often there comes a huge responsibility to other people, and all too often there are other people who take control of your professional life.

"You're rushing from gig to gig, no sleep, drinking, bad food, travel, flights, totally exhausted, managers having you travelling through the night to save money ..."

There's also the competition, the other singers or players, waiting to get their chance. For many performers, there are critics, directors, managers, all watching and commenting on the performer's every move. As one singer put it, "word can get around that maybe you didn't feel well one time or something, and you could get a reputation for being unreliable. Coping strategies for stress and pressure in the job of being a performer are so important. In other jobs, when you're done, it doesn't get written about in national papers or international magazines. A performer has to try to please the critic, the theatre boss, the director, the conductor, the audience, not to mention coping with the inner critic. It's a miracle anyone has the guts to get up and perform!"

As if that wasn't enough! There are other factors that can be distracting. There are the technical aspects – acoustics, sound and electrical equipment. There is the set-up – where will you be positioned in relation to the audience or co-performers, to water, music stands, seats, speakers, and so on.

There's responsibility to others. Responsibility to others can mean different things depending on the performer and the performance. In music performance, there is often a feeling of responsibility to the audience and to the composer of the music. There is a strong desire for people to enjoy the music, to communicate with the audience, to convey the meaning of the music, to convey the composers' wishes. There can also be a feeling of responsibility to your co-performers, to parents and family, to teachers and mentors. For professional musicians, there is often the immense responsibility to other people whose salaries depend on their performances – how well they play, whether they draw audiences and then maintaining that audience, how often they perform and where they perform.

*"When we tour in Canada, we can be playing to thousands in a venue, standing ovations, signing autographs. Then we come home, and I'm asked if I want to do some **** gig. So, we have to tour. We have to keep going away. Not only is it nice to have an audience who want to hear you, but we have to pay the bills."*

Internal or external?

Many of these factors are external 'distractors', and are outside of the performer's control most of the time. There is nothing that can be done about them – whether it's irritating co-performers, money-saving managers, or bad venues. What is within your control is how you think about them, how important you perceive them to be, how much time and importance you give to them cognitively and emotionally and the strategies you use to help you cope.

Internal distractions include a vast array of possible thoughts and feelings (see Chapters 4 and 5 for more on this). All can vary in how seriously you perceive them, the importance they have for you, and how deeply they affect your performance and preparation for performance. It is possible to prepare for them. It is possible to use strategies and tips to help cope with the distractions.

To do: strategies for effective focus[10]

Make the decision to concentrate

We do actually have to make the decision to concentrate. It's not going to happen by chance. Your response to that might be that of course you're focused on the performance, that you couldn't think about anything else if you tried. But as I said earlier, you have to be concentrating on the actual thing, the actual task that you are doing as you do it. You may often be focusing on the 'wrong thing', some other aspect that is connected to the performance, but not on the actual doing of the skill that you are doing.

Make the decision to focus on what you are doing as you do it. This might require you to practise that. When you are practising your mind might wander. Start becoming aware of this happening, and practise re-focusing, practise bringing your mind back to where it should be – on the movements you are making, your breathing, the musical expression.

Become aware of what it is that usually distracts you

In practise sessions, start to be aware of what distracts you. Are you distracted by your thoughts? Does your mind wander? Is it other noises or other people that distract you? or do you become distracted by negative thoughts about your playing? Become aware of what it is and then you can practise focusing your mind and your mental spotlight on what you actually want to focus on.

Practise focusing on one thought at a time

Start to practise focusing on one thing at a time. Try not to let other thoughts and distractions interfere with what you have decided to focus on. Sometimes it actually takes pressure to make us do that, the pressure of an upcoming performance. It's amazing how single-minded we can become when we really have to.

Focus on doing exactly what you are thinking

You are really only focused when you are doing exactly what you are thinking, when your thoughts and actions are the same. As you know, you can sometimes play music that you have practised without even thinking about what you are doing.

To do this you may have to focus in on the exact actions, the exact movements your body has to make in order to make the music. Or perhaps you can focus in on the music, hear the music, sing it in your head and focus on that.

To say 'hear the music' might sound obvious, but it can be easy to become so concerned with the technical execution of playing the music that you stop hearing the actual sounds you are making. So focus on the sounds, focus on the music, listen to the sounds you are producing, and even hear them in your head at the same time as playing them.

Focus on factors within your control

Focus on your body, your breathing, the movements you are making, the music you are making. So many other things can distract you that you have no control over – external disruptions, noises, people. Practise focusing on what you have control over, and ignoring what you can't do anything about.

Focus outwards, focus on the sound of the music, when you get nervous

When we are nervous, our thoughts run riot, and our body doesn't necessarily do what we want it to do. So in this situation, you have to actively direct your thoughts outwards, *away from yourself.*[11] Focus on the music, sing the music in your head, listen to the music you are making, feel the emotion or musical intention that you want to express.

You may find it helpful to find someone in the audience who makes you feel good, it may help to make eye contact, smile, move. If you tend to become paralysed or tense when you get nervous, feel the music and move.

Practise re-focusing

Having started to become more aware during your practise sessions of when your mind wanders, start practising to re-focus yourself. Be aware. And direct your thoughts back to the music, back to the movements you are making.

Use trigger cues

When practising music you are going to perform, look for places or passages where you might find it easier to re-focus. Mark these places, on the sheet music or in your mind. Draw smiley faces or focus faces, an emoticon, maybe use a word or an image that might make you smile, or bring you back to the music. Draw them on your music or etch them in your head, imagine them when you come to that spot. Link these trigger cue passages to something that reminds you to bring your mental spotlight back to this passage, back to the music, this moment in time, this bodily feeling.

Get your focus directed where it should be *before* the performance

Get your mental spotlight onto what it should be on prior to the performance. Focus on the music, not on what could go wrong, or who will be in the audience or the applause (or shame!) at the end. The worrier, or analyser, or the diligent musician in you might think it's necessary to go over every possible pitfall before a performance. What many musicians and athletes find useful is to give themselves a cut-off point, after which no more analysing, no more negative thinking is allowed. So do all the negative thinking you have to do up until a certain point. After that, put your focus on the music, on mental practice, on visualisation, on positive self-talk (see Chapters 5 and 8). Hear the music in your head, sing the music in your head, and don't let yourself be distracted by anything that should have ended before the cut-off.

Use imagery, visualisation, and mental practice

So I just mentioned doing visualisation and mental practice. You can read more about this and do the exercises in Chapter 8 that is specifically about mental practice and visualisation. But just to explain briefly, visualise yourself in the venue, in the performance setting. Use positive visualisation to imagine the setting, the audience, your co-performers. Imagine the feelings and thoughts you will have and imagine yourself coping with it, smiling, playing. Go through the motions in your head of starting to play, hear the music as you play it. Imagine yourself playing it as you have practised it, as you want it to sound. Do this from the first person perspective, from inside your own body and mind, not from the perspective of the audience. Mentally practise specific passages or mentally practise from beginning to end if you can or have time to. See yourself playing the notes, making the sounds, be aware of your breathing, feel your body, name the notes inside your head, say the words, make the actions with your fingers, or diaphragm, or lips and mouth.

Using these techniques focuses your mental spotlight on what you have to do, and will help you to ignore any other distracting thoughts or feelings that are trying to get into your conscious thinking.

Use simulation

In sport psychology, simulation is the idea that if you re-create situations that are as close to the performance situation as possible you can train your focus more effectively. It has also been found by researchers to be effective in music performance situations.[12]

This can be done using visualisation techniques, as described above. Make your own dress rehearsal situation. Imagine the setting (see the above paragraphs), imagine how you will feel, summon up all the emotions related to the performance, put on the clothes you will wear, imagine you are in the venue, and perform the music. Even if you have to do it on your own without your co-performer(s). This is a technique that the great violinist Itzhak Perlman has used when he is preparing for performance.[13]

It is also effective if you can get to practise your performance in the venue you are going to be performing in, or find a setting that is similar to the one you will be performing in. There might not be an audience, but you get to do a practise performance in the setting.

Another way of doing this is organising practise performances in front of friends and family. This is an absolute must. Do it as many times as you can make them listen to you! Do it even if you feel you aren't ready. You might find you are pleasantly surprised by how well you play, even when not feeling quite ready, and importantly, it might make you aware of places in the music that need more practise. As I explain in the chapter on memorising – sometimes our kinaesthetic memory (muscle memory) can be prone to letting us down when we become nervous. It takes a practise performance to give us the chance to become aware of those places where our memory is relying on kinaesthetic memory only. So, mistakes in front of friends are a good thing. Try to welcome the opportunity and use it. As musicians often say – 'bad rehearsal, good performance'.

Some coaches (in sport) recommend practising a performance in all sorts of stressful and disruptive situations in order to train concentration. Musicians also do this. In recommending this kind of method, my own violin teacher told me how his teacher in the Menuhin Academy in Switzerland insisted he wake himself in the middle of the night, go out into the snow and play through his concerto(s) in preparation for performances. That might seem extreme, but you get the idea of putting yourself in adverse conditions and practising the performance.

Have a routine

Many musicians and sportspeople recommend having a routine.[14] In sport, this often means a routine of thoughts and actions taken prior to the execution of a skill such as a serve in tennis or penalty shots in football or rugby. Musicians recommend having a routine prior to the performance. Chapter 10 has more on routines and how to put together your own pre-performance routine, but to briefly explain for now, a pre-performance routine tends to involve positive self-talk, visualisation and imagery, mental practice, physical practise, a rest, exercise, dietary preferences, getting ready, getting dressed, mantras, and cut-offs points for anything unhelpful. These are all small parts that make a routine and most importantly help the performer to get focused on the music and on the performance in a positive way.

You can make your own pre-performance routine, one that suits you and your needs. Everyone's routine is different, although they usually constitute at least one and sometimes all of the things I listed above. How many of each of those things are done or how long they are done for varies from one musician to another.

Key tips from this chapter

- We are always focused on something. It might be the wrong thing.
- You can direct your mental spotlight; you are in charge of what you focus on.
- Immerse yourself in the music – all aspects of it, the notes, the fingers, the words, the breathing, the expression, to take yourself out of self-conscious mode.
- There are many possible distractions; they can be internal or external.
- Even the experts get distracted and become focused on something other than the music.
- Accept that this happens and be prepared for distraction.
- Use the strategies to help cope with distractions.
- External distractions are usually not in your control.
- What is in your control is how you think about those distractions, and being prepared – having practised the strategies to help you deal.
- 'Choking' happens. If it has happened to you, you're not alone – it can happen to anyone.
- Practise the strategies.

8 Mental practice, imagery, and visualisation

"I do most of my practice away from the instrument", "I do mental practice … I used to call it 'learning my words while I'm out running' … now it's called 'mental practice'!".

Mental practice is an extremely powerful learning technique. The fastest progress is made when we use mental practice as well as actual physical practising.

When we carry out mental practice or visualisation and imagery, we are using our imagination. Mental practice, visualisation, and imagery can be described as what we do when we use our senses and our imagination to picture an ideal outcome, to create or re-create a real experience.

Research in cognitive neuroscience has shown that mental practice is very similar to actual physical practice.[1] The same regions of the brain are activated when we *imagine* doing an activity, as are activated when we actually do that activity. Even parts of the brain that are involved in controlling physical movement are activated when we *imagine* movement. When we use imagery in mental practice and visualisation, there is neural activation in the brain areas that are involved in sensory, perceptual and emotional information as well as mental processing of cognitive information. Mental practice, or the imagining of movements, is referred to in neuroscience as being 'functionally equivalent' to the actual physical movements. In other words, as far as the brain is concerned, the functions of imagining and doing are very similar. The neural activation that occurs during imagining is equivalent to the actual physical experience, during actual physical practice.[2]

This means that carrying out mental practice is a really effective learning tool. However, when being used as a specific tool for practice and improvement, mental practice is not necessarily a simple task or easy thing to do.

This is mainly because mental practice is knowledge-based – it uses information and knowledge that we already have in order to create the actual experience in our minds. Mental practice does not involve making up information or imagining something that is not real. It is based on our knowledge and therefore it can be quite testing or challenging.

Carrying out mental practice can vary in difficulty for different people. We all differ in our ability to imagine, to see, hear, and feel in our minds and so practice may be required to improve your ability.

How do mental practice and use of imagery and visualisation differ?

Mental practice and visualisation are two different techniques and so they differ in what they involve and how we can use them as effective tools.

> *"I run through it in my head ... what exactly are my fingers doing here."*

Mental practice involves using specific and often complex knowledge about a specific task and using all the senses that are involved in performing that specific task in order to re-create that task. This might be performing a piece of music, or some aspect of technique and can include practising the execution of musical expression and emotion. The senses most involved in musical mental practice are visual, auditory, and kinaesthetic – imagining the physical feel of doing something. Kinaesthetic memory or knowledge is often referred to as muscle memory or muscle knowledge, and this is what you might have heard it called before.

Musicians most often talk about using mental practice to memorise, to test their memory, to practise passages that are technically demanding, and to rehearse the musical or emotional expression. So basically, they use mental practice to practise everything.

> *"I can name every note, every finger", "I would go through the map of the piece in my head", "I practise in my head how I want it to sound, the phrasing, the dynamics".*

Joshua Bell, international soloist said, "To turn around the negativity, I visualise positive scenarios. Sometimes visualising a passage going correctly before it happens can really help".[3]

Using visualisation and imagery involves imagining a scene, the situation that you are going to be in, capturing in your imagination as many of the aspects of that situation as you can, and imagining each of those aspects with a positive outcome. The situation may be one that involves imagining a scene you know well, perhaps a venue you've been in before, with people that you know in the audience and co-players that you've played with before. But more likely, each of those elements will vary – you may be trying to imagine a situation you have little knowledge of, other than the music you are going to play, the people you are playing with and the memory of how you tend to feel in performance situations. Even still, visualisation can work as a strategy for coping.

> *"I imagine what it will be like to be up there", "I knew the venue well, so over and over I visualised myself going on and walking across the stage and being in*

the venue, and I went through it all in my head ... so I suppose there was an affirmation that I'd done it, I was already successful, I'd already sung well and now all I had to do was go through the motions of it", "I go through everything in my head – the preparing backstage, the actual steps to the instrument, you can mentally put yourself through it", "I try to recreate the situation beforehand ... And then I play, as if it's the actual performance".

Expert musicians use visualisation to help them imagine their concert venue and concert experience. They use it in order to imagine positive outcomes, but most often musicians use visualisation to imagine the feelings they will have in relation to a particular venue, performance, and audience, to conjure up all the emotions that they are likely to feel in the real situation and then they either carry out mental practice of the music using the visualisation of the performance venue, or they actually physically practise, using the visualisation of the performance venue and the emotions they expect to feel.

In Chapter 7, I mentioned that Itzhak Perlman is reported to use imagery and visualisation to prepare for performances and have used imagery and visualisation to prepare, and then use his living room to run through the recital programme, imagining the audience of Carnegie Hall.[4]

Mental practice: key factors to remember for effective mental practice

1. The first and possibly most important is that mental practice is carried out from inside your own body, viewed from your own perspective, the first-person perspective. This might sound obvious, but it can be quite easy and not particularly effective to imagine ourselves from a distance, in a venue, possibly on a stage, being 'brilliant'. This is viewing ourselves from a third person perspective, from someone else's point of view. This is a hazy, imagined scenario where yes, you might be viewing and hearing yourself in a very positive image, which is good for positive thinking, but it is not adequate for actual, effective, knowledge-based mental practice and may not be based on the reality of a situation. So mental practice must be carried out from the first-person perspective.

2. Mental practice is knowledge-driven. It is based on the information and knowledge that you have, either in your memory or on a page in front of you; it is not based on pure imagination or pretence.[5]

3. Use all the senses that are involved in the actual execution of the task, of the piece of music, the scale, the technical study.

    For musical mental practice you will most likely be using three senses most of the time – visual, auditory, and kinaesthetic. You might be 'seeing' the music in front of you, seeing your fingers and hands execute the skills, 'hearing' the sound of your playing, and 'feeling' the feel of playing, the breathing, relaxation, and tension of your muscles, the posture in your body. You should also imagine and re-create the emotional expression of the music.

4. Use detailed, vivid, 3D, first person, colour images.[6] Practise seeing, hearing, and feeling as vividly and with as much detail as you possibly can. This will get better and easier the more you do it.

   See, hear, and feel the beginning, middle, and end of every note, phrase and physical movement both musically and technically.

5. Practise! The more you do it the more skilled you will become at feeling, seeing, hearing the music, the imagery, the sensations and emotions associated with the movements. The more skilled you become, the more easily and naturally this will surface when you imagine and when you play.

6. When physically playing, become more aware of the all of the feelings, sounds, sensations, and movements required.

When to use mental practice

Always combine mental practice with physical practising. If this is new to you, start by setting aside five minutes of practise time to try mental practice. Or identify a couple of passages that you could practise mentally, one in which the musical expression is the goal, and one where achieving something more technical is the goal, and start practising your ability to carry out mental practice. You can use it during practise time – combine physical and mental practice.

When you have other free time. It's ideal for waiting time – on a bus, in the car, walking – instead of taking out your phone to use social media or play games, do some mental practice.

During physical practising – use just before executing a skill, a passage, a phrase, a technically challenging passage.

If you have limited practice time, do mental practice anywhere and anytime you get the chance. Keep the sheet music or score or recording nearby so you can check it.

If you're having a bad day for physical practising – everyone has days when they feel physically tired or tense and it's just not going well for you. Whilst it can be good to persevere through these practice sessions, sometimes it's wise to keep it short and mental practice is ideal on these days.

Before going to sleep – before sleep is an ideal time for consolidating memory, checking over what you know, what you remember from your practice session. This is especially so if you are tossing and turning on the nights before a performance or a lesson, or an important rehearsal. Set aside a specific amount of time and do some work in your head, some mental practice. Then knowing that it's done, this will also aid your ability to sleep.

What to use mental practice on

Mental practice can be used for practising:

- Technical skills and passages that are technically challenging.
- Expressive aspects of a piece of music.

- Memorising – memorising the notes of the music, expression, counting, rhythm (see the following section on memorising).
- Coping with the emotions you might feel during an actual performance – for this you might combine the use of visualisation and mental practice, as I will explain below in the section on visualisation.

Memory

Mental practice really challenges our memory and knowledge of a piece of music. Whether you are practising technical aspects, expressive aspects or memorising notes/chords/switches/words, your memory of the knowledge of the music is being used. So perhaps it is helpful to know a little more about memory and the types of memory involved in music performance.

Classical music, some jazz music, some pop music, and some traditional music is learnt from a score. Often this means that the music score has to be known from memory and performed from memory. Even music that has been learnt by ear or has been composed or improvised and has been learnt organically, cognitively, and kinaesthetically over time by the musician, has to be memorised and reproduced from our memory.

This takes time, and often happens naturally over time, when learning a piece or a song without the player even realising that it is happening. Players sometimes use repetition to learn from memory, then testing their memory by playing through. A lot of this work can be done mentally, away from the instrument itself. It is particularly important to check and consciously commit the music fully to memory using mental practice.

How memory works

It is currently assumed by psychologists and neuroscientists that there are three different memory stores in the brain – the sensory memory store, the short-term working memory, and the long-term memory store.[7] The sensory memory store is the first store where all information goes and is held only for a short time. Most of the information that comes through our senses is forgotten within seconds. If the sensory information is attended to by us, it is then transferred into our short-term working memory store. The short-term memory store holds information that we are currently using in our day to day life, interactions, experiences. We work out money transactions, remember lists, phone numbers, email addresses, carry out conversations, make plans. It is information that we are 'working on' in the present, hence the name 'working memory'. Sometimes the information being worked on is new information, sometimes it is information that has been pulled from the long-term memory store. In order for information to be transferred to the long-term store, it must be used, repeatedly used, worked on, and committed to long-term storage. This information can be taken back into the short-term store and used from time to time whenever it's needed, but if not used for a long time the knowledge degrades, disintegrates, the neural networks linking that information gradually fade away.

There are two overall types of knowledge stored in memory. These are called declarative knowledge and procedural knowledge.[8]

Procedural knowledge is the 'how to' knowledge of *how* to carry out an action, or function. In music, procedural knowledge includes the actual *how* to make the sounds, perform the notes, the chords, the expressive instructions, the rhythm. Procedural knowledge underlies your ability to physically play the music. It includes the co-ordination of the physical movements needed to produce the music and comes about as a result of repetition of physical movements over days, weeks, years.

Declarative knowledge is knowledge of rules, structures, plans – it is the knowing *that* or *why* something is what it is. It is the knowledge of understanding. So, in music, the declarative knowledge would include knowledge of musical rules of harmony, notes, keys, chord patterns, expressive instructions, rhythm, sequences of notes, patterns, and sequences of movements that are necessary to execute a particular passage, expressive intent or to produce a particular sound.

Musicians use both types of knowledge stored in long-term memory. But there are often times when a musician, usually a young or less experienced musician, does what they do without knowing how they do what they do, particularly in relation to the physical co-ordination that brings about particular skills, sounds, or expression. This means that they have procedural knowledge without having the declarative knowledge to back it up. Procedural knowledge is based on kinaesthetic memory, the type of memory that is most likely to break down in music performance.

Apart from these two main types of knowledge, knowledge and memory has also been categorised in other terms. There are five common types of knowledge relevant to music performance, all stored in the long-term memory, but used or worked on in the short-term working memory whenever required.

Kinaesthetic memory

The physical playing of a piece of music, a song, or a sequence of notes in a melody or harmony is usually transferred into memory using *kinaesthetic* memory. This is often referred to as muscle memory. Through repetition and over time, the physical act of playing the music becomes automatic, the knowledge of how to do it stored using kinaesthetic memory.

This can't be done in the first place, without using auditory knowledge, and/or visual knowledge, and conceptual knowledge.

Visual

We use visual knowledge and memory of notated music on a page or screen. We also have a visual knowledge of how it looks when we play a physical instrument outside of our body, watching our fingers, or arms, or body reach for notes and chords, create expressiveness, produce the sound.

Auditory

We have an auditory memory of the sounds we created and also of sounds we imagined and wish to create. We use auditory memory also when we remember how we heard the music created or produced by someone else.

Conceptual

Conceptual memory is our knowledge of the structure of the music, our analysis of the music – whether we know we've done it or not, knowledge of structural sections, key changes, important features, important expressive moments, the names of notes, dynamic instructions. Basically – the rules.

Episodic

We also use episodic knowledge when playing music – that is the associations we have given to the music that might be emotional or sentimental. We use this kind of memory when we express emotions through the music or communicate emotion and expression to others.

The brain stores mental representations (a type of image) of all our knowledge and because of the brain's ability to store mental representations we have a huge capacity for storing knowledge in memory. An entire song or piece of music is represented mentally as a whole, but also, every note, movement, sound, feeling, and sequence of actions has a corresponding representation in the brain.

Use all types of memory

Since all these types of knowledge and memory are used in music performance, it is important to be aware of them and to use all of them to your advantage. The more the music is played and rehearsed kinaesthetically, visually, and aurally, and even conceptually, the better and stronger the mental representations will be and the more committed to long-term memory they will be. This makes it easier for your brain to use the information and to shift seamlessly from one type of knowledge to another. The more you do it the faster, more efficient, and more agile the brain becomes.

This might seem obvious, but often we rely on only one type of memory. Kinaesthetic memory (or muscle memory) is the one most relied upon by students, particularly young and less experienced students. This is because as we learn a song or piece of music, we gradually come to know it and it becomes automatic – the movements, the sounds, the rhythm. We get to a point where we can play through a piece from beginning to end without having to look at the music score or listen to it. Young musicians tend to think this means the music is learnt, it is known, it is memorised.

However, when we go to perform, often there are breakdowns in memory, even when we were sure we knew it so well. When under pressure, kinaesthetic memory is the most prone to breakdown of all the memory types. This is because when we get nervous, we become alert and focused. When we get very nervous, we become hyper-alert and suddenly every move we make, every note we have to play comes under intense scrutiny, our own scrutiny, and so every note and every movement must be very clearly known in another format than kinaesthetic memory.

What was an automatic process, learnt, and remembered kinaesthetically, in our muscles, comes into our consciousness and we become very aware of it. What previously had been something we could do easily without even thinking about it, immersed totally in the music when standing in our own practice room, now with nerves and hyper-alertness becomes something we are highly aware of, aware of what we are doing and how we are doing it. It is no longer easy because our mind, our very conscious and alert mind, can start to question everything we are about to do, every (once-automatic) movement your muscles are about to make.

After an experience like that, musicians often report that they had no idea what was coming next, what the next note was even, or if they were playing it the right way, the right length, with the right finger. When playing in a group or when improvising, one can easily start to question every aspect of playing – "how long is my bit, how many times am I to play this section, when is my solo". A singer might forget the words or question when to come in or when to harmonise or improvise.

> "We went on stage, the audience was right beside me, able to touch me if they'd
> wanted to and I wasn't expecting that ... I went totally blank until the last
> song ... I had no idea what I was doing. And yet we had played these songs a
> thousand times!"

Sometimes musicians report forgetting or making errors in the 'easy bit', the part they thought they knew so well they didn't need to practise it. But this 'easy' part, having been practised the least and thought about the least because it was easy, means that all memory types were less used than when the 'harder' parts were practised. The easy part wasn't broken down into different aspects, no trial and error on ways to play it, no rote repetition over days and at the last minute, and in general was less analysed in various ways by the conscious processing mind.

Sport psychologists call this 'choking' (see Chapter 7). So when we get nervous and we become highly alert to our actions and those around us, we cannot rely completely on the automatic nature of kinaesthetic memory. We need to check on all our memory types, use all the types of knowledge we have stored, use all forms of knowledge to our advantage when preparing for performance. Use auditory memory, conceptual memory, visual memory, and kinaesthetic memory.

Rehearsal, or practice can be done physically with the instrument and it can also be done mentally, away from the instrument. Memorising is most effectively and efficiently done when both types of practise are carried out.

Simon Fischer, violinist, teacher, and author said, "Once you can visualise an entire piece note-by-note, without hesitation, you will never worry about your memory when playing that piece".[9]

Mental practice is the key to memorising and checking your memory effectively. Through mental practice, you take all the knowledge that has become automatic in the learning process and check that you can remember every note. By using mental practice you get to take all the knowledge you have learnt back out of unconscious and automatic processing and bring it into full conscious awareness in order to check that you really know it. "The places in your mental rehearsal where you hesitate, wondering what the next notes, bowings or fingerings might be, are the points at which you are most likely to have memory slips" (Simon Fischer, 2017).[10]

Doing this means that you are much less likely to question yourself in that moment of feeling highly alert and conscious of every aspect of your playing in the middle of a performance. Even if you do, you will know that you know it well and will feel confident that you can get through it.

By practising using all memory types and using mental practice as well as physical practise, you become faster and more efficient at bringing information, knowledge that you've stored during your hours of practise from long-term memory into working memory. You will become better and faster at accessing notes, sequences, melodies, patterns, rhythms, dynamics, expressive features, phrasing in your long-term memory, and using them in short-term working memory. The brain's role in performing is a processing system that has many parts working together, all of which can be used to help you perform better, memorise better, and ultimately make you better prepared and feel more confident.

Keys to memorising

- Use four types of memory, all the time, consistently – kinaesthetic, visual, auditory, conceptual.
- Get to know which is your strongest and capitalise on it. Although most young players rely on kinaesthetic memory, everyone is different and you might find that remembering the look of the music on the page is something you're really good at. Or you might find that when you focus on hearing the music in your head, that this is where your strength lies. Actually we all tend to be a bit overly focused on our visual sense. Hearing the music in your head – for practise purposes is the key to mental practice. But also hearing the music in your head whilst you play, singing along with yourself as you play, is a really good strategy for taking focus away from the feeling of nerves and to help focus your attention on the music.
- Use mental practice. Mental practice is *the* key to memorising music. When you use mental practice, there is no physical playing and so you are not able to fall back on the kinaesthetic memory. In order to mentally practise the physical, you really have to know the music – the notes, the movements and physical coordination necessary to make the notes.

Read the section above on mental practice, and the following tips for memorizing, which all make use of mental practice.

- Make time in your daily routine for memorising and for mental practice. Don't just expect it to happen with physical practice. Make time and set goals for your mental practice time.

Auditory memorising

- Be able to sing (in your head) from beginning to end with no interruptions, no break downs.
- Sing the harmonies, the other parts, important accompanying motifs.
- Know the part of the other player, when you are not playing. Don't just rely on counting. Be able to sing it, in your head.

Conceptual memorising

- Know the structure of the piece or song. This might seem obvious, but you need to check that when you are not looking at the music, or playing the music, or listening to your co-players or accompanist, that you know the structure, so that you are not second-guessing yourself when you become nervous.
- Analyse the music. This doesn't have to be complicated – just make sure you know the important melodies, key changes, time changes, rhythmic patterns, section boundaries, chord progressions, mood changes, any important structural features.
- Make mental notes of and know all the chords and switches.
- Whilst imagining yourself playing – be able to name every note as you play (mentally, without the instrument) and be able to name or number every finger. Know every bow change and style, every breath, position shift, any patterns (depending on your instrument).

Kinaesthetic memorising

- Be able to imagine playing the music, all the notes without the instrument from beginning to end.
- Imagine or mime.
- You can physically play out without the instrument, or you can just imagine physically playing each note.
- Know the feeling of every note, every breath, every bow, every chord, every phrase or passage, every dynamic, all expressive interpretations.

Visual memorising

- Make an image in your mind of the layout of the page.
- Try to see each page in your mind's eye.

- Note the position of important structural features and changes.
- Note the beginnings and ends of sections, rests, changes of keys/times/dynamics/mood.

Checking

- When you start doing this, you will forget notes, chords, words. There will be whole sections even that you don't know well enough to mentally practise.
- Have the music score, directions, or a recording of it nearby, so that when you come to a point where you can't remember something, the next note, position, a breath, bow, switch, or finger, you can check.
- It is really important not to ignore this bit that you don't know. Don't just carry on, or distract yourself by doing something else.
- When you are practising mentally – the thing you can't remember, or the place where you forget is a weak spot. This must be checked and practised mentally. Practise in your head. Go back over this bit. Repeat. In your head. You can practise it physically also.
- Combine mental practice with physical practising, particularly in the early days of mental practice. When you can't play something mentally, and you go to your instrument to actually physically play it, you will go to it with a whole different or new awareness and focus on the detail of what you are playing and what you need to do in order to play the music.

Does this seem excessive? Maybe. But it is what experts do when preparing to perform. If they feel the need to do it, then you should do it too.

What you are doing, as described earlier, is bringing musical knowledge, that you have come to play automatically, back into your conscious awareness. This is information that has become so automatic for you that you are no longer conscious of doing it or even knowing it anymore.

In order to be totally prepared for the highly conscious or self-conscious state of performing, you need to check on the music and notes that you have come to play unconsciously and automatically. Because sometimes in a self-conscious state of performance, what was once automatic, comes into full conscious awareness.

When you start to carry out this kind of memorising and mental practice, it can take a long time. It can even seem like quite hard work. As you get more practised at doing it, it becomes easier and faster. Also, with each piece of music, depending on how complex it is for you, it can be slow when you start but by the time the performance comes about, you can do it more efficiently and faster.

One musician said that when he first starts to mentally memorise a piece it can take hours to go through it, but by the time the performance is nearing, he can go through it very quickly and easily. So, don't shy away from doing mental practice because it is hard at first. Keep doing it. Keep practising it. You'll get better at it and ultimately, once you can do it, you will be extremely confident about how well you know your music.

To do: mental practice exercise 1

This is a mental practice exercise of a major scale as an initial exercise and example of how mental practice can be employed to practice scales, but similar exercises can also be employed with studies and pieces.

Start with a scale, let's take the scale of B major. Read through the guide below. You can start to imagine playing the notes as you read, but read it once or twice through before trying to do the mental practice on your own.

I'm going to name the notes of the first octave and then you can continue on your own. Try to imagine playing the scale the way you would usually play the scale, so three octaves or three and a half, or four, whatever it is that you usually play.

The tempo is really slow to start with. Imagine playing a minim for each note for the first time you play the scale in your head. As you read you will find that the tempo gradually increases on each mental playing of the whole scale. Go at your own speed, take your time and when you descend the scale just play a long note and start the scale again. Then you are going to repeat the scale over a few times.

So close your eyes if you like, and imagine that you have your instrument in your hands and that you're about to start playing minims ... B ... C# ... D# ... E ...F# ... G# ... A# ... B ... continue on up the scale .... Long minims slowly ... you can hear every note that you are playing ... You can feel your fingers playing each and every note ... Imagine the feel of the instrument ... Hear the notes ... the fingerings that you need to use ... anywhere you may have any difficulty just go over the few notes a couple of times if you like ... be sure of every note you play ... Picture the notes if you like on a page in front of you ... hear the sound you are making ... the tuning of each note ... Imagine playing every note correctly ... with a clear sound ... knowing exactly what your fingers are doing ... Everything is very steady ... your breathing is steady and calm ... your body feels relaxed and comfortable ... Your shoulders are free ... you're making a nice, even, smooth sound ... if you're using vibrato it's nice and even and free ... your arms feel heavy and your shoulders are free ... Just relax into the notes ... and the next time you come back down to the bottom of the scale, in your own time, you're going to increase the tempo to play crotchets and you're going to slur two crotchets at a time ... so we're moving the tempo forward to double speed but it's still quite slow ... you're still feeling every finger playing every note ... Evenly ... smooth ... relaxed ... you're making a beautiful sound ... you can say the name of the notes as you play ... your posture is straight and relaxed ... feel every note ... hear every note ... every note in tune ... sounding exactly how you would want it to sound ... seeing yourself playing ... your breathing is relaxed .... Your muscles are soft and relaxed ... all your energy is going into playing every note smoothly and evenly ... Put a little emphasis on the first of every two notes ... see the music on an imaginary page in front of you ... so you can almost see the music ... you're playing every note in tune ... your tone is even ... your embouchure is stable ... your fingers are playing every note evenly and precisely but relaxed and free ....

The next time you come down to the bottom of the scale, again in your own time, you're going to increase the tempo again to four quavers to each slur, so you're playing double tempo again ... Put a little emphasis on the first of every four notes ... and start hearing yourself crescendo as you go to the top of the scale and decrescendo as you descend the scale again ... your shoulders and neck are relaxed ... Your arms feel heavy ... the little emphasis on the first of every four notes makes an almost lilting feel to the scale ... the notes are ringing out exactly as you would want them to be played ... your tuning is precise ... your sound is beautiful, even ... you can see the notes on the stave on the music ... your vibrato is free and even ... you can see and hear yourself playing each and every note ... your breathing is relaxed ... your rhythm is even ....

The next time you come down to the bottom of the scale you're going to increase the tempo again to eight semiquavers to every slur, so double the tempo again ... the scale is really flowing now ... one note flowing beautifully into the next ... hear yourself, imagine yourself crescendo-ing to the top of the scale and decrescendo as you come back down the scale ... a little emphasis on the first of every eight notes, the first note of each slur ... everything, your muscles are soft and relaxed ... your shoulders are relaxed ... you're feeling confident and playing exactly as you would want it to sound ... your tuning is precise ... imagine your fingers are moving easily and fluidly ... your sound is beautiful ... the notes are ringing out ... even ... smooth ... Fluid ... ease ... The next time you come to the bottom of the scale, you're going to end the scale, play a long note and finish ....

Now you can increase that tempo again when you are practising on your own .... until you are playing the notes as fast as you can play, comfortably but pushing yourself a little out of your comfort zone of tempo.

Having done that, now go to your instrument and do exactly the same exercise only this time physically play the scale. How was it? You may be surprised at how well you play it. There may be parts that need more mental practice, or perhaps as the tempo increases it became more difficult. Go back and repeat the mental practice of the exercise. Or take the tempo you found difficult to physically play and mentally practise again at that tempo.

Some people like to do this exercise with the metronome, so you can set the tempo for each increase of speed. Try another scale or exercise. Perhaps adapt it – so that it is similar to the above exercise here, but you are practising it in the style in which scales are generally practised by you, for your instrument.

To do: mental practice exercise 2

Take a passage, piece, song, or solo that you have been working on. Start to play through it mentally. Can you hear the notes? Probably. Can you see your fingers playing the notes? Hold a mental image of this. You can move your fingers as you do this. Can you name the notes or the chords as you play them? Can you hear yourself sing the words? How far do you get in the song or piece before you are unsure of a note, a fingering, a word? Check your score, sheet music or recording for notes, chords or words. It might be helpful to go to your instrument for help, there might be a muscle memory there that can jolt your memory. But don't stop mental practice at that point. Carry on mentally practising. Repeat the bit you hadn't been able to remember, a few times. And keep going. Work your way through the passage or song. Always use the sheet music or instrument to help you, but always return to the mental practice. This might be a slow process at first, but you will find it really effective for learning and remembering.

This kind of practise is really suitable for note learning or memorising. When you can mentally practise the notes, you can add mentally practising how you want it to feel, how you want it to sound and the creative ideas you want to express.

When imagining yourself playing the notes, imagine that you are playing exactly as you want to, your body relaxed, your hands and arms in just the ideal position for executing great technique and also great sound and expression. Your posture is just how you want it to be, your fingers are just the right feel, your mouth and throat are moist and relaxed, your lips feel just right, your breathing is relaxed and consistent, your diaphragm is supporting your voice as you need it to. Whatever it is that your instrument requires, you imagine doing it and feeling just exactly the way you want to.

After mental practice, physically play the music using your instrument. It doesn't have to be immediately, but the same day preferably.

To do: a visualisation and imagery exercise

Part 1

Imagine the challenging situation that you are going to be in. The venue, the people in the audience, your co-performers. Imagine the waiting area, backstage. Imagine getting ready. Try to imagine and conjure up the emotions that you will experience at each of the moments – arriving, waiting, taking out your instrument, preparing, warming up. Imagine your final preparations of getting dressed, or checking you feel comfortable. Imagine your breathing exercises, even do a breathing exercise.

Imagine what your thoughts will be about the performance. Try to imagine all the thoughts you would have in that situation and feel every emotion that you might have. Conjure up the emotions. Create the experience of waiting in your head. Feel all the emotions. Let yourself feel all of it.

Picture yourself walking into the room, the concert room, the exam room, the recital hall, or onto the stage. See the people, faces that might be in the audience, imagine the smell, hear the sound of the room, the welcome, whatever form that might take. Try to imagine every step of the walk. Use as much detail, and vivid imagery as you can. Imagine the thoughts you might be having at that time. Imagine greeting your audience, your co-players or any communications that might occur between you and any other people in the room or venue. Imagine the emotions you might be feeling as vividly as you can feel them. For some, conjuring up these emotions can be easily done, for others it is harder.

This can all be done as slowly as you like, taking time and with as much detail as you can. Really try to put yourself through all the thoughts and emotions that are possible for you to have in the performance situation.

Part 2

There are two options.

1. Either pick up your instrument or prepare to sing, and play or sing through your programme of music
2. Or, now carry out a mental performance, having summoned all the emotions that you might feel in the performance situation, mentally sing or play through your music, beginning to end.

So you either play or sing through your programme for real and you have the experience of performing whilst coping with and managing some of the emotions you might feel in the real situation.

Or you can imagine what it would be like to perform, do a full mental rehearsal of the performance, whilst having summoned up all the emotions that you might feel in the real situation. Now you can mentally test your knowledge and your memory of the music you are going to play or sing. This puts your mental practice to the test and gives you the opportunity to imagine, think, and feel through how you might perform in this condition of feeling the anxiety and excitement of the performance situation.

Perform from beginning to end of your programme of music, whether you are doing it physically or mentally. In fact, do this on more than one occasion; do it as often as possible.

I cannot stress enough how highly effective this is for the practice of settling yourself, managing the emotions, and practising playing with all the emotions that you might feel.

Key tips from this chapter

- Mental practice differs from visualisation and imagery.
- Mental practice is a highly efficient and effective way to practise.
- When we imagine playing or singing, what happens in the brain is very similar to what happens in the brain when you actually play or sing; that is why it works.
- Be able to mentally play or sing through all music you're are going to perform before a performance. If you really know it, you will be able to do this. If you don't really know, this will highlight the notes, sections or the words, that you don't know well enough.
- Do mental practice! Every day.
- Mental practice helps block out other negative thoughts, it focuses your mind on the music and when you do it, it gives you supreme confidence in your preparation.
- Using visualisation and imagery is a brilliant technique for practising how you will feel and practising coping with those feelings in a performance situation.
- Using visualisation and imagery helps you imagine and feel all the emotions, feelings and even physiological sensations that are involved prior to performance.
- Mental practice and visualisation should be done from the first-person perspective, not as though you are watching or hearing yourself from the audience perspective.
- Use all of the types of memory when preparing for performance. Kinaesthetic memory (muscle memory) is the most prone to breakdown – don't rely on it alone.

9 Calming the body and mind

"I do some yoga breathing exercises that is like very fast in and out breathing with the diaphragm. Very fast. And then it just gives this rush of oxygen to the brain, and you feel after that that you don't have to breathe for a while", "I do breathing and a small bit of yoga. A bit of positive thinking and singing".

One of the many, many things that stood out to me when I interviewed musicians was how useful breathing exercises are to singers, wind players and brass players of all genres of music. When I talked to musicians about their routines before performances, and about things they like to do in the hours before a performance, all singers, wind players, and brass players talked about doing breathing exercises as part of their preparation process. For some it was a regular part of physical preparation that was done almost without thinking about it; others were quite meticulous about doing it and focused on it as an important part of both physical and psychological preparation. It was clear either way that taking care of their breathing was extremely important to experts who use their breath to produce music.

It was quite noticeable how rarely breathing was mentioned by string players and keyboard players. Singers, wind players, and brass players all find breathing exercises really useful, not just in preparing for how they would actually produce the sounds they would make in their music, but in preparing for performance psychologically and physically.

In comparison, string players and keyboard players could learn something really important from this. Although their sound and their music is not produced by breath, breathing is still (obviously) a basic requirement for being able to produce the music, and it is fundamental to relaxation in the body and muscles, to pacing oneself, and calming the mind and body in preparation for producing sound using their breath.

There are many ways of taking care of breathing and muscle relaxation that are also very effective. Musicians spoke about various kinds of exercise, and various ways of calming the body or managing their breathing, for example, walking, yoga, running, meditation, mindfulness meditation, the Alexander Technique, and osteopathic treatment ... whatever form of management that appealed to the individual.

But musicians and music students are busy people, and many don't have time to join classes or take lessons that would benefit their breathing and calm their body. Maybe it's the same for you.

So, in this chapter, I want to discuss some techniques that you can do on your own, in your own time, anywhere. This chapter will show you how to do various breathing exercises, a progressive muscle relaxation exercise, and a mindfulness meditation exercise.

You can try these techniques and experiment with them. Try to incorporate at least one into your daily life. As with the other management techniques in this book, the more routinely you do the exercises, the more benefit they will be. A one-off breathing exercise can be helpful on the day of a performance, but its impact will be so much more effective if you have practised the exercise before the day of a performance, and the more you practise the more benefit it will be.

Just a little small-print reminder here – these techniques are very effective for those who have practised and prepared their music technically and musically. No amount of breathing and muscle relaxing is going to wave a magic wand over lack of preparation and practice.

Breathing

Regulated, controlled breathing has hugely beneficial effects on the body and mind. It's an age-old idea, but there is now a considerable amount of evidence backing common sense knowledge that regulated breathing helps calm the body. Research is showing that self-regulation of breathing can have highly beneficial effects on the nervous system, effects that calm the body and mind.

In the last twenty years in particular, research from neuroscience, psychology, physiology, and medicine has uncovered a complex network of activity in the brain and body involving hormones, neurons, neurotransmitters, the vagus nerve, the hypothalamus, the pituitary gland, the thalamus, the amygdala, the frontal cortex, all intricately contributing to the workings of the autonomic nervous system and the fight or flight system.[1]

What researchers are finding, time and again, is that self-regulated breathing, diaphragmatic breathing specifically, has a direct and significant impact on this complex system with outcomes that include significant effects on anxiety, stress, depression, post-traumatic stress disorder, pain, blood pressure, seizure conditions, and you'll be happy to know ... on performance enhancement.[2]

How breathing impacts on the fight or flight system

The autonomic nervous system is part of the nervous system and it incorporates the sympathetic nervous system and the parasympathetic nervous system (see Figure 9.1). The sympathetic nervous system is responsible for preparing us to act when we perceive threat, danger, and stressful situations. The parasympathetic nervous system is responsible for relaxing the body following threat and stress.[3]

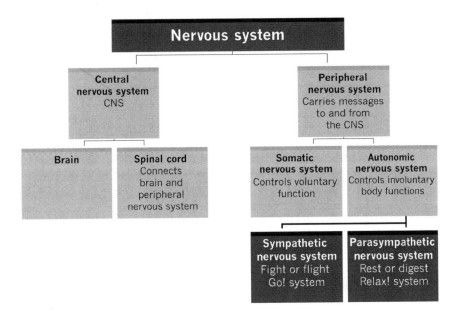

Figure 9.1 The nervous system

The sympathetic nervous system involves a system of neurotransmitters, hormones, and information processing that gets the body ready to either fight or flee. It makes us more alert, more energetic, increases heart rate, blood pressure, and breathing. The eyes dilate, activity is inhibited in the bladder and bowels, the muscles tense, the heart beats faster – we are ready to act.

The parasympathetic nervous system restores and nourishes the body following threat, danger, or stress. The muscles relax, the intestines start to work again, the heart rate slows, the glands are activated again (see Figure 9.2), and the body is restored to a relaxed state and replenished.

The two systems are sometimes referred to as the Go! (sympathetic nervous system) and Relax! (parasympathetic nervous system) systems. They work together to preserve homeostasis in the body. In times of danger or stress, they work together to prepare us to act and then recover us afterwards.

During persistent stress over long periods of time, the Go! system is constantly active and the body is in a constant state of hyperarousal. This can have detrimental effects on our health and wellbeing in general.

The parasympathetic system, the Relax! system, can decrease stress and anxiety, but will only do so if the brain perceives that stress and threat is over, or if we 'trick' it into thinking that the threat is gone. This means that with the right strategies, even when your body is being told by the brain to get ready for threat, you can harness the Relax! system in order to lessen levels of anxiety and stress.

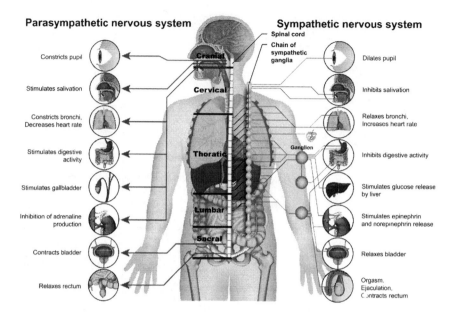

Figure 9.2 The bodily functions affected by the sympathetic and the parasympathetic nervous system

The stress you feel activates the autonomic nervous system, it works without your voluntary control – so you could almost think that it has a mind of its own. The Go! system makes you sweat, shake, dry, and tense just when you don't want it to during performance. This involuntary nervous system reacts in response to your brain's perception of threat. Conversely, once your brain perceives the threat to have gone away, the Relax! system restores calmness and relaxation. Your muscles relax, the heart rate decreases, breathing slows, and other bodily functions are restored. You can learn ways, strategies or tricks to encourage the Relax! system to calm everything down.

One of those tricks is diaphragmatic breathing. It's not just that taking a few moments of calm and quiet to breathe deeply will decrease your heart rate, relax your muscles, give your body and mind time and space to quieten a little. It is also because diaphragmatic breathing directly activates the Relax! system of the autonomic nervous system.

Activating the vagus nerve and the Relax! system

It is currently thought that diaphragmatic breathing directly impacts on the fight or flight system via the vagus nerve.

Diaphragmatic breathing activates the vagus nerve.[1] The vagus nerve activates the Relax! system and because it is connected to many organs of the body it causes a widespread calming of body functions.[5] This activation of the Relax! system, the calming of the body and bodily functions then results in messages being sent to and from the brain, via the vagus nerve, allowing the body to relax and the perception of threat to decrease. So, diaphragmatic breathing actually leads to widespread calming of the body and reduction of the sense of threat.

The vagus nerve is a long nerve that 'wanders' through the body, connecting various organs (see Figure 9.3) – the throat muscles, the heart, lungs, stomach, liver, and intestines – with the brain (specifically the *locus coeruleus* in the brain stem). Messages about all sensory and motor information are conveyed via the vagus nerve from the organs of the body to the brain and from the brain to the body.

Where the vagus nerve meets the brain stem, connections then project to other parts of the brain conveying information about the state of the body. Some of those brain areas include the hypothalamus (a very small but crucial centre that regulates feeding, fighting, fleeing, and mating), the thalamus (the central relay station for all sensory information), the amygdala (the source of

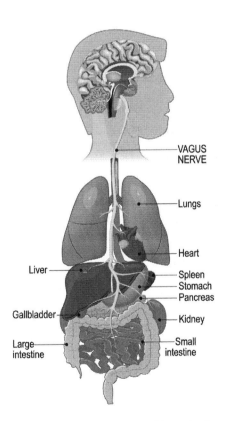

Figure 9.3 The vagus nerve and its projections to the body and brain

fear and other emotions), the hippocampus (a central location for learning and memory), the frontal cortex (where all your cognitive processing of information occurs – your perception of threat, problem solving, decision making, analysing, social functioning), the somatosensory cortex (centre for processing all sensory information), and the motor cortex (where movement is controlled and produced).[6]

Numerous studies have shown that diaphragmatic breathing enhances vagal nerve activity, which directly sets the Relax! system in motion and thereby decreases the response of the sympathetic nervous system, the Go! system. The vagus nerve is directly involved in calming the fight or flight system.

The messages sent back to the brain via the vagus about how the body is responding and coping subsequently impact on your perception of the threat, your decisions about what to do, the emotions you feel, your coping, your analysis of the situation, how you behave and the quality of your motor action and co-ordination. Because it connects so many areas of the body and brain, activation of the vagus nerve can lead to widespread inhibition of the fight or flight system, thereby decreasing all the symptoms of the fight or flight response, and reducing all symptoms of panic and anxiety.

How to do diaphragmatic breathing

When we breathe normally, we tend to breathe at different rates within a minute, and those rates speed up and slow down. Frequency of breathing rate can vary as much as from nine to twenty-four breaths per minute; although it probably is more likely to be between nine and fourteen breaths per minute for most people most of the time.[7]

With diaphragmatic breathing, you can reduce the rate of breathing and you can reduce the variability. This reduces the dominance of the Go! system during times of stress or performance anxiety and enhances the dominance of the Relax! system.

Diaphragmatic breathing is slow, deep breathing and there are a number of breathing exercises recommended in the research and in the mainstream media. You can try all or as many as you like, experiment a bit and I would say, find which works best for you.

Some experts recommend breathing in through the nose and out through the mouth, others recommend breathing in through the mouth and out through the mouth. Some recommend breathing in through one nostril and then breathing out through the other nostril, closing each alternate nostril with finger and thumb.

Do whatever is comfortable for you; it is the slow, deep, regulated breathing that has the desired impact on your nervous system.

It is helpful to imagine that there are three sections to the lungs during breath inhale and exhale – upper lungs, mid lungs, and lower lungs. Make sure to breathe to the lower lungs, you should see your stomach rise on inhalation. Imagine the lower lungs filling up first. Some experts recommend that you imagine oxygen filling the lower torso, the chest, and spreading up to the brain.

To do: slow, deep breathing

Breathe slowly in through your nose. Imagine filling your entire lungs from the bottom up until you can't fit any more air. Then breathe out slowly through your mouth. Do this five times, or spend about 60 seconds doing it. With your hand on your tummy, notice your lungs and tummy pushing outwards. Breathe in 'calm', breathe out 'stress', breathe in positive thoughts, breathe out negative thoughts. You can add a positive affirmation.

Not very difficult, was it? You could probably easily spend more time doing this. But if you start with one minute, and repeat it several times a day, that would be greatly beneficial to your Relax! system. Doing one minute of these deep breaths several times a day, is quick, easy and quite manageable for the novice self-regulating breather. You can do this any time anywhere.

Sudarshan Kriya Yoga breathing or SKY technique

Sudarshan Kriya Yoga (SKY) breathing is another technique for which there is evidence of its extremely positive effects on the Relax! system and negative emotional states, particularly anxiety.[8] It differs from other breathing techniques because it combines cycles of slow breathing with cycles of fast inhale and exhale of breath. Just like other breathing exercises, the slow breathing cycle activates the vagus nerve and the Relax! system, but in this technique, the fast cycles of breathing activate a mild response from the Go! system, that seems to provide energy and boosts tolerance of stress. This is similar to some breathing techniques that are popular in mainstream media that recommend fast breathing cycles for stress tolerance. However, the positive effects of this SKY technique on negative emotional states have been verified by research, whereas others may not have been validated, as yet.

To do: SKY breathing technique

The SKY technique involves alternating cycles of slow deep, breathing and fast, deep breathing.

Take six slow, deep breaths filling the lungs, in and out. Breathe in through the nose and out through the nose.

Next, take about 30 fast deep breaths in and out, filling the lungs, at a rate of approximately 30 breaths per minute. The breaths in and out should flow without time inbetween the exhale and the inhale.

Repeat six slow, deep breaths in and out. Repeat 30 fast, deep breaths in and out. If you can, do cycles of each. It is recommended that you breathe in and out through the nose, particularly on the slow breath cycle. But I find that through the mouth is fine for the fast breaths – it's important that you do whatever you find comfortable. Be aware that fast breathing cycles can cause a feeling of light-headedness or dizziness. Only do when sitting or lying down and don't do whilst driving or cycling.

Ujjayi breathing technique: 'to be victorious'

Ujjayi breath is grounded in yoga breathing and if you are not as yet engaging in yoga practice you can still benefit a lot from doing a version of this yoga practice. Ujjayi means 'to be victorious' and at times when you need to do an 'emergency' restoration of calm, and gain an emergency feeling of 'victorious-ness', this version of Ujjayi breathing method is highly effective.[9] It is often and ideally carried out using alternate nostrils for the breath in and the breath out. It is quick, easy, easy to do anywhere and very effective.

To do: 4-4 breathing exercise

Breathe in deeply for four counts through the nose and breathe out for four counts through the nose, mouth gently closed. This is not slow breathing – counting should be at a rate of around one second per count. Fill the lungs on each breath. Breathing is continuous, and breath does not have to empty entirely on the exhale.

True Ujjayi breath is carried out by breathing in through one nostril and out through the other, closing each alternate nostril with your thumb and ring finger. If this is uncomfortable, or you are in a public place, you can simply breathe in and out through the nose or in through the nose and out through the mouth.

Repeat the cycles of breathing eight or ten times.

Pranayama breathing and the 4-7-8 breathing technique

The 4-7-8 breathing technique has gained much popularity in recent years, and originates in *pranayama* breathing, which is the practice of breathing control in yoga.[10] The *Ujjayi* breath technique above is one of the techniques in the practice of pranayama. Pranayama is about becoming aware of your breathing and awakening 'prana' or vital energy.

To do: the 4-7-8 breathing technique

Breathe in through your nose, counting to four as you do so. Hold your breath for a count of seven. Release your breath through your mouth for a count of eight. It is often recommended that as you exhale the breath, make a 'whoosh' sound as the air is released.

Repeat this cycle at least four times and up to eight times. Lie down or sit, just make sure you have good posture and release all tension.

'Emergency' breathing-relax combo

You can combine the 4-4 breath technique (see the Ujjayi breathing technique above) with an 'emergency' version of a muscle relaxation exercise. This is particularly useful if parts of your body are shaking or if some part of your body is likely to shake. So for example, if you shake during performance, progressive muscle tensing and relaxing is very effective before performance.

Relaxation exercises involve a purposeful tensing and relaxing of each muscle in the body, usually starting with the feet and working your way towards the face. See the exercise below.

To do: emergency breathing-relax combo

Begin an emergency relaxation-breathing combo with eight breaths of four in and four out exercise. So, breathe in deeply for four counts through the nose and breathe out for four counts through the nose, or mouth if more comfortable. This is not slow breathing – counting should be at a rate of around one second per count. Fill the lungs on each breath. Breathing is continuous, and breath does not have to empty entirely on the exhale.

Next, tense all the muscles you can in your legs and buttocks for five seconds. Do it again. Then tense as many of your upper body muscles as you can in one go – arms, shoulders, fists, torso (but not the face). Don't hurt yourself doing it! So just tense them as much as doesn't actually hurt, for five seconds and relax them. Do it again. Again, tense your legs and buttocks one more time. Then again, tense the muscles of your upper body one more time.

This can be quite effective for situations when your body is tense and you don't have time to do full relaxation or breathing exercises. If your body is tense to the point of shaking, this is a good emergency combo.

You can repeat the breathing cycles following the muscle tense and relax.

Many of the breathing techniques that are evidence-based and have been found to be highly effective for stress and anxiety arise from yoga and meditation practices. Many performers find yoga useful and it can become part of a lifestyle routine for being 'fit' as a musician.

Progressive muscle relaxation

Progressive muscle relaxation is very effective when used in combination with other strategies.[11] You can focus on areas that are most likely to cause problems for you during performance, and perhaps give these areas more attention than other areas. However, tension in any muscle group of the body tends to spread to other muscle groups, and so it is advisable to cover all muscle groups.

To do: progressive muscle relaxation exercise

Starting with your lower body, tense the muscles of your feet and toes, for five or more seconds, whilst breathing in. Then relax the muscle group whilst breathing out.

Move to your calf muscles, tense this muscle group for five or more seconds, whilst breathing in. Then relax the muscle group whilst breathing out. Become aware of how you feel during each tensing and relaxing of the muscles.

Move up your body gradually, the thighs, the buttocks, the abdomen and stomach, the shoulders, the arms, the hands and the face, alternating tension and relaxation of each muscle group in turn with each inhale and exhale of breath.

If you are doing the exercise before performance and you tend to shake when you are nervous, focus on the muscle group which is most likely to shake during performance. Do that muscle group again at the end. For most performers this will be the legs or the hands and arms, although for some performers, particularly brass and wind players, it is the jaw and face that require additional focus.

Mindfulness meditation

Many people find meditation really useful, and you might like to try it. In addition to its ever-increasing popularity, the research on mindful meditation has shown significantly positive results.

Mindfulness meditation has many benefits – as well as the effects on body and mind – it is quite simple to do; it can be carried out as quickly as in a couple of minutes, and can be done anywhere. It doesn't require a lot of your time, although as you become more practised doing it, you may want to spend longer engaging in it. It may require some persistence, and not just for one day; however, if you persist by making it part of your daily routine there are great rewards.

Research consistently shows that meditation practised on a regular basis has many positive effects.[12] Mindfulness meditation has been shown to decrease anxiety and depression, and is also used very effectively by people who are working to maintain low levels of anxiety or depression, following treatment.[13]

As well as being happier and having more satisfying relationships,[14] people who meditate have been shown to enjoy lower stress levels, reduction of chronic stress, reduction of impact of pain, strengthened immune system, faster reaction times, and strengthened mental and physical stamina.[15] Mindfulness improves memory, creativity, and enhances likelihood to experience flow.[16] It has a positive impact on the underlying thought patterns of stress and anxiety, the kind of underlying thoughts that may not lead you to have chronic and persistent anxiety or depression, but that nevertheless impact consistently on your thoughts about yourself and possibly about your music performance.

In order to work effectively, it does require that you practise – regular, committed practise. Although many people say they feel better from the day they started to 'practise' meditation, it can take time to feel comfortable with and to experience its full benefit.

Doing mindfulness meditation

In our everyday life, thoughts come and go, but sometimes, a negative thought wanders into our mind and instead of letting it go, we hold onto it, think about it, and it starts to become bigger than it should have. Not only does it become bigger, it even prevents us from having other thoughts, it takes over and new thoughts, more positive thoughts have a hard time interrupting our focus on this negative idea.

The key to understanding how to carry out mindfulness meditation is this – you don't have to empty your mind of all those nagging thoughts – that is quite a difficult thing to do, especially for the beginner. Instead, let the thoughts come to you, whatever thought comes, be aware of it, accept it, and let it move on.[17] You will find that another thought will come along. Again, be aware of it, accept it, accept that you think or feel this, and allow it to move away. Another thought might come, or perhaps the first thought will come back. Let it be, accept it, and let it go. If you are struggling to sit still or struggling with letting a thought go, focus in on your breathing and feel yourself drawing your breath in and out again.

During mindfulness meditation, observe yourself and your thoughts without criticism; be compassionate to yourself. Notice your thoughts and feelings – and notice how they shift. By doing this, you can become aware of negative thought patterns before they flood your mind without your noticing and overwhelm you.

Perhaps you will become aware of a negative pattern of thinking, or some particular thought that keeps returning. You can challenge these thoughts later, at a time when you are not trying to meditate. Chapter 5 discusses strategies for challenging and changing negative thoughts.

As we saw in Chapter 4 on emotions, how we feel – your emotions and your moods – has a major impact on your thoughts. This can mean that what might be a momentary feeling of sadness or gloominess, disappointment, anger or feeling a bit down on yourself, if left unchecked, can grow unnecessarily, impacting on your thoughts about yourself. With one thought leading to another, thoughts snowballing and gathering momentum, turning from momentary emotions to more persistent feelings of unhappiness, sadness, anger, or loss of self-esteem. These feelings in turn, affect our thoughts, perhaps leading to us dredging up memories and sad or negative thoughts, and all the while we are becoming more sad, angry or negative. They affect how we view our day, the people around us, the challenges we face, and our ability to cope. This cycle works the same with all emotions and thoughts – whether they are sad or happy, stressed or angry, tense or satisfied.

Because we develop 'patterns' of thinking, often quite negative patterns of thinking about ourselves, a whole system, or a cycle of habitual feelings that we are so used to feeling can be triggered in a moment by a passing feeling or thought, a passing memory, or by a song, a piece of music, a person, the image of a place, or an object. Even the image of your instrument or instrument case, your sheet music, or your music stand can trigger a whole network of thoughts and feelings, and depending on how you've been feeling about your music and your-self, depending on the patterns of thinking you have developed, this can be very powerful either negatively or positively.

We all have an inner critic and listening to the inner critic too much can lead to a lot of analysing, questioning, and doubting ourselves. Instead of analysing our thoughts and feelings, mindfulness helps us to be aware, and to *not* analyse. In awareness, we can just sense things, allow our senses to simply experience. The mind can process this awareness and this experience of sensing without having to analyse and question and critique everything. In the processing, according to mindful meditation principles, we can become more accepting, more compas-sionate towards ourselves and more patient.

Also, in allowing our brains to 'sense', we will experience more clarity, without having to consciously make ourselves understand. Clarity will come to us through quiet mindful meditation, helping us to understand and be clearer about our goals and how to achieve them.

Mindfulness meditation is about observing, becoming aware and paying attention to those momentary moods or thoughts, acknowledging them, accepting them and observing them move on.[18] Mindfulness meditation allows us to become aware of the negative thought patterns and the cycles of thoughts and emotions, before they snowball. In a way, mindfulness gives us control of these fluctuations.

To do: exercise – take a minute to be mindful of your current state

One minute meditation exercise

Sit still – in a chair, back straight, with your hands in your lap. Close your eyes.

Focus on your breath … Become aware of the in and out of your breath and focus on it. Direct your attention to it. You don't need to change your breathing, just breathe how you breathe.

Your mind might wander. Bring your attention back to your breathing. You might grow fidgety, moving around in your seat. Bring your attention back to your breathing. Simply accept that your mind wandered and that's fine. No criticism.

You might go through various thoughts or states of unease ... bring your mind back to your breathing each time. The minute might seem endless ... Attend to your breathing. Even a sense of relaxation or stillness might come to you ... and leave you again. Whatever you feel, let yourself feel it, bring yourself back to your breathing and just notice that whatever it is, it passes. Accept and allow.

After a minute open your eyes and carry on with your day.

Even in this one minute, particularly if you are not used to meditating, or being mindful, or even sitting still for as long as a minute, you will probably notice yourself battling through some of the seconds and through some of your thoughts. Within that one minute you will notice how your thoughts and even your emotions shift. They come and go as if of their own doing.

Once you have added mindfulness meditation to your daily routine, start trying to extend the length of time you can meditate for – two minutes, three, five, ten. You will find that with practice, you can achieve longer sessions, and you may even enjoy it.

Mindfulness helps to break habits. It provides us with a few moments of purposeful breaking of repetitive habits of thinking. It encourages us to let the thoughts come, be aware of them, but to allow them to move on and be replaced by other thoughts.

So, in mindfulness meditation, don't expect that your mind should be empty. That is perhaps something that will come with time and practice. Instead, let the thoughts come and let them go. You might be surprised by what floats in when you let the foremost thoughts float away.

As with all the strategies in this book, whilst some people notice immediate benefits when they find a strategy that works for them, in order to get the greatest benefit, you should practise strategies in advance of a performance. I have heard music students say, "I tried that on the day of my gig, but it didn't work for me". As I've already said in this book, that's a bit like saying I practised the music on the day of the gig and it didn't work, so I'm not going to practise again. When something doesn't work on the day, what it actually means is that you should start practising sooner. Get into the habit of carrying out mindful meditation as part of your routine.

Key tips from this chapter

-   Create your own programme of strategies to calm body and mind.
-   Controlled, self-regulated breathing exercises are highly effective for combatting anxiety and music performance anxiety.

- Breathing activates the vagus nerve, which directly sets the Relax! system in motion. Because the vagus nerve connects so many areas of the body and brain, activation of the vagus nerve can lead to widespread inhibition of the fight or flight system, thereby decreasing all the symptoms of the fight or flight response.
- Find the technique that suits you, and you can adapt it to suit whatever version of it works best for you.
- Use it daily, incorporate it into daily routines.
- Remind yourself to carry out your chosen breathing exercise.
- You can combine regulated breathing with mindfulness meditation, if you like.
- Mindfulness meditation is highly effective – use it!
- Mindfulness meditation breaks patterns of thought, and is very effective at breaking patterns of negative thinking.
- Progressive muscle relaxation is very effective when combined with the other strategies. It is highly effective for reducing shaking, so if there are muscles in your body that tend to shake during performance, use this technique prior to performance.

10 Pre-performance routines

"The habit of the routine just sort of settles you", "I have a very well worked out routine that I go through every time".

The day of a performance is approaching. You have practised for the performance, whether it's a recital, concert, exam, or a competition, you've done what you can and now it's crucial for your psychological preparation that you make a plan for the day itself.

As we saw in Chapter 3, expert musicians have pre-performance routines – they vary greatly, some are very detailed, others incorporate just one or two things that they feel they must do in order to be ready to perform.

In the world of sport and sport psychology, pre-performance plans and routines are commonplace.[1] They are used for getting the athlete emotionally, cognitively, and physically ready. Sport psychologists recommend that even things that have never gone wrong before should be thought about and accounted for, because anything can happen when we are under pressure. Even experts can forget something when they're heading to a performance.

At its most basic function, a routine for preparation will reduce uncertainty – it will ensure you don't forget to bring something, that you arrive in good time, or that you remember to eat. But the central aim of a having a routine is that it will help you to achieve your optimal mental state. If you have carried out the IZOF exercise in Chapter 4, you will know which emotions and what arousal level of those emotions are ideal for you when you are performing (and if you haven't done it already, do it now). The IZOF will help you to have a clear understanding of your own unique blend of emotions, the blend of emotions that are optimal for you. Once you know this, then you know which emotions and what level of emotion you are working to reach by the time of the performance.

A routine is also like a little cocoon that you can rely on to safeguard you against the negative effects of pressure. By having a routine, you can focus on each step of the routine and on factors that you can control. Your routine will help to decrease anxiety levels around getting ready and having everything you need in order to perform.

You can aim to develop a number of steps that incorporate actions that you can take control of in order to reach the mental state that you desire. Each step, each part of the day leading up to a performance will contain actions that will be building blocks to your ideal zone of optimal functioning. Each step and each of the strategies you use will be linked to building up the emotions you need to feel by the time of performance. You will plan each part of the day, and you will plan to carry out positive self-talk, use a number of mantras that you repeat, use imagery and visualisation, mental practice, and decide on the strategies you will use for managing your physiological arousal levels.

There are times when optimal emotion levels and an optimal mental state just seem to happen. But you can take control, not leave it to wishful thinking, and simply hope that it happens. You can actually take the steps to control the likelihood of it happening.

There are a number of factors that you should consider, some are very practical – sleep, eating, relaxation, exercise, practising, what you will wear, getting dressed for the performance, travel. Some are more obviously psychological – thought and emotion management strategies, mental practice, imagery and visualisation, positive self-talk, cut-off time for negative thoughts, mantras, breathing and relaxation exercises. However, even planning the practical elements is important for psychological preparation. If you prepare well, it helps to avoid any last-minute panic; it builds your self-confidence and reduces your levels of anxiety.[2]

Have an overview of the day

Think about how the day will unfold, if your performance is early in the day or the evening, work out how much time you have and what you can fit in to the time. Think out a structure for the day and consider when you will eat, will you have a nap, will you take some exercise – a walk, run, or yoga, do you need time alone and when will that be, when will you practise and what kind of practise will you do, when will you shower, shave, get dressed, put on make-up, what will you wear, when will you meditate or take time to breathe, how are you travelling to the performance, what time do you want to arrive at, and what time do you need to begin the journey. Have an actual structure and a flexible time allotment for each of those things.

Planning your pre-performance routine for the day

Performance routines should be individual and flexible. A pre-performance plan is not something rigid but as well as having a time structure for obvious things that you absolutely need to do (eating, resting, practising, travelling) it should also include a number of factors – factors that are physiological, mental, and technical.[3]

Physiological factors include eating, resting or napping, physiological arousal management such as breathing, exercise, relaxation techniques, warm-up, acclimatisation to the venue, possibly even recovery from travel.

Mental factors include what you need to bring, general organisation, dressing, focusing, coping strategies such as mental practice, imagery, breathing, self-talk, mantra, quiet time, cut-off for negative thoughts.

Technical factors include practising and what type of practice, what to wear, getting to the venue – travel and travel time, rehearsal, sound check, acoustics check.

These are specific needs that can all be addressed in the plan for your routine. What you should also consider is what *outcome* you want to achieve from each of the things that you do. By outcome, I mean – how do you want to feel on carrying out each of the things you need to do, each of the actions you decide to take. Do you want to feel a little more relaxed? Or confident? Or excited? Or enthusiastic? Motivated? Hopeful? Aggressive?

Attach a coping strategy to each activity

Attach a specific coping strategy to each step of or to as many steps of the day as you can and attach a desired emotion or blend of emotions to each step of the day, each part of your plan.

Example: Linking activity and strategy

- Showering/shaving/dressing/make-up – repeat your mantra(s).
- Travelling – mental practice, immersing yourself in the music.
- Arriving at venue – your cut off: no more negative thoughts allowed.
- Relaxation/meditation/walk – free yourself from all of it, have a break from thinking about it, pretend it's a regular day for 15 minutes, escape!
- Eating – positive self-talk, reasons why it's going to be great.
- Set a time for imagery and visualisation – practise feeling the emotions you will feel, then play or imagine performing.
- Practising time – be in the moment.
- Slow practise – calm the body and reassure the mind.
- Breathing – repeat your mantra with each breath, or breathe in positive thoughts breathe out negative thoughts.
- Doing some other activity – time off from thinking about the performance, distract yourself with some other activity or work.

If you feel you need to run through all the worst possible scenarios – then plan when are you going to allow yourself to do this for the *last* time and do it. Do it well, and make the decision that you won't be doing it again before that performance.

To do: planning sheet[4]

Add in the times for carrying out each activity

Time	Activity (physical, practical)	Mental activity (strategies)
	Wake up	
	Relaxation exercise	Relax and breathe
	Walk/exercise/yoga	Breathe, positive self-talk
	Eat	Mental practice
	Warm-up body and instrument	In the moment, calm and reassure
	Practising – what type: slow	In the moment, calming
	Practising – what type: other music	Refocus mind
	Mental practice time	Absorb and focus: check memory/knowledge/expression
	Listen to other music	Shift focus
	Relaxation exercise	
	Imagery and visualisation time	Practise the feeling
	Practise: short	Play, whilst feeling
	Other activity (TV, read, chat)	Not thinking about it
	Nap/rest	Refresh
	Eat	
	Showering/shaving/make-up/dressing	Mantras
	Travel	Mental practice
	Warm-up	
	Rehearse in venue	
	Sound check/acoustic check	
	Dressing	
	Other activities you want to add:	Other strategies:

Ask yourself

• How long you will sleep, will you have a nap? How do you want to feel after the nap?
• What you will eat and when? How do you want to feel after you eat?
• How long will you practise for and what will you practise? Include warm up time and consider playing music other than what is to be performed on the day.
• Exercise – will you take a walk, or yoga, or meditate, or something more strenuous? When will you do it, for how long and how do you want to feel after it?

- Breathing – when will you carry out a breathing exercise and how long for?
- Meditation, quiet time, or prayer – when and how long for? What thoughts do you want to have and how do you want to feel after it?
- Positive self-talk and mantra – have you selected one or two mantras? Use your mantra. How do you want to feel at various points in the day?
- Cut-off point – at what point will you no longer allow negative thoughts to stay in your head? Perhaps you want to give some acceptance of them up until a particular point in the day, after which you will replace all negative thoughts as soon as they occur to you.
- What you will wear? Is it laid out, prepared, clothes ironed, shoes ready? When will you do this? How do you want to feel as you put on your clothes, put on make-up, shave, brush or comb your hair?
- How will you travel there and how long will it take? Which part of your routine will you carry out whilst travelling – mental practice, visualisation, positive self-talk?
- Will you spend time with other people? If it is helpful for you, do. When and how long will you spend? If it is not helpful for you, plan how you will find time to be on your own.
- Mental practice – effective mental practice. Make sure to include parts that you feel less confident of, so you can check with the score or with other players, as well as parts that you love and feel confident about. On the day of performance, it may not be helpful to do technical practice – that's up to you and what works for you. Consider doing only mental practice for expression.
- Imagery and visualisation – imagine yourself and the emotions you want to feel when you walk out in front of the audience, and as you play.

These are the common factors in many routines. You will most likely have something of your own to include that is unique to you. That's good – remember to plan how long you will do it for and how you want to feel during and after it.

The plan is not rigid. It is flexible and fluent. One part of the routine might overlap with another. But have a general plan of what you want to do, how and where you are going to do it, how long you are going to do it for, and how you want to feel during and after are each thing. Don't worry if it doesn't quite happen the way you thought, be flexible. The point is to keep focused. Your mental practice, visualisation, and positive self-talk can be done anywhere, at any time and will help you to control your attention, your thoughts, and your emotion.

Putting together a routine can involve trying out strategies and finding out what exactly works for you and when it works for you. Make a note of times when something did not work for you and plan for not incorporating that aspect in future.

Not everything can be planned or controlled. But some things can. Over time you will work out what the controllables are and what strategies works best for you.

What do the experts do?

Everyone, even the experts, has at some point got to get up, get dressed, and travel to a venue, and work out a time plan for doing that. But what actions do experts take that are necessary and beneficial to their mental preparation? Do they use strategies to achieve an optimal mental state? Do they have rituals or routines? If you've read Chapter 3 you know already that they do.

The pre-performance routines of experts vary quite a bit. Whilst one person may have a very detailed routine for mental preparation, another might have just one or two things they like to carry out before performance. Routines differ as much as "as long as I have a nap or alone time, I'm fine. But I *must* have that" to "about a week before ... I would have all my panic, dreams, classic panic attacks ... go through all the possibilities of what could happen, I'd have one day of being jittery ... I practise a lot, I do a lot of mental practice ... and then I become completely calm ... I start to practise different music, new repertoire, I listen to different music, and do only slow practice on the day ...".

The routines of experts tend to include practising and specific type of practice, rest or sleep, alone time, food/diet, exercise, positive thinking, breathing and relaxation exercises, use of imagery and visualisation, taking it easy/slow pace, listening to other music, dressing and make-up, venue activities (which include getting quiet time alone, slow pace, rehearsal).

The type of rest or sleep depends on the individual, some people just rest, others like to have a nap. "The most important thing for me is to have a nap in the afternoon". Food intake varies too – some people don't eat much just before a performance but make sure to have something that sustains them earlier in the day and have a snack before performing. "I don't eat much just before, I'd eat early and then have something light, maybe a banana".

Positive thoughts are important, even for the expert. "I imagine the good vibes of the audience", "I do a bit of positive thinking and singing ... singing to let it out", "I try to think as many positive thoughts as possible". Experts also use positive visualisation and imagery "I imagine myself doing it and doing it right". All of the singers, wind players, and brass players mentioned doing breathing exercises "I do a breathing exercise ... it slows the heart rate down", "I focus on my breathing". And many of these experts (wind/brass/voice) have particular specific individual routines that they have tried and tested for getting their voice, throat, face, lips, or jaw feeling ready. "I have very specific things that I do ... I want everything to feel nice, the lips, the chops, get the mouthpiece to feel right on my face, that's why I have the routine I have."

For exercise, experts like to do different things – some do yoga, some go for a walk, others like to have a short run, or just do some exercises they have become accustomed to doing, even just jumping up and down on the spot. However, there are expert musicians who don't do any exercise at all! So if that's like you, then that's ok, but it is worthwhile to experiment with exercise of some kind yourself, in order to find out if and what works for you. Any exercise you do on the day of a performance does need to be light, and should be thought about and tried out well in advance of a performance. Don't go doing something you've never attempted prior to the big day – no 5k runs or lifting weights or strenuous yoga for the very first time.

Some people like to try to do everything slowly, taking their time to do things, and keeping their physical activation slow and calm if possible. "I do everything very slowly", "I'm very slow and measured about everything I do". Many listen to other music, "I listen to something that is similar in meaning or in atmosphere to what you want to create", "listening to music is inspiring".

Dressing, shaving, or putting on make-up is a key time for focusing or for getting into the right frame of mind. "I don't shave in the morning; in the evening I want to feel fresher", "putting on make-up is an important time for focusing", "I find dressing really nerve wracking".

And many experts say that it is crucial for them to get time alone. "I'm not particularly social during the day of a concert", "I avoid any confrontations … quiet time is mine, don't come near me!", "I prefer to be in the dark", "silence is one of the most important things". Some get this time alone during the day and perhaps go walking in order to be alone and have quietness. For some, it's important to have it once they arrive at a venue, "I go in and shut myself off and prepare".

How to practise or what to practise on the day of a performance also varies depending on the expert. Most experts like to go easy on practising on the day, for example, "I try to leave well enough alone", "I don't push it too far", "I practise but not over-practise". Many do slow practise "I take it easy and do slow practise", "I would take out the bits I'm anxious about and practise really slowly". But others say, "the worst thing to do is take out the instrument and look at bits you're worried about". Some experts would recommend practising early and then leaving it "I do a few hours practise and then go away from it, so that the instrument is fresh when I pick it up", "I don't think it's good to practise right up until the minute you go on", "I practise as soon as I get up, then leave it until later".

In general, the experts have well worked out routines for how they like to practise and what kind of practice works for them. "I have a well worked out practise routine", "I practise a little, then I practise at the venue, touching lightly on the instrument, having some sort of touch with the different pieces", "having practised in the morning, I do warm-up at the venue, just to make sure my hands are warmed up physically", "throughout the day I have my breathing exercises, I check on words … mentally, I want my throat to feel right and so I take it easy and my exercises are most important".

Many experts talk about feeling right with the instrument and often refer to feeling 'instrumentally fit'. Some have routines to make that happen, "my face has to feel right … That's what my routine is for". Others say it might happen or it might not, "there is a physical feeling of it feeling 'right' when you pick up the instrument … some days it just feels right". Others believe it comes from general everyday practice, "first and foremost, [it's important] being at one with your instrument. I associate that with being fit … and that's the discipline of everyday".

Even the experts believe in being very well prepared and thinking through every aspect of their performance, including what happens just before a performance or on the day of important performances. The level of detail and planning may vary depending on the expert but it also varies depending on the level of challenge, the importance of a performance, or the repetitiveness of on-going performances for example, during a tour. There are always going to be times when there isn't time for all aspects of a routine, or when so many performances have been done that the routine becomes less necessary or the routine needs to change, in order to psych up a 'bored' musician rather than calm down a 'nervous' musician.

You may not have heard much before about the discipline and planning that expert musicians involve themselves in when it comes to planning and carrying out routines. But you might well have heard rumours escaping from the music business of alcohol and drugs! Yes, it's sometimes true, irrespective of the genre of music, that there is intake of alcohol and/or drugs by some expert musicians. However, most experts would recommend that aspiring performers don't do either of these, and particularly important not to do so prior to performances. Many musicians find that alcohol or drugs can have a negative impact on their performance and would be fearful of generating an addictive pattern in their pre-performance behaviour.

> *"Doing this kind of work, you end up an emotional mess, and some end up drinking a lot and taking drugs."*

There is a medically prescribed and legal medication that some musicians use, or have used at times, that eases the physical manifestations of nerves.[5] Beta blockers have also been used in some sports and are illegal in many competitive sports because of their performance enhancing quality. Beta blockers should only be taken under a medical doctor's consultation and prescription. The main reason that musicians take beta blockers prior to performance is that they slow the heart rate, and so calm the body, therefore easing symptoms such as shaking, sweating, nausea. Such is the secrecy surrounding the use of beta blockers particularly in the world of classical music, that beta blockers have been referred to by psychologists as 'the musician's underground drug'.[6] Generally, experts who have said that they have tried or used beta blockers, say that they didn't know what else they could do to alleviate their symptoms, and that they found them useful at times when they were more stressed than usual, or for a period of time after which they stopped using them, "I do occasionally take a beta blocker yea, but sometimes I have to admit to having a drink", "I don't take them but I know people who do and I also know people who have a drink or a smoke … it happens", "I did use beta blockers at one point when I seemed to be having a phase of difficulty coping with the physical side of nerves … but then I didn't need to anymore, I found other ways of coping".

There are other random things that experts find useful, each individual having their own solution to being 'ready' to perform; for example, seeing the big picture, "knowing there's something bigger than yourself out there … takes the pressure off", "keep it realistic", or having a sense of belonging "as soon as I start to play, I know I'm back where I should be", "once I'm on stage, it's 'yes I'm where

I belong'", having trust or faith, "I had a sense of trust", or saying a prayer, "I pray to a spiritually higher power". Communicating with the audience is helpful for some, "I love talking to the audience", "if I can have a little bit of conversation with the audience, or a little bit of feedback, then it makes it much easier for me". Remembering that you could have fun can be powerful too, "we wanted to have a bit of fun", "if I can have a good laugh that helps breaks the ice".

The very last thing many experts try to do before they walk out on stage, is 'let go'.

Letting go!

> *"Just do it. Don't be careful! Don't hold back!", "you have to let go of all attachments, all concerns", "I just have to go for it … it might be brilliant or I might fail".*

How do you let go? It's a big question, and it really only has a short little answer – you just do it. Sometimes this is referred to as the 'feck it moment'![7]

Two things are key – first, you actually have to make the conscious decision to let go and take the risk, and the second is preparation – you are able to let go because you are confident that you have done all the preparation that it was possible for you to do. Most experts feel it is only possible for them to let go when they feel totally prepared. When talking yourself into letting go, you need to feel that you have done all the work you can, that you know as much as you can, that you have prepared in every way possible.

> *"You must feel that you are totally secure. And then you can be free to let go, to create", "what allows you to have those sort of experiences is that you have left no stone unturned in the preparation", "anything that was in my control I had covered", "preparation is everything".*

Yes, possibly you could go on practising and preparing. The inner critic in you might never feel prepared enough, but you have to rationalise this a bit, if you have indeed worked hard and done what you can. You have to reassure yourself, with positive self-talk and using mental practice to check over parts of the music that you doubt your ability to play or remember.

It happens to all musicians that they might have prepared to the best of their ability, but still feel there are parts they don't know well enough, or technical passages that they don't feel sure of and wish they had had more time to practise. When experts have to perform without enough rehearsal time or practice time, they are often going into performance situations feeling not quite fully prepared, with their inner critic chastising them. But they use positive self-talk, positive mantras, they rationalise their thinking, and challenge their negative thoughts. You can do the same.

So, the final moment will come when you have to let go. You've done the work, done the best you can and now all you can do is leave the worry and concern behind, step into the moment and 'just go for it'.

In making this conscious decision, you talk yourself into it, 'psych' yourself up so that it is possible to do it. Using a mantra is helpful for this. You have to talk yourself into leaving the fear behind. Leave the worry outside the room. Tell yourself to do that, in the hours and minutes prior to performance. Transport yourself as you walk out or in, onto the stage area.

It will feel like a risk, a big risk, but you perhaps will already feel like you are taking some risk just performing in the first place. You need to accept that there is a huge risk involved, and that that is ok. It may feel like you are putting yourself out there without a safety net.

> *"It was do or die, I just had to let go and go for it", "there is always a bit of the unknown coming … you don't know what's going to happen in the next moment", "there's nothing to fall back on, you're totally putting yourself out there".*

Before expert musicians experience flow, we've seen that they experience heightened emotional, cognitive and physiological arousal, increased absorption and focus on the music, intrinsic motivation for the music, and feel they are facing great challenge. These lead to a sense of risk being taken – no kidding! But when this is combined with the confidence inspired by the high levels of preparation they have carried out, and the clear knowledge of knowing exactly what they want to do, they are 'allowed' or compelled to 'let go', to give themselves over, let go of their inhibitions and their self-consciousness, and so they free themselves to the experience of flow.[8]

It can feel very uncomfortable to take this risk, this leap of faith in yourself. You have to be willing to face the discomfort, feel the discomfort and do it anyway. Some expert musicians say that they don't like to let go of control, that this is not pleasant or easy for them. So, for some, letting go is harder than for others.

When the point in time comes for taking risk and letting go, you cannot allow negative thoughts enter your head. You make a conscious decision to not allow yourself to think a negative thought about yourself. When a negative thought comes into your head, you must immediately let it go, replace it with a positive thought, with your mantra. Do not let that negative thought gather any power. Don't think about it or hold onto it. Let it go. Hopefully, if you have been practising the stop! and replace technique, this will have become easier for you.

'Just go for it' is a phrase and mantra that expert musicians use a lot. It is one of the most common pre-performance mantras.

> *"I just thought 'risk it, go for it!' ", "it was sink or swim kind of feeling and you just have to take the risk", "I really want to do this, I can do it", "I've done the work, I know the stuff", "I just decided I'm going to go for it, if it doesn't work out, 'there we go!' ".*

Common 'let go' and 'take the risk' mantras used by musicians

* 'Put everything into it! I've nothing to lose'
* 'Go for it! Don't be afraid to fail'

- 'Risk it! Go for it!'
- 'Don't be careful, don't hold back'
- 'It might be brilliant'
- 'It's not about me, it's not about me'
- 'You can do it! You can do it!'
- 'I really want to do this and I can do it!'

Take one for yourself, and use it.

Key tips from this chapter

- Create your own individual and personal routine.
- Include an overall view of the day of the performance.
- Have a plan for the whole day.
- Your routine should include three kinds of activities – physical, practical, and mental activities.
- Attach coping strategies to as many of the activities as possible.
- Think about how you would like to feel at each point of the day, or during each activity.
- Practise coping strategies before the performance day, so that you are not trying things out for the first time that day.
- Have a cut-off for negative thoughts … no more negative thoughts allowed after this cut-off.
- There comes a point when everyone has to take the risk and 'just do it!'

11 Putting it all together

In this book I have described how it feels for musicians to experience flow from their own very personal perspective and often in their own words. I described how they set up the conditions to increase the likelihood of flow happening and the lengths that musicians go to in order to perform their best. Their preparation – musical, psychological, and physical – enables them to sometimes experience flow, to always perform at their best and to have really positive experiences of performance in general. In the past we've had very little detailed knowledge of *what* exactly it is that expert musicians do to prepare, but for all student performers, music teachers, aspiring musicians, amateur musicians, and other professional performers, it is extremely beneficial to know.

Knowing *what* the experts do is highly useful; but to understand *how* they do it, requires more information. In the book I have brought together my research with key findings from decades of practical knowledge that has sprung from areas of academic and experimental research – areas of sport psychology, cognitive psychology, performance psychology, emotion theory and research, motivation theory and research, neuropsychology, biopsychology, clinical psychology, psychotherapy, music psychology, music education, and cognitive neuroscience. Drawing on these disciplines helps us to know more about how the brain works, our thought processes, how body and brain interact, and how we can manage those interactions in our search for more positive experiences of performance, for peak performance, and peak experience during performance.

There are some points I would like to emphasise particularly to student musicians or young aspiring performers in my conclusion to this book.

Preparation

Practise! Practise! Practise!

> *"No stone left unturned", "when I go out to play, I want it to be just about the music. I would be totally in the music, and the technical side of it should be totally automatic. I don't think about that at all. I have it all totally worked out before going out to play".*

Perhaps it is stating the obvious to say what I'm about to say here – preparation is fundamental to feeling ready to perform, being able to perform, to having positive experiences of performance and to having peak experiences of performance.

I'm saying it because – first, there may be students reading who haven't realised just how much preparation is required, or who don't realise that experts don't just magically become experts without a lot of hard work. In our instant celebrity culture, and with TV competitions such as *The X Factor, The Voice, Britain's Got Talent, America's Got Talent*, it can appear as though 'talented' people get spotted and discovered if they can just be lucky enough to be in the right place at the right time, or on the right show at the right time. The hard work and hours or years of practising and rehearsing that *many* of these contestants have consistently carried out is rarely disclosed or voiced in these programs and this can be very misleading.

Second, I'm saying it because professional musicians don't often find it easy to share with each other how much practice they do or the specific kind of practice they do. I know there are experts out there who carry out dedicated preparation but aren't aware of how much others are doing.

Third, I'm saying it because this book describes and details the psychological strategies that are helpful for enjoyable and successful performances. It has not provided information on how to carry out the specifics of instrumental practice and effective instrumental practice strategies. However, that does not mean that the book is suggesting that practise is not important.

It is crucial to put in the technical and musical work. Psychological strategies won't conceal inadequate work. What they will do is maximise your performance potential when you have already done the work, and you want to perform at your best, at that specific moment in time. Just doing that is hard enough, without feeling that you don't know the music well enough or that you are underprepared.

As we saw in Chapter 3, expert musicians have said that when they had their best and most enjoyable performances, they had prepared to the point of automatisation, they had left "no stone unturned". We have seen the lengths they go to – the preparation, the memorising – not just of the music, but of every aspect including the stage set up. Experts do it! So, if you ever thought you were being a bit over the top about getting prepared or being overly attentive to detail, it might be consoling to know that you are in good company. To students reading – remember that added to the preparation that experts put in, they also have years of experience of practising, preparing, performing, and getting their heads in the right space and they still continue to do it for important, special or particularly challenging performances. Furthermore, it's easier for them to do it than it is for you the student, with all their experience and practice behind them. So, it may be the case that whatever amount of practice and preparation the experts do, perhaps you have to double that, or triple it even. In general, keep in mind the 10,000 hours rule – that it takes 10,000 hours to become an expert.[1] Where are you on getting those hours done? Getting close? Maybe not close yet?

If you are experiencing a high level of performance anxiety, you may feel that you do prepare and practise as much as possible most of the time. You are feeling anxiety because you care, and that's a good thing. Performers who don't care, don't feel anxiety. It is unlikely that they enjoy performances, and they certainly don't experience flow. Even though you feel you have prepared well, possibly you still feel as though you aren't ready, you possibly think you aren't good enough, that there are bits you can't play or should have practised more, and still you feel you can't manage to perform as well as you can in your practice room. Be compassionate towards yourself. If you are a student, remember you are learning. You're not perfect – and you're not supposed to be perfect, as a student. If you are a professional musician, you are most likely growing and developing as an artist too. There's always more to learn. Everyone has stages in their life or times of life when other personal issues are stressful and distracting. However, here in this book I have described strategies that perhaps you have not employed yet, strategies that will help you achieve more positive experiences and achieve the level of performing of which you know you are capable.

You are more likely to feel good about performing, to feel 'ready' to perform and to *manage* performance anxiety when you feel that you are really on top of things musically – feeling musically competent. As well as feeling that you are prepared, you should also aim to look after both your physical health and your psychological health and wellbeing. Physical health requires that you eat well, you sleep well, and you feel 'fit' – to whatever level is comfortable for you. Physical health, particularly in the days prior to a performance, is imperative, and tends to be underrated by student performers. Psychological health requires you to be aware of yourself, your thoughts, emotions, and your vulnerabilities, to be compassionate towards yourself, and to carry out activities and psychological strategies that will enhance your psychological health.

If you are the performer who is feeling apathetic and struggling to care, who doesn't feel either anxiety *or* joy when you perform, you can also use the strategies to enhance your performance experiences. Motivation and your reasons for performing, playing or singing are probably at the crux of the problem for you and you should explore that (see Chapter 6 for more on this). Another possibility is that you are not challenged enough and you need to look for new opportunities to stretch yourself – possibly new music, new people around you, new goals, or new ways of playing, singing, or performing (Chapter 6). Like any other player or singer who is struggling with some aspect of performance, take the ten steps, carry out every one of those steps, before you make any decisions to give up or give in.

Practise performing

Taylor Swift, singer/songwriter, once said, "In my opinion the only way to conquer stage fright is to get up on stage and play. Every time you play another show, it gets better and better".[2]

Most student musicians and some professional musicians spend a lot more time practising than performing. Sport psychologists talk about the practise:performing ratio, because this is also an issue for athletes to be aware of in sport.[3] Sport psychologists look at the number of days of the year that someone trains and compare to the number of days of performance. You might spend three months before you get an opportunity to perform, and so you might find that you have a practice:performance ratio of about 91:1. But the ratio might be even more disparate than this.

Some young music students spend from September until competition season, or until an exam, practising without having a performance opportunity. This means that for some, between September and March your performance ratio could be 195:1. What do you think the chances are that you can perform at your best, or exactly how you want to, with this amount of performance experience?

Practising performance is just as important as practising repertoire. How can you do this? Get your friends together to listen to you. Ask family to listen to you. Before you do that, *imagine* that you have a performance – use visualisation and imagery. Set a date and a time and imagine the performance, imagine how you will feel before a performance, summon up all the emotions and thoughts you might feel (see Chapter 8). Record yourself; again, sometimes it's helpful to set a time for a performance for your recording. Watch your videos and learn from them. Arrange virtual performances – ask a friend or a family member to watch you and listen to your performance online, using one of the many apps that are available to us. When asked to play for someone in a casual setting, do it. Take the chance. You will probably think that you won't play or sing as well as you played in your practice room, that you're not ready, but perhaps you can use it as an opportunity to learn. Or you could sing something easy that you know well, a nice tune or song that someone might just enjoy. Or sing something you already know you sing well. And mostly, people just want to enjoy your music, not criticise small errors that only you notice.

Psychological strategies

"I have read a lot about psychology and performance stuff. I had to. And I was interested to. I read about mental practice and visualisation in particular. Actually I had already been doing those in my own way. But it was nice to find out that other people were doing it too, it wasn't just my own obsessiveness."

Use the psychological strategies and practise them. Don't think that you can or *should* be able to perform without them. And you won't be alone in using strategies. Expert performers are using them too.

Some people find a strategy that works for them immediately. But more usually it takes time to learn, practise and build on strategies, to make them your own and to allow them to be as effective as they can be.

Highly effective as they are, do not expect magic. If you experience anxiety, don't expect that suddenly you won't be anxious anymore once you start using strategies. You will most likely continue to feel anxious, or nervous, or apprehensive. As you saw in Chapter 4, nerves actually help you perform better, annoying as that might be. So, you need those nerves, but the strategies will help you to cope, help you manage those thoughts and emotions, and help you harness the nervousness to enable you to perform your best and to enjoy performing more.

The strategies break the cycle, break unhelpful habits of thinking and behaving; they prevent the sympathetic nervous system (the Go! system) from going into overdrive, by helping to keep the body calm.

Small steps

It's about taking small steps at first, breaking the cycle, doing even little things, that will have a ripple effect on how you think, feel and behave.

Don't overwhelm yourself. Don't be perfectionist about trying to get all the strategies mastered. Take it step by step. Start by just doing one thing, one strategy each day. Keep a diary on your phone, tablet, or notebook, noting what you've done and how it felt or what you could do to improve.

It is essential to practise the strategies. So, yes, I said don't overwhelm yourself at first, don't be perfectionist about it; but do an appropriate amount of practising of the strategies you choose and that you find effective. Build up a routine of doing mental practice every day. If you wait until the day of a performance to carry out mental practice or visualisation, or any strategy for that matter, it will probably help you somewhat on that day. But the effectiveness will be staggeringly *limited* compared to how each of those strategies could enhance your performance state if you were to practise them, make them your own, and make them part of your preparation routine in days, weeks, months before a performance.

The day of a performance, or any time when we are stressed and/or anxious, is a time when we are *least* likely to have the state of mind to be able to effectively carry out impromptu breathing exercises or mental practice, or any unfamiliar strategy. That is one of the reasons why it is important to have practised them previously. So that on the day of a performance, you don't have to think about the mechanics of how exactly to use the management tools, because you have done it previously and practised it. It or they have become a habit, a well-practised habit that work(s) effectively and almost automatically.

Making mistakes ... failing

"Try again. Fail again. Fail better."

This famous quote by Irish writer Samuel Beckett has become 'meme-ified' in recent years.[1] Just as the media and popular culture has become interested in how to be an expert, scientifically and psychologically we are also gaining knowledge about how experts become experts. Just as experts will often say that hard work (not talent, by the way), is what got them to the level they have achieved, we often hear stories in the media about experts in all sorts of domains talking about mistakes, about losing, about failures they experienced, what they learnt from that, how they carried on and how it made them better than ever. Anyone who is great at something, has made mistakes, has failed in some way.

"You have to get to a place in your mind and your heart and your spirit that you are OK with failing and failing better. That's a very hard place to get to." This was the response of the first female conductor of 'the Oscars' orchestra, Eímear Noone

(2020),[5] when she was asked "How do you keep your cool in front of 30 million people?" We actually don't learn a lot that is beneficial from winning or succeeding. Like Beckett, Michael Jordan, American sprinter and four-time Olympic gold medal winner, has also been 'meme-ified, when he said, "I've failed over and over, and that is why I succeed" (Michael Jordan, NBA basketball champion).[6]

If you feel like you are failing, if you feel that you are not performing well, instead of giving up or giving in, ask yourself, "What can I learn from this? How can this help me to improve?"

Chris Martin, singer/songwriter and lead singer of Coldplay, said, "I think everything we've done is sh**. That's why I keep trying to do new stuff. That's what fires you up to do the next thing".[7]

Whilst this may have been his *perception* at the time of speaking, it's obviously not an opinion that is shared by many. As well as perhaps noting the self-criticism of this expert (it's not just you!), it is really interesting to recognise in what he says 'the journey' he was on and that giving up or giving in was not an option, purely because he thought what he had done wasn't good enough.

You are on a journey. Don't write off individual bad performances as some kind of personality defect. It's not 'you'. It's how you prepared. Or it's part of the journey you are on. See the journey for what it is. You are learning and with each time you perform badly, or not as well as you hoped you would, look at what you can learn from it, what you can do differently in your preparation next time, what you can change about how you prepare, musically, psychologically, physically.

Evaluate your performances

It is so important to properly evaluate your performances, to analyse what exactly happened. It can be all too easy to simply write off a performance, without really looking at what happened. It's only natural – there are some performances we wish we could delete from memory. But you can learn a lot from analysing what went wrong for you. The answers will be in your preparation and your psychological preparation. Likewise, when you perform well or enjoy a performance, it's also important to evaluate the performance.

Sport psychologists recommend that evaluation is done as soon as possible following a performance, in order to maximise the benefits of good performances and to minimise any damaging effects when the performance did not go the way you wanted, when you didn't play how you hoped you would. Don't spend a long time doing it, particularly in cases of bad performance. Analyse what happened, and pinpoint what you can focus on to enhance future performances.[8]

Evaluate your performance plan and your preparation. Ask four key questions:

1. Did you cover everything?
2. What had you planned to do but didn't?
3. What did you do that you hadn't planned to do?
4. What were the factors that caused the most disruption to your performance?

Then move on!

Resilience, mental toughness, 'grit'

In the last number of years, words that have become 'buzz words' in the media and popular intelligence are resilience, mental toughness and most recently 'grit'. They have made their way to popular intelligence because they have originated in psychological, sociological, or sport research. They are intriguing concepts to us because many of us want to know how to be tougher, how to persist when things are hard, how to be less affected by struggles and challenges, and even, how to survive. Some people seem to cope well in the face of struggle and hard times. They seem calm, or as if they are floating through and we want to know how or why.

Is it because they have 'grit'? Some special ability that allows them to 'stick it out', to persevere no matter what? The concept of 'grit' is a relatively recently explored concept and so there is still much debate amongst psychologists about what exactly it is and on-going investigation about whether it really exists on its own as an idea, trait, or ability. Two of the assumptions are that grit means having perseverance and being consistent in effort. Grit has been linked to traits, abilities or 'strengths' such as conscientiousness, courage, resilience, toughness, self-control, to name a few.[9]

But the problem with the idea of 'grit' is it doesn't seem to help us with *why* some people persevere or manage to be consistent or have 'grit', whilst others don't. The most likely reason is that the real mechanism for grit and the basis of it is actually motivation. Having motivation to achieve, having intrinsic motivation, having something that you love to do, having passion for something makes it easier to have grit, to persevere and to consistently put in effort. It's even enjoyable to do so much of the time.

Resilience is our capacity to cope with adversity, and the use of coping skills is key to coping. How well we manage our emotional responses will determine our level of resilience. How we manage is determined by our use of coping skills. In order to be able to use coping skills effectively, we have to have some awareness about our emotional state.[10]

So resilience is something you can develop. You can develop it as a result of life experiences and struggles, and your use of strategies to help you cope with those struggles. Resilience is one of the crucial underlying abilities of the survivor, the performer, the success story, the expert. In relation to your music performance, you can develop resilience by being aware of your emotions and emotional state and by acquiring and using a range of coping skills or psychological strategies to help you manage your emotions.

You may have heard the term 'mental toughness' talked about in the field of sport. Just like having resilience, in sport there seem to be some people who float through the struggles, challenges, or obstacles placed in their way. Again, we all want to know *how* they do it. Sport psychologists have identified that people who may be 'mentally tough' are first and foremost aware of their mental states, and their emotions and are able to identify and use coping strategies that will help them. Further to that, mental toughness may include being consistently confident, focused, determined, and in control when under pressure.[11]

Sport psychologists have had difficulty finding consistent evidence for the existence of mental toughness. Even so, the label is commonly used, we all have an idea of what it might mean and we would quite like to have it!

Like resilience, awareness of your emotions and use of coping skills or psychological strategies to cope and manage are at least two of the keys to developing mental toughness. So, if mental toughness or resilience are abilities you would like to acquire, become more aware of your emotions, and take on the challenges you are faced with using coping skills and psychological strategies to enable you to better manage and enhance your performance. It's that simple. (See Chapters 4, 5, 6, 7, 8, 9 and 10 on how to do this.)

The ten steps to peak performance and more positive experiences of performance

The ten steps to peak performance are the ten processes that I found musicians engage in most often before they experience peak performance and flow during performance. These ten steps lead to better performance, more enjoyable performances, and even to flow. I recommend that you, like the experts, do all of these steps too. It will change your experience of performing.

1. Feel challenged. This is a good thing. It excites us, motivates us, scares us! and drives us to push ourselves out of our comfort zones to learn and have new, exciting experiences. So, take on the challenge. Accept it as a challenge and do it (see Chapters 1, 4, and 5).

2. Prepare. Be more prepared than you ever thought it possible to be. Do the practise, the hours of work that are necessary. Do good practise. Use practice strategies, don't rely on all your old ways of practising, look for new and inventive methods. Do what your teacher advises, explore with your friends how they practise, inform yourself about how experts practise, and about what research shows is effective. Leave no stone unturned (see Chapter 2).

3. Use mental practice. This is *the* most effective learning tool we have at our disposal. I cannot emphasise enough how important and effective it is. Use it! It is *the* way to accomplish just about anything you want in your performances – get focused, beat performance anxiety, practise technical, and expressive elements of your performance (Chapter 8).

4. Use imagery and visualisation. Imagery and visualisation are wonderful strategies to help you focus, to prepare you emotionally, and to get into your optimal performance state (Chapter 8).

5. Engage in positive self-talk and have a mantra. Stop the negative critic in your head, or at least give it a good battle of wits. Negative thoughts can snowball into catastrophisation, both before performance and/or during performance. You can stop it by challenging your thoughts, by engaging in positive self-talk and by having a positive mantra (Chapter 5).

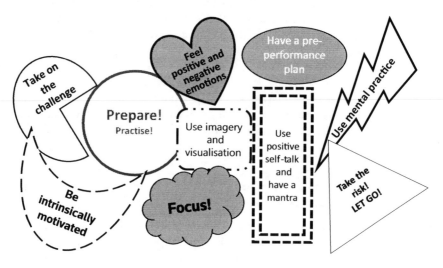

Figure 11.1 The ten steps to peak performance and flow

6. Focus! Make the decision to focus. Immerse yourself in the music, the expression, the notes, the harmony, the chords, the meaning (Chapters 7 and 8). This will block out other distractions and negative thoughts, as well as help with learning the music, technically and expressively.

7. Have a pre-performance plan (and use it!). This should include all the mental strategies that you have previously decided work for you and have practised, as well as exercises that enhance your levels of physiological arousal to the optimum (Chapter 9 and 10).

8. Feel negative and positive emotions. Be aware of how you feel. Analyse your past performances. Accept how you feel. Allow yourself to feel both negative and positive emotions. It's a rollercoaster. Go with it (Chapter 4).

9. Be intrinsically motivated. Love the music (or at least find something to love in it). Remind yourself why you are doing this, if you've forgotten even momentarily (Chapter 6).

10. Take a risk and let go! Go for it. Don't hold back. Let go of all your worries and concerns. Throw yourself into it and just do it (Chapter 10).

> *"The hard bit is getting into it before you perform, working up to it, being on your own in your dressing room and waiting for somebody to come 'ok here we go, we're ready'. That's frightening. That space of time when you come into the venue, to the conductor's room and you get dressed, just waiting for the knock on the door",*
> *"I have plenty of negative thoughts. I would feel quite humble about my ability*

... I have worked quite hard at getting rid of those negative thoughts and at being positive ... Now, when I go on stage, I don't let myself think anything negative. Now it's a habit, it's not a huge effort anymore ... I just do it. I don't let anything negative enter my mind. I always think 'yes, I can do it' ", "I just try to be as honest as I can. I try to put myself out there. You have to not be afraid to fail – take the chance, risk it".

Be yourself, and be ok with that. Find your own voice and, if you've already found it, be ok with it. *Accept.* Accept yourself and how you feel. Accept your journey. Make mistakes. Put in the work. Use the psychological strategies. Practise them daily. Change your thoughts – they're just thoughts, not facts! You create your own reality. Be honest and genuine about your music and about yourself.

Do what you love, or find the love in what you do, take on the challenge, be prepared to prepare to the point of automatisation, feel negative and positive emotions, *accept* that you feel negative as well as positive emotions, or perhaps you need to remind yourself that you feel *positive* emotions as well as the negative ones, do the mental practice, use imagery and visualisation, do positive self-talk, use a mantra, do some exercise (breathing, walking, yoga, meditation) that lowers your physiological arousal levels, have a pre-performance routine. Then, don't be afraid to fail, take the risk, put yourself out there emotionally, musically, and psychologically, let go, and just do it.

> When I'm on stage I've got a job to do. Sometimes it's exhilarating, the most euphoric feeling you could ever have. It's like "wow I'm so on a ledge up here, this could all go really wrong, really quickly, with whatever I say or whatever I do". That's such a powerful thing, that the wind in my sails is that I could fail, I could fall flat on my face in front of so many people. And that feels brilliant!
>
> Robbie Williams, singer/songwriter[12]

> [A concerto] is like a journey ... it is difficult but don't think about it. Just think about the music, sometimes the structure of the piece, sometimes the colours, so you focus on different elements of the piece. And somehow you feel very comfortable after several passages pass. And then *all* the world is yours somehow. It's the best feeling and that is why I'm addicted to play recitals or concerts. Without these feelings I'm missing something in real life. It's crazy, right? but its true.
>
> Lang Lang, international concert pianist[13]

The information and strategies in this book will assist you in bringing about more positive experiences of performance. Whether you experience flow or not, I hope that you will find the strategies effective and empowering, and that you will find yourself to be more in control of your own psychological performance states. I hope that, like the expert musicians, you too can enjoy more positive experiences of performance, more peak performance and, possibly even the occasional (or frequent) added ecstasy and freedom that comes with experiences of flow.

Notes

Introduction

1 Maslow, I. (1954). *Motivation and personality.* New York: Harper and Row; Maslow, I. (1962). *Toward a psychology of being.* Princeton, NJ: D Van Nostrand Co. doi:10.1037/ 10793-000.

2 Csikszentmihalyi, M., & Csikszentmihalyi, I. S. (Eds.). (1992). *Optimal experience: Psychological studies of flow in consciousness.* Cambridge University Press; Csikszentmihalyi, M. (2002). *Flow: The classic work on how to achieve happiness.* London: Random House; Csikszentmihalyi, M., & Nakamura, J. (2018). Flow, altered states of consciousness, and human evolution. *Journal of Consciousness Studies, 25*(11–12), 102–114; Csikszentmihalyi, M., Montijo, M. N., & Mouton, A. R. (2018). Flow theory: Optimizing elite performance in the creative realm. In S. I. Pfeiffer, E. Shaunessy-Dedrick, & M. Foley-Nicpon (Eds.), *APA handbooks in psychology®. APA handbook of giftedness and talent* (pp. 215–229). Washington, DC: American Psychological Association. doi:10.1037/0000038-014.

3 Jackson, S. A., & Csikszentmihalyi, M. (1999). *Flow in sports.* Champaign, IL: Human Kinetics; Jackson, S. A., Ford, S. K., Kimiecik, J. C., & Marsh, H. W. (1998). Psychological correlates of flow in sport. *Journal of Sport and Exercise Psychology, 20*(4), 358–378. doi.org/10.1123/jsep.20.4.358.

4 Apter, M. J. (2001). *Motivational styles in everyday life: A guide to reversal theory.* Washington, DC: American Psychological Association. doi:10.1037/10427-000.

5 Becker, J. (1994). Music and trance. *Leonardo Music Journal, 4,* 41–51. doi:10.2307/ 1513180; Becker, J. (2004). *Deep listeners: Music, emotion, and trancing.* Bloomington and Indianapolis: Indiana University Press.

6 Rouget, G. (1985). *Music and trance: A theory of the relations between music and possession.* University of Chicago Press.

7 Werner, K. (1996). *Effortless Mastery.* New Albany, IN: Jamey Aebersold Jazz.

8 Martin, J. J., & Cutler, K. (2002). An exploratory study of flow and motivation in theater actors. *Journal of Applied Sport Psychology, 14*(4), 344–352. doi:10.1080/ 10413200290103608.

9 Ericsson, A., & Pool, R. (2016). *Peak: How all of us can achieve extraordinary things.* London: Penguin Random House.

10 Gladwell, M. (2008). *Outliers: The story of success.* New York: Little, Brown and Company.

11 Ericsson, K. A., Krampe, R. T., & Tesch-Römer, C. (1993). The role of deliberate practice in the acquisition of expert performance. *Psychological Review, 100,* 363–406. doi:10.1037/0033-295X.100.3.363; Ericsson, A., & Pool, R. (2016). *Peak: How all of us can achieve extraordinary things.* London: Penguin Random House.

12 Sinnamon, S. (2008). *Musicians in flow: An empirical investigation of the peak performance experiences in novice and expert performers.* University College Dublin.
13 Moran, A. P. (2016). *The psychology of concentration in sport performers: A cognitive analysis.* Exeter: Psychology Press. doi:10.4324/9781315784946; Moran, A., & Toner, J. (2017). *A critical introduction to sport psychology: A critical introduction* (3rd ed). New York: Routledge. doi:10.4324/9781315657974.
14 The Yehudi Menuhin School, A specialist music school in Stoke d'Abernon, Cobham, Surrey, UK.

1 Music performance

1 Werner, K. (1996). *Effortless Mastery.* New Albany, IN: Jamey Aebersold Jazz.
2 Csikszentmihalyi, M., & Nakamura, J. (2018). Flow, altered states of consciousness, and human evolution. *Journal of Consciousness Studies, 25*(11–12), 102–114; Csikszentmihalyi, M. (2008). *Flow: the psychology of optimal experience.* New York: Harper Perennial Modern Classics.
3 Csikszentmihalyi, M., & Csikszentmihalyi, I. S. (Eds.). (1992). *Optimal experience: Psychological studies of flow in consciousness.* Cambridge University Press; Csikszentmihalyi, M., Abuhamdeh, S., & Nakamura, J. (2014). Flow. In *Flow and the foundations of positive psychology* (pp. 227–238). Dordrecht: Springer. doi:10.1007/978-94-017-9088-8_15. Csikszentmihalyi, M. (2008). *Flow: the psychology of optimal experience.* New York: Harper Perennial Modern Classics; Csikszentmihalyi, M., & Nakamura, J. (2018). Flow, altered states of consciousness, and human evolution. *Journal of Consciousness Studies, 25*(11–12), 102–114.
4 Jackson, S. A., & Csikszentmihalyi, M. (1999). *Flow in sports.* Human Kinetics.
5 Araujo, M. V., & Hein, C. F. (2016). Finding flow in music practice: An exploratory study about self-regulated practice behaviours and dispositions to flow in highly skilled musicians. In L. Harmat, F. Andersen, F. Ullen, J. Wright, & G. Sadlo (Eds.), *Flow experience: Empirical research and applications* (pp. 23–36). Dordrecht: Springer. doi:10.1007/978-3-319-28634-1_2.
6 Csikszentmihalyi, M., Abuhamdeh, S., & Nakamura, J. (2005). Flow. In A. J. Elliot, & C. S. Dweck (Eds.), *Handbook of competence and motivation* (pp. 598–608). New York: The Guilford Press.
7 Lehmann, A. C., Sloboda, J. A., Woody, R. H., & Woody, R. H. (2007). *Psychology for musicians: Understanding and acquiring the skills.* Oxford University Press. doi:10.1093/acprof:oso/9780195146103.001.0001; McPherson, G., Davidson, J. W., & Evans, P. (2017). Playing an instrument. In G. McPherson (Ed.), *The child as musician: A handbook of musical development* (pp. 401–421). Oxford University Press; Hallam, S., Cross, I., & Thaut, M. (Eds.). (2011). *Oxford handbook of music psychology.* Oxford University Press. doi:10.1093/oxfordhb/9780199298457.001.0001; Chaffin, R., & Lemieux, A. F. (2004). General perspectives on achieving musical excellence. In A. Williamon (Ed.), *Musical excellence: Strategies and techniques to enhance performance* (pp. 19–39). Oxford University Press.
8 Ericsson, K. A., Krampe, R. T., & Tesch-Römer, C. (1993). The role of deliberate practice in the acquisition of expert performance. *Psychological Review, 100,* 363–406. doi:10.1037/0033-295X.100.3.363; Ericsson, K. A. (2014). *The road to excellence: The acquisition of expert performance in the arts and sciences, sports, and games.* London and New York: Routledge. doi:10.4324/9781315805948.

2 What flow feels like

1 Csikszentmihalyi, M. (1997). *Finding flow: The psychology of engagement with everyday life*. New York: Basic Books. doi:10.5860/choice.35-1828; Jackson, S. A., & Csikszentmihalyi, M. (1999). *Flow in sports*. Champaign, IL: Human Kinetics; Sinnamon, S., Moran, A., & O'Connell, M. (2012). Flow among musicians: Measuring peak experiences of student performers. *Journal of Research in Music Education, 60*(1), 6–25. doi:10.1177/0022429411434931; Martin, J.J., & Cutler, K. (2002). An exploratory study of flow and motivation in theater actors. *Journal of Applied Sport Psychology, 14*, 344–352. doi:10.1080/10413200290103608; Araujo, M. V., & Hein, C. F. (2016). Finding flow in music practice: An exploratory study about self-regulated practice behaviours and dispositions to flow in highly skilled musicians. In L. Harmat, F. Andersen, F. Ullen, J. Wright, & G. Sadlo (Eds.), *Flow experience: Empirical research and applications* (pp. 23–36). Dordrecht: Springer. doi: 10.1007/978-3-319-28634-1_2; Harmat, F., Anderson, F. O. Ulen, F., Wright, J., & Sadlo, G. (2016). *Flow experience: Empirical research and application*. Dordrecht: Springer. doi:10.1007/978-3-319-28634-1; Harmat, L., de Manzano, Ö., Theorell, T., Högman, L., Fischer, H., & Ullén, F. (2015). Physiological correlates of the flow experience during computer game playing. *International Journal of Psychophysiology, 97*(1), 1–7. doi:10.1016/j.ijpsycho.2015.05.001; Chirico, A., Serino, S., Cipresso, P., Gaggioli, A., & Riva, G. (2015). When music "flows". State and trait in musical performance, composition and listening: a systematic review. *Frontiers in Psychology, 6*, 906. doi:10.3389/fpsyg.2015.00906.

2 Csikszentmihalyi, M., & Nakamura, J. (2018). Flow, altered states of consciousness, and human evolution. *Journal of Consciousness Studies, 25*(11–12), 102–114; Csikszentmihalyi, M. (2008). *Flow: the psychology of optimal experience*. New York: Harper Perennial Modern Classics; Fritz, B. S., & Avsec, A. (2007). The experience of flow and subjective well-being of music students. *Horizons of Psychology, 16*(2), 5–17. Martin, J. J., & Cutler, K. (2002). An exploratory study of flow and motivation in theater actors. *Journal of Applied Sport Psychology, 14*(4), 344–352. doi:10.1080/10413200290103608.

3 Fong, C. J., Zaleski, D. J., & Leach, J. K. (2015). The challenge–skill balance and antecedents of flow: A meta-analytic investigation. *The Journal of Positive Psychology, 10*(5), 425–446. doi:10.1080/17439760.2014.967799.

4 Hemery, D. cited in Jones, S. (1995, December 11). Inside the mind of perfection. *The Independent*, p. 10 (Sport).

5 Katwala, A. (2016). *The Athletic brain: How neuroscience is revolutionising sport and can help you perform better*. London: Simon & Schuster.

6 Jackson, S. A., & Csikszentmihalyi, M. (1999). *Flow in sports* (p. 26). Champaign, IL: Human Kinetics.

7 Jones, S. (1995, December 11). Inside the mind of perfection. *The Independent*, p. 10 (Sport). As cited in Moran, A. (2012). Thinking in action: Some insights from cognitive sport psychology. *Thinking Skills and Creativity, 7*(2), 85–92. doi:10.1016/j.tsc.2012.03.005

8 Sinnamon, S., Moran, A., & O'Connell, M. (2012). Flow among musicians: Measuring peak experiences of student performers. *Journal of Research in Music Education, 60*(1), 6–25. doi:10.1177/0022429411434931.

9 Csikszentmihalyi, M. (2002). *Flow: the classic work on how to achieve happiness* (p. 69). London: Random House.

10 Araujo, M. V., & Hein, C. F. (2016). Finding flow in music practice: An exploratory study about self-regulated practice behaviours and dispositions to flow in highly skilled

musicians. In L. Harmat, F. Andersen, F. Ullen, J. Wright, & G. Sadlo (Eds.), *Flow experience: Empirical research and applications* (pp. 23–36). Dordrecht: Springer. doi:10.1007/978-3-319-28634-1_2; Tan, L., & Sin, H. X. (2019). Flow research in music contexts: A systematic literature review. *Musicae Scientiae*. Advance online publication. doi:10.1177/1029864919877564; Bakker, A. B. (2005). Flow among music teachers and their students: The crossover of peak experiences. *Journal of Vocational Behaviour, 66*(1), 26–44. doi:10.1016/j.jvb.2003.11.001.

3 How musicians prepare for peak performance

1 Sinnamon, S., Moran, A., & O'Connell, M. (2012). Flow among musicians: Measuring peak experiences of student performers. *Journal of Research in Music Education, 60*(1), 6–25. doi:10.1177/0022429411434931. Sinnamon, S. (2008). *Musicians in flow: An empirical investigation of the peak performance experiences in novice and expert performers.* University College Dublin.

2 Newell, K. M. (1991). Motor skill acquisition. *Annual Review of Psychology, 42*(1), 213–237. doi:10.1146/annurev.ps.42.020191.001241.

3 Hanin, Y. L. (2000). *Emotions in sport.* Champaign, IL: Human Kinetics; Hanin, Y. L. (2000). Individual zones of optimal functioning (IZOF) model. *Emotions in Sport*, 65–89. Champaign, IL: Human Kinetics.

4 Managing your emotions

1 Dwyer, K. K., & Davidson, M. M. (2012). Is public speaking really more feared than death? *Communication Research Reports, 29*(2), 99–107. doi:10.1080/08824096.2012.667772.

2 Seinfeld, J. (1998). *I'm telling you for the last time.* Retrieved on 30th March, 2020, from www.youtube.com/watch?v=J020Hmu7P-g.

3 James, I. (1988). Medicine and the performing arts. The stage fright syndrome. *Transactions of the Medical Society of London, 105*, 5–9.

4 Kenny, D. (2011). *The psychology of music performance anxiety.* Oxford: Oxford University Press. doi:10.1093/acprof:oso/9780199586141.001.0001 Kenny, D. T. (2006). Music performance anxiety: Origins, phenomenology, assessment and treatment. *Journal of Music Research, 31*, 51.

5 Mascarenhas, D. R. D., & Smyth, N. C. (2011). Developing the performance brain: Decision making under pressure. In D. J. Collins, A. Button, & H. Richards (Eds.), *Performance psychology: A practitioner's guide.* London: Elsevier. doi:10.1016/B978-0-443-06734-1.00017-1.

6 Henry, K. (2019) Jonny Sexton exclusive. *Real Health Podcast, Irish independent.* Retrieved on 4th August, 2019, from www.independent.ie/life/health-wellbeing/fitness/real-health-podcast-johnny-sexton-exclusive-you-get-nervous-you-get-butterflies-you-think-why-do-i-do-this-38338693.html.

7 Pinel, J. P. J., & Barnes, S. (2017). *Biopsychology.* London: Pearson.

8 Ellis, A. (1962). *Reason and emotion in psychotherapy.* New York: Stuart; Beck, A. T. (1967). *Depression: Causes and treatment.* Philadelphia: University of Pennsylvania Press; Rodgers, S., & Tajet-Foxell, B. (2011). Emotional issues in peak performance. In *Performance psychology: A practitioner's guide* (pp 301–318). London: Elsevier. doi:10.1016/B978-0-443-06734-1.00021-3.

9 Button, C., MacMahon, C., & Masters, R. (2011). 'Keeping it together': Motor control under pressure. In D. J. Collins, A. Button, & H. Richards (Eds.), *Performance psychology: A practitioner's guide*. London: Elsevier. doi:10.1016/B978-0-443-06734-1.00013-4.

10 This article also contains a longer version of the MPAI: Kenny, D. T., & Osborne, M. S. (2006). Music performance anxiety: New insights from young musicians. *Advances in Cognitive Psychology, 2*(2–3), 103–112; doi:10.2478/v10053-008-0049-5. Osborne, M. S., Kenny, D. T., & Holsomback, R. (2005). Assessment of music performance anxiety in late childhood: A validation study of the Music Performance Anxiety Inventory for Adolescents (MPAI-A). *International Journal of Stress Management, 12*(4),312. doi:10.1037/1072-5245.12.4.312.

11 Matei, R., & Ginsborg, J. (2017). Music performance anxiety in classical musicians – what we know about what works. *BJPsych International, 14*(2), 33–35. doi:10.1192/S2056474000001744; Papageorgi, I., Creech, A., & Welch, G. (2013). Perceived performance anxiety in advanced musicians specializing in different musical genres. *Psychology of Music, 41*(1), 18-4 1. doi:10.1177/0305735611408995; Kenny, D. T. (2006). Music performance anxiety: Origins, phenomenology, assessment and treatment. *Journal of Music Research, 31*, 51; Fehm, L., & Schmidt, K. (2006). Performance anxiety in gifted adolescent musicians. *Journal of Anxiety Disorders, 20*(1), 98–109. doi:10.1016/j.janxdis.2004.11.011; Wilson, G. D., & Roland, D. (2002). Performance anxiety. In Parncutt, R., & McPherson, G. (Eds.), *The science and psychology of music performance: Creative strategies for teaching and learning* (pp. 47–61). Oxford University Press. doi:10.1093/acprof:oso/9780195138108.003.0004; Van Kemenade, J. F., Van Son, M. J., & Van Heesch, N. C. (1995). Performance anxiety among professional musicians in symphonic orchestras: a self-report study. *Psychological Reports, 77*(2), 555–562. https://doi.org/10.2466/pr0.1995.77.2.555; Cox, W. J., & Kenardy, J. (1993). Performance anxiety, social phobia, and setting effects in instrumental music students. *Journal of Anxiety Disorders, 7*(1), 49–60. doi:10.1016/0887-6185(93)90020-L; Salmon, P. G. (1992). *Notes from the green room: Coping with stress and anxiety in musical performance*. Hoboken, NJ: John Wiley & Sons; Wesner, R. B., Noyes Jr, R., & Davis, T. L. (1990). The occurrence of performance anxiety among musicians. *Journal of Affective Disorders, 18*(3), 177–185. doi:10.1016/0165-0327(90)90034–6; Fishbein, M., Middlestadt, S. E., Ottati, V., Straus, S., & Ellis, A. (1988). Medical problems among ICSOM musicians: overview of a national survey. *Medical Problems of Performing Artists, 3*(1), 1–8.

12 Cooper, C. L., & Wills, G. I. (1989). Popular musicians under pressure. *Psychology of Music, 17*(1), 22–36. doi:10.1177/0305735689171003.

13 Kenny, D. T., & Osborne, M. S. (2006). Music performance anxiety: New insights from young musicians. *Advances in Cognitive Psychology, 2*(2–3), 103–112. doi:10.2478/v10053-008-0049-5.

14 DSM-V American Psychiatric Association. (2013). *Diagnostic and statistical manual of mental disorders* (5th ed.). Arlington, VA: American Psychiatric Publishing. doi:10.1176/appi.books.9780890425596.

15 Matei, R., & Ginsborg, J. (2017). Music performance anxiety in classical musicians – what we know about what works. *BJPsych International, 14*(2), 33–35. doi:10.1192/S2056474000001744.

16 Hewitt, P. L., & Flett, G. L. (1996). *The multidimensional perfectionism scale*. Toronto: Multi-Health Systems Inc; Hewitt, P. L., Flett, G. L., & Ediger, E. (1995). Perfectionism traits and perfectionistic self-presentation in eating disorder attitudes, characteristics, and symptoms. *International Journal of Eating Disorders, 18*(4), 317–326. doi:10.1002/1098-108X(199512)18:4<317::AID-EAT2260180404>3.0.CO;2-2.

17 Hewitt, P. L., Flett, G. L., & Ediger, E. (1995). Perfectionism traits and perfection-istic self-presentation in eating disorder attitudes, characteristics, and symptoms. *International Journal of Eating Disorders*, *18*(4), 317–326. doi:10.1002/1098-108X(199512)18:4<317::aid-eat2260180404>3.0.CO;2-2; Sinden, L. M. (1999). *Music performance anxiety: Contributions of perfectionism, coping style, self-efficacy, and self-esteem* (Doctoral dissertation, ProQuest Information & Learning); Kenny, D. T., Davis, P., & Oates, J. (2004). Music performance anxiety and occupational stress amongst opera chorus artists and their relationship with state and trait anxiety and perfectionism. *Journal of Anxiety Disorders*, *18*(6), 757–777. doi:10.1016/j.janxdis.2003.09.004.

18 Yerkes, R. M., & Dodson, J. D. (1908). The relation of strength of stimulus to rapidity of habit-formation. *Neural. Psychol.*, *18*, 459–482. doi:10.1002/cne.920180503.

19 Csikszentmihalyi, M., & Nakamura, J. (2018). Flow, altered states of consciousness, and human evolution. *Journal of Consciousness Studies*, *25*(11–12), 102–114. Csikszentmihalyi, M. (2008). *Flow: the psychology of optimal experience*. New York: Harper Perennial Modern Classics; Csikszentmihalyi, M. (2002). *Flow: The classic work on how to achieve happiness*. London: Random House.

20 Csikszentmihalyi, M. (2008). *Flow: the psychology of optimal experience*. New York: Harper Perennial Modern Classics; Csikszentmihalyi, M., Abuhamdeh, S., & Nakamura, J. (2005). Flow. In A. J. Elliot, & C. S. Dweck (Eds.), *Handbook of competence and motivation* (pp. 598–608). New York: The Guilford Press; Jackson, S. A., & Csikszentmihalyi, M. (1999). *Flow in sports*. Champaign, IL: Human Kinetics.

21 Csikszentmihalyi, M. (2008). *Flow: the psychology of optimal experience*. New York: Harper Perennial Modern Classics; Csikszentmihalyi, M. (2002) *Flow: The classic work on how to achieve happiness*. London: Random House.

22 Hanin, Y. L. (2000). Individual zones of optimal functioning (IZOF) model. *Emotions in Sport*, 65–89. Champaign, IL: Human Kinetics; Hanin, Y. L. (2007). Emotions in sport: Current issues and perspectives. *Handbook of Sport Psychology*, *3*(3158), 22–41. doi:10.1002/9781118270011.ch2; Hanin, Y. L. (2000). *Emotions in sport*. Champaign, IL: Human Kinetics.

23 Robazza, C., Pellizzari, M., & Hanin, Y. (2004). Emotion self-regulation and athletic performance: An application of the IZOF model. *Psychology of Sport and Exercise*, *5*(4), 379–404. doi:10.1016/S1469-0292(03)00034-7.

24 Hanin, Y. L. (2000). Individual zones of optimal functioning (IZOF) model. *Emotions in Sport*, 65–89. Champaign, IL: Human Kinetics.

25 Lazarus, R. S., & Lazarus, R. S. (1991). *Emotion and adaptation*. Oxford University Press on Demand; Lazarus, R. S., Kanner, A. D., & Folkman, S. (1980). Emotions: A cognitive–phenomenological analysis. In R. Plutchik, & H. Kellerman (Eds.), *Theories of emotion* (pp. 189–217). New York: Academic Press. doi:10.1016/B978-0-12-558701-3.50014-4; Lazarus, R. S., & Folkman, S. (1984) *Stress, appraisal, and coping* (p. 141). Dordrecht: Springer.

26 Lazarus, R. S., & Folkman, S. (1984) *Stress, appraisal, and coping*. p.141. Dordrecht: Springer; Richards, H. (2011). Coping and mental toughness. In D. J. Collins, A. Button, & H. Richards (Eds.), *Performance Psychology: A practitioner's guide* (pp. 281–300). London: Elsevier; Biggs, A., Brough, P., & Drummond, S. (2017). Lazarus and Folkman's psychological stress and coping theory. *The handbook of stress and health*, 349-36. doi:10.1016/B978-0-443-06734-1.00020-1.

27 Richards, H. (2011). Coping and mental toughness. In D. J. Collins, A. Button, & H. Richards (Eds.), *Performance psychology: A practitioner's guide* (p. 283). London: Elsevier. doi:10.1016/B978-0-443-06734-1.00020-1.

5 Managing your thoughts

1 Lazarus, R. S., & Folkman, S. (1984). *Stress, appraisal, and coping* (p. 141). Dordrecht: Springer. Richards, H. (2011). Coping and mental toughness. In D. J. Collins, A. Button, & H. Richards (Eds.), *Performance psychology: A practitioner's guide* (pp. 281–300). Elsevier Health Science. doi:10.1016/B978-0-443-06734-1.00020-1; Biggs, A., Brough, P., & Drummond, S. (2017). Lazarus and Folkman's psychological stress and coping theory. *The Handbook of Stress and Health*, 349–364. doi:10.1002/9781118993811.ch21; Ward, J. (2014). *A student's guide to cognitive neuroscience* (pp. 135–164). New York: Psychology Press. doi:10.1080/17588928.2014.976381.

2 Ward, J. (2014). *A student's guide to cognitive neuroscience* (pp. 135–164). New York: Psychology Press; Ashby, F. G., & Isen, A. M. (1999). A neuropsychological theory of positive affect and its influence on cognition. *Psychological Review*, 106(3), 529–550.

3 Ashby, F. G., & Isen, A. M. (1999). A neuropsychological theory of positive affect and its influence on cognition. *Psychological Review*, 106(3), 529–550; Pinel, J. P. J., & Barnes, S. (2017). *Biopsychology*. London: Pearson; Wacker, J. (2018). Effects of positive emotion, extraversion, and dopamine on cognitive stability-flexibility and frontal EEG asymmetry. *Psychophysiology*, 55(1), e12727. doi:10.1111/psyp.12727; Vago, D. R., & David, S. A. (2012). Self-awareness, self-regulation, and self-transcendence (S-ART): A framework for understanding the neurobiological mechanisms of mindfulness. *Frontiers in Human Neuroscience*, 6, 296. doi:10.3389/fnhum.2012.00296; Sapolsky, R. (2003, November). Stress and plasticity in the limbic system. *Neurochemical Research*, 28(11), 1735–1742. doi:10.1023/A:1026021307833.

4 Beck, A. T. (1967). *Depression: Causes and treatment*. Philadelphia: University of Pennsylvania Press; Beck, J. S., & Beck, A. T. (2011). *Cognitive behavior therapy: Basics and beyond*, 2nd edition. Guildford Press.

5 Rodgers, S., & Tajet-Foxell, B. (2011). Emotional issues in peak performance. In *Performance psychology: A practitioner's guide* (p. 306). London: Elsevier. doi:10.1016/B978-0-443-06734-1.00021-3.

6 Fredrickson, B. (2010). *Positivity: Ground breaking research to release your inner optimist and thrive*. New York: Random House. Also see website: www.positivityratio.com.

7 Ellis, A. (2000). *How to control your anxiety before it controls you*. New York: Citadel Press; Dryden, W., & Ellis, A. (2001). Rational emotive behaviour therapy. In K. S. Dodson (Ed.), *Handbook of Cognitive-Behavioral Therapies* (pp. 295–348). New York: Guilford Press; Ellis, A. (1962). *Reason and Emotion in Psychotherapy*. New York: Stuart.

8 Beck, J. S. (2011). *Cognitive behavior therapy: Basics and beyond* (2nd ed.). New York: Guilford Press; Rodgers, S., & Tajet-Foxell, B. (2011). Emotional issues in peak performance. In *Performance psychology: A practitioner's guide* (pp. 301–318). London: Elsevier. doi:10.1016/B978-0-443-06734-1.00021-3; Williams, C. J. (2001). *Overcoming depression: a five areas approach*. London: Arnold.

9 Eagleson, C., Hayes, S., Mathews, A., Perman, G., & Hirsch, C. R. (2016). The power of positive thinking: Pathological worry is reduced by thought replacement in generalized anxiety disorder. *Behaviour Research and Therapy*, 78, 13–18. doi:10.1016/j.brat.2015.12.017; Wolpe, J. (1973). The practice of behavioural therapy. Pergamon general psychology series. Beck, A. (1976). *Cognitive therapies and the emotional disorders*. New York: International Universities Press.

10 Dryden, W., & Ellis, A. (2001). Rational emotive behaviour therapy. In K. S. Dodson (Ed.), *Handbook of Cognitive-Behavioral Therapies* (pp. 295–348). New York: Guilford Press;

Ellis, A. (1962). *Reason and emotion in psychotherapy*. New York: Stuart. Maltby, J., Day, L., & Macaskill, A. (2017). *Personality, individual differences and intelligence*. London: Pearson.
11 Dryden, W. (2006). *Getting started with REBT: A concise guide for clients*. London: Routledge; Malkinson, R. (2010). Cognitive-behavioral grief therapy: The ABC model of rational-emotion behavior therapy. *Psihologijske teme*, *19*(2), 289–305.
12 Dryden, W., & Ellis, A. (2001). Rational emotive behaviour therapy. In K. S. Dodson (Ed.), *Handbook of Cognitive-Behavioral Therapies* (pp. 295–348). New York: Guilford Press; Beck, J. S. (2011). Cognitive behavior therapy: Basics and beyond (2nd ed.). New York: Guilford Press; Mind Tools Content Team. (n.d.). Cognitive restructuring: Reducing stress by changing your thinking. *Mind Tools*. Retrieved on 23rd January, 2020, from www.mindtools.com/pages/article/newTCS_81.htm.
13 Katie, B., & Mitchell, S. (2008). *Loving what is: How four questions can change your life*. Random House; Smernoff, E., Mitnik, I., Kolodner, K., & Lev-ari, S. (2015). The effects of "The Work" meditation (Byron Katie) on psychological symptoms and quality of life—a pilot clinical study. *Explore*, *11*(1), 24–31. doi:10.1016/j.explore.2014.10.003. Dryden, W., & Ellis, A. (2001). Rational emotive behaviour therapy. In K. S. Dodson (Ed.), *Handbook of Cognitive-Behavioral Therapies* (pp. 295–348). New York: Guilford Press; Mind Tools Content Team. (n.d.). Cognitive restructuring: Reducing stress by changing your thinking. *Mind Tools*. Retrieved on 23rd January, 2020, from www.mindtools.com/pages/article/newTCS_81.htm.
14 Walter, N., Nikoleizig, L., & Alfermann, D. (2019). Effects of self-talk training on competitive anxiety, self-efficacy, volitional skills, and performance: An intervention study with junior sub-elite athletes. *Sports*, *7*(6), 148. doi:10.3390/sports7060148; Richards, H. (2011). Coping and mental toughness. In Collins, D. J., Button, A., & Richards, H. (Eds.), *Performance psychology: A practitioner's Guide*. London: Elsevier. doi:10.1016/B978-0-443-06734-1.00020-1; Hardy, J. (2006). Speaking clearly: A critical review of the self-talk literature. *Psychol. Sport and Exer*, *7*, 81–97. doi:10.1016/j.psychsport.2005.04.002; Van Raalte, J. L., Vincent, A., & Brewer, B. W. (2017). Self-talk interventions for athletes: A theoretically grounded approach. *Journal of Sport Psychology in Action*, *8*(3), 141–151. doi:10.1080/21520704.2016.1233921.

6 Motivation

1 Deci, E. L., & Ryan, R. M. (2000). The "what" and "why" of goal pursuits: Human needs and the self-determination of behavior. *Psychological Inquiry*, *11*(4), 227–268. doi:10.1207/S15327965PLI1104_01. Ryan, R. M., & Deci, E. L. (2000). Intrinsic and extrinsic motivations: Classic definitions and new directions. *Contemporary Educational Psychology*, *25*(1), 54–67. doi:10.1006/ceps.1999.1020.
2 Ryan, R. M., & Deci, E. L. (2000). When rewards compete with nature: The undermining of intrinsic motivation and self-regulation. In C. Sansone, & J. M. Harackiewicz (Eds.), *Intrinsic and extrinsic motivation: The search for optimal motivation and performance* (pp. 13–54). New York: Academic Press. doi:10.1016/B978-012619070-0/50024–6.
3 Ryan, R. M., & Deci, E. L. (2000). The darker and brighter sides of human existence: Basic psychological needs as a unifying concept. *Psychological Inquiry*, *11*(4), 319 338. Deci, E. L., & Ryan, R. M. (Eds.) (2004). *Handbook of self-determination research*. New York: University Rochester Press. doi:10.1207/S15327965PLI1104_03. Standage, M., & Ryan, R. M. (2019). Self-determination theory in sport and exercise. *Handbook of Sport Psychology* (4th ed., pp. 352–378). Hoboken, NJ: Wiley.

4   Austin, J., Renwick, J., & McPherson, G. (2006). Developing motivation. In G. McPherson (Ed.), *The child as musician: A handbook of musical development* (pp. 213–238). Oxford: Oxford University Press. doi: 10.1093/acprof:oso/9780198530329.003.0011.

5   Evans, P. (2017). Motivation. In G. McPherson (Ed.), *The child as musician: A handbook of musical development* (pp. 325–339). Oxford: Oxford University Press. doi:10.1093/acprof:oso/9780198744443.003.0017; Dweck, C. S. (2017). *Mindset: Changing the way you think to fulfil your potential* (6th ed.). London: Robinson.

6   Dweck, C. S. (2008). *Mindset: The new psychology of success.* London: Random House Digital.

7   Austin, J., Renwick, J., & McPherson, G. (2006). Developing motivation. In G. McPherson (Ed.), *The child as musician: A handbook of musical development* (pp. 213–238). Oxford: Oxford University Press. doi:10.1093/acprof:oso/9780198530329.003.0011; Dweck, C. S. (2017). *Mindset: Changing the way you think to fulfil your potential* (6th ed.). London: Robinson; O'Neill, S. A. (2006). Positive youth musical engagement. In G. McPherson (Ed.), *The child as musician: A handbook of musical development* (pp. 461–474). Oxford University Press. doi:10.1093/acprof:oso/9780198530329.003.0023.

8   Hayes, N. (2018). *Your brain and you: A simple guide to neuropsychology.* London: Teach Yourself Publications; Kolb, B., & Wishaw, I. Q. (2015). *Fundamentals of neuropsychology.* New York: Worth Publishers.

9   Low, L. K., & Cheng, H. J. (2006). Axon pruning: An essential step underlying the developmental plasticity of neuronal connections. *Philosophical Transactions of the Royal Society B: Biological Sciences, 361*(1473), 1531–1544. doi:10.1098/rstb.2006.1883.

10 Deci, E. L., & Ryan, R. M. (Eds.) (2004). *Handbook of self-determination research.* New York: University Rochester Press.

11 Evans, P. P. (2015). Self-determination theory: An approach to motivation in music education. *Musicae Scientiae, 19*(1), 65–83. doi:10.1177/1029864914568044; O'Neill, S. A. (2006). Positive youth musical engagement. In G. McPherson (Ed.) *The child as musician: A handbook of musical development* (pp. 461–474). Oxford: Oxford University Press. doi:10.1093/acprof:oso/9780198530329.003.0023; O'Neill, S., & McPherson, G. (2002). Motivation. In McPherson, G., & Parncutt, R. (Eds.), *The science & psychology of music performance: Creative strategies for teaching & learning* (pp. 31–46). Oxford: Oxford University Press.

12 Evans, P. (2015). Self-determination theory: An approach to motivation in music education. *Musicae Scientiae, 19*(1), 65–83. doi:10.1177/1029864914568044; Tucker, O. G. (2018). Positive teacher influence strategies to improve secondary instrumental students' motivation and perceptions of self. *Update: Applications of Research in Music Education, 36*(3), 5–11. doi:10.1177/8755123317733109.

13 Nicholls, J. G. (1984). Achievement motivation: Conceptions of ability, subjective experience, task choice, and performance. *Psychological Review, 91*(3), 328. doi:10.1037/0033-295X.91.3.328; Nicholls, J. G. (2017). Conceptions of ability and achievement motivation: A theory and its implications for education. In *Learning and motivation in the classroom* (pp. 211–238). London and New York: Routledge. doi:10.4324/9781315188522-11. Note on the concept of 'ego' goals. In current literature, the concept of 'ego' goals is referred to as 'performance' goals. I have maintained the older label 'ego' goals so as not to confuse the discussion of performance with the use of the label 'performance' goals.

14 Duda, J. L., Appleton, P. R., Stebbings, J., & Balaguer, I. (2017). Towards more empowering and less disempowering environments in youth sport: Theory to

evidenced-based practice. In *Sport psychology for young athletes* (pp. 81–93). London and New York: Routledge. doi:10.4324/9781315545202-8; Standage, M., & Treasure, D. C. (2002). Relationship among achievement goal orientations and multidimensional situational motivation in physical education. *British Journal of Educational Psychology*, *72*(1), 87–103. doi:10.1348/000709902158784; Sinnamon, S. (2008). *Musicians in flow: an empirical investigation of the peak performance experiences in novice and expert performers*. University College Dublin; Standage, M., & Ryan, R. M. (2019). Self-determination theory in sport and exercise. *Handbook of sport psychology* (4th ed., pp. 352–378). Hoboken, NJ: Wiley.

15 Lang, L. (2015). Lang Lang's three secrets for a calm, composed on-stage performance. *Classic FM*. Retrieved from www.classicfm.com/artists/lang-lang/news/teaching-app on 29th June 2020.

16 Duda, J. L. (2005). Motivation in sport: The relevance of competence and achievement goals. In A. J. Elliot, & C. S. Dweck (Eds.), *Handbook of competence and motivation* (pp. 318–335). New York: The Guilford Press.

17 Standage, M., & Treasure, D. C. (2002). Relationship among achievement goal orientations and multidimensional situational motivation in physical education. *British Journal of Educational Psychology*, *72*(1), 87–103. doi:10.1348/000709902158784; Standage, M., & Ryan, R. M. (2019). Self-determination theory in sport and exercise. *Handbook of sport psychology* (4th ed., pp. 352–378). Hoboken, NJ: Wiley.

18 Csikszentmihalyi, M., Abuhamdeh. S., & Nakamura, J. (2005). Flow. In A. J. Elliot, & C. S. Dweck (Eds.), *Handbook of competence and motivation* (pp. 598–608). New York: The Guilford Press; Sinnamon, S. (2008). *Musicians in flow: an empirical investigation of the peak performance experiences in novice and expert performers*. University College Dublin.

19 Eilish, B. (2019). Carpool Karaoke. *The late late show with James Corden*. Retreived 20th December, 2019, from www.youtube.com/watch?v=uh2qGWfmESk.

20 Csikszentmihalyi, M. (2002). *Flow: The classic work on how to achieve happiness*. London: Random House.

21 Roberts, G. C., Treasure, D. C., & Balague, G. (1998). Achievement goals in sport: The development and validation of the perception of success questionnaire. *Journal of Sports Sciences*, *16*(4), 337–347. doi:10.1080/02640419808559362.

22 Heider, F. (1958). *The psychology of interpersonal relations*. New York: Wiley. doi:10.1037/10628-000.

23 Rotter, J. B. (1954). *Social Learning and Clinical Psychology*. Englewood Cliffs, NJ: Prentice-Hall; Rotter, J. B. (1966). Generalized expectancies of internal versus external control of reinforcements. *Psychological Monographs*, *80* (whole no. 609). doi:10.1037/10788-000.

24 Rotter, J. B. (1954). *Social learning and clinical psychology*. Englewood Cliffs, NJ: Prentice-Hall; Rotter, J. B. (1966). Generalized expectancies of internal versus external control of reinforcements. *Psychological Monographs*, *80* (whole no. 609). doi:10.1037/10788-000.

25 Austin, J., Renwick, J., & McPherson, G. (2006). Developing motivation. In G. McPherson (Ed.), *The child as musician: A handbook of musical development* (pp. 213–238). Oxford: Oxford University Press. doi:10.1093/acprof:oso/9780198530329.003.0011; Evans, P., & McPherson, G. E. (2015). Identity and practice: The motivational benefits of a long-term musical identity. *Psychology of Music*, *43*(3), 407–422. doi:10.1177/0305735613514471.

26 Dweck, C.S. (2017). *Mindset: Changing the way you think to fulfil your potential* (6th ed.). Robinson; Ericsson, A., & Pool, R. (2017). *Peak: How all of can achieve extraordinary things*.

London: Penguin Random House; Kremer, J., & Moran, A. P. (2012). *Pure sport: Practical sport psychology*. London and New York: Routledge. doi:10.4324/9780203934494.

27 McPherson, G. E., & McCormick, J. (2006). Self-efficacy and music performance. *Psychology of Music*, *34*(3), 322–336. doi:10.1177/0305735606064841; Bonneville-Roussy, A., Lavigne, G. L., & Vallerand, R. J. (2011). When passion leads to excellence: The case of musicians. *Psychology of Music*, *39*(1), 123–138. doi:10.1177/0305735609352441; Yusuf, M. (2011). The impact of self-efficacy, achievement motivation, and self-regulated learning strategies on students' academic achievement. *Procedia-Social and Behavioral Sciences*, *15*, 2623–2626. doi:10.1016/j.sbspro.2011.04.158; Skaalvik, E. M. (1997). Self-enhancing and self-defeating ego orientation: Relations with task and avoidance orientation, achievement, self-perceptions, and anxiety. *Journal of Educational Psychology*, *89*(1), 71. doi:10.1037/0022-0663.89.1.71; Skaalvik, E. M. (1997). Self-enhancing and self-defeating ego orientation: Relations with task and avoidance orientation, achievement, self-perceptions, and anxiety. *Journal of Educational Psychology*, *89*(1), 71. doi:10.1037/0022-0663.89.1.71.

7 Concentration and focus

1 Moran, A. (2011). Concentration. In D. J. Collins, A. Button, & H. Richards (Eds.), *Performance psychology: A practitioner's guide* (pp. 319–336). London: Elsevier. doi:10.1016/B978-0-443-06734-1.00022-5.

2 Moran, A. (2011). Concentration. In D. J. Collins, A. Button, & H. Richards (Eds.), *Performance psychology: A practitioner's guide* (pp. 319–336). London: Elsevier. doi:10.1016/B978-0-443-06734-1.00022-5.

3 Moran, A. P., & Sinnamon, S. (2019). Music and the mind series: Focus, with Liz Nolan. *Lyric fm*. Retrieved 18th March, 2020, 14.40, from https://soundcloud.com/rtelyricfm/music-and-the-mind-episode-4-concentration-and-focus.

4 Van Hooff, J., & Goldstein, E. (2018). *Cognitive psychology* (pp. 84–117). Boston, MA: Cengage Learning; Eysenck, M. W., & Keane, M. T. (2015). *Cognitive psychology: A student's handbook* (pp. 155–206). London and New York: Routledge. doi:10.4324/9781315778006.

5 Moran, A. (2011). Concentration. In D. J. Collins, A. Button, & H. Richards (Eds.), *Performance psychology: A practitioner's guide* (pp. 319–336). London: Elsevier. doi:10.1016/B978-0-443-06734-1.00022-5.; Moran, A. (2010). Concentration/attention. In *Routledge handbook of applied sport psychology* (pp. 516–525). London and New York: Routledge.

6 Moran, A. P. (2016). *The psychology of concentration in sport performers: A cognitive analysis*. London and New York: Routledge; Kremer, J., & Moran, A. (2008). Pure sport: Practical sport psychology. London and New York: Routledge. doi:10.4324/9781315784946;

7 Beaumeister, R. F. (1984). Choking under pressure: self-consciousness and the paradoxical effects of incentives on skilled performance. *J Pers. Soc. Psychol*, *46*, 610–620. doi:10.1037/0022-3514.46.3.610.

8 Mascarenhas, D. R. D., & Smyth, N. C. (2011). Developing the performance brain: Decision making under pressure. In D. J. Collins, A. Button, & H. Richards (Eds.), *Performance psychology: A practitioner's guide*. London: Elsevier. doi:10.1016/B978-0-443-06734-1.00017-1.

9 Sinnamon, S. (2008). *Musicians in flow: An empirical investigation of the peak performance experiences in novice and expert performers*. University College Dublin.

10 Moran, A. (2011). Concentration. In D. J. Collins, A. Button, & H. Richards (Eds.), *Performance psychology: A practitioner's guide* (pp. 319–336). London: Elsevier. doi:10.1016/B978-0-443-06734-1.00022-5; Williams, J. M., & Leffingwell, T. R. (2002). Cognitive strategies in sport and exercise psychology. In J. L. Van Raalte, B. W., & Brewer (Eds.), *Exploring sport and exercise psychology* (2nd ed.), 75–98. Washington, DC: American Psychological Association. doi:10.1037/10465-005.

11 Williams, J. M., & Leffingwell, T. R. (2002). Cognitive strategies in sport and exercise psychology. In J. L. Van Raalte, & B. W. Brewer (Eds.), *Exploring sport and exercise psychology* (2nd ed., pp. 75–98). Washington, DC: American Psychological Association. doi:10.1037/10465-005

12 Aufegger, L., Perkins, R., Wasley, D., & Williamon, A. (2016). Musicians' perceptions and experiences of using simulation training to develop performance skills. *Psychology of Music, 45*, 417–443. doi:10.1037/10675-000.

13 This example about Itzak Perlman using imagery and visualisation technique for replicating performance conditions in order to practise performance is cited in Hays, K. F., & Brown, C. H. Jr (2004). *You're on! Consulting for peak performance* (pp. 102–103). Washington, DC: American Psychological Association. doi:10.1080/10413200.2010.491780.

14 Mesagno, C., & Mullane-Grant, T. (2010). A comparison of different pre-performance routines as possible choking interventions. *Journal of Applied Sport Psychology, 22*(3), 343–360. doi:10.1080/10413200.2010.491780.

8 Mental practice, imagery, and visualisation

1 Pearson, J. (2019). The human imagination: The cognitive neuroscience of visual mental imagery. *Nature Reviews Neuroscience, 20*(10), 624–634. doi:10.1038/s41583-019-0202-9; Pilgramm, S., de Haas, B., Helm, F., Zentgraf, K., Stark, R., Munzert, J., & Krüger, B. (2016). Motor imagery of hand actions: Decoding the content of motor imagery from brain activity in frontal and parietal motor areas. *Human Brain Mapping, 37*(1), 81–93. doi:10.1002/hbm.23015; Wakefield, C., Smith, D., Moran, A. P., & Holmes, P. (2013). Functional equivalence or behavioural matching? A critical reflection on 15 years of research using the PETTLEP model of motor imagery. *International Review of Sport and Exercise Psychology, 6*(1), 105–121. doi:10.1080/1750984X.2012.724437; Moran, A., Guillot, A., MacIntyre, T., & Collet, C. (2012). Re-imagining motor imagery: Building bridges between cognitive neuroscience and sport psychology. *British Journal of Psychology, 103*(2), 224–247. doi:10.1111/j.2044-8295.2011.02068.x; Holmes, P., & Calmels, C. (2011). Mental practice: Neuroscientific support for a new approach. In D. J. Collins, A. Button, & H. Richards (Eds.), *Performance psychology: A practitioner's guide* (pp. 231–244). London: Elsevier. doi:10.1016/B978-0-443-06734-1.00016-X; Holmes, P., & Calmels, C. (2008). A neuroscientific review of imagery and observation use in sport. *Journal of Motor Behavior, 40*(5), 433–445. doi:10.3200/JMBR.40.5.433-445; Holmes, P., Collins, D., & Calmels, C. (2006): Electroencephalographic functional equivalence during observation of action. *Journal of Sports Sciences, 24*(06), 605–616. doi:10.1080/02640410500244507.

2 Holmes, P., & Calmels, C. (2011). Mental practice: Neuroscientific support for a new approach. In D. J. Collins, A. Button, & H. Richards (Eds.), *Performance Psychology: A Practitioner's Guide* (pp. 231–244). London: Elsevier. doi:10.1016/B978-0-443-06734-1.00016-X.

3 Bell, J. (2015). 'I often have to battle negative thoughts on stage', says violinist Joshua Bell. The Strad, Nov, 2015. Retrieved from www.thestrad.com/i-often-have-to-battle-negative-thoughts-on-stage-says-violinist-joshua-bell/2970.article on 29th June 2020.

4 Story about Itzak Perlman, cited in Hays, K. F., & Brown, C. H. Jr (2004). *You're on! Consulting for peak performance* (pp. 102–103). Washington, DC: American Psychological Association.

5 Van Hooff, J., & Goldstein, E. (2018). *Cognitive Psychology* (pp. 84–117). Boston, MA: Cengage Learning.

6 Fischer, S. (2004). *Practice*. London: Edition Peters; Fischer, S. (1997). *Basics*. London: Edition Peters. Retrieved on 23rd January, 2020, from www.simonfischeronline. com/uploads/5/7/7/9/57796211/203_may_mental_rehearsal.pdf.

7 Goldstein, E. B. (2011). *Cognitive psychology: Connecting mind, research and everyday experience* (3rd ed., pp. 114–237). Boston, MA: Cengage Learning.

8 Abraham, A., & Collins, D. (2011). Effective skill development: How should athletes' skills be developed? In D. J. Collins, A. Button, & H. Richards, H. (Eds.), *Performance Psychology: A Practitioner's Guide* (pp. 207–230). London: Elsevier. doi:10.1016/ B978-0-443-06734-1.00015-8.

9 Fischer, S. (2017). Cited in 7 ways to harness mental practice for musicians. *The Strad*. Retrieved on 28th January, 2020, from www.thestrad.com/7-ways-to-harness-mental-practice-for-musicians/168.article.

10 Fischer, S. (2017). Cited in 7 ways to harness mental practice for musicians. *The Strad*. Retrieved on 28th January, 2020, from www.thestrad.com/7-ways-to-harness-mental-practice-for-musicians/168.article.

9 Calming the body and mind

1 Lehrer, P. M., & Gevirtz, R. (2014). Heart rate variability biofeedback: How and why does it work? *Frontiers in Psychology, 5*, 756. doi:10.3389/fpsyg.2014.00756; Jerath, R., Crawford, M. W., Barnes, V. A., & Harden, K. (2015). Self-regulation of breathing as a primary treatment for anxiety. *Applied Psychophysiology and Biofeedback, 40*(2), 107–115. doi:10.1007/s10484-015-9279-8; Pinel, J. P. J., & Barnes, S. (2017). *Biopsychology*. London: Pearson.

2 Khalsa, S. B. S., Shorter, S. M., Cope, S., Wyshak, G., & Sklar, E. (2009). Yoga ameliorates performance anxiety and mood disturbance in young professional musicians. *Applied Psychophysiology and Biofeedback, 34*(4), 279. doi:10.1007/s10484-009-9103-4; Brown, R. P., & Gerbarg, P. L. (2005). Sudarshan Kriya Yogic breathing in the treatment of stress, anxiety, and depression: part II—clinical applications and guidelines. *Journal of Alternative & Complementary Medicine, 11*(4), 711–717. doi:10.1089/acm.2005.11.711; Bhimani, N. T., Kulkarni, N. B., Kowale, A., & Salvi, S. (2011). Effect of Pranayama on stress and cardiovascular autonomic function. *Indian J Physiol Pharmacol, 55*(4), 370–7; Brown, R. P., & Gerbarg, P. L. (2005). Sudarshan Kriya yogic breathing in the treatment of stress, anxiety, and depression: part I—neurophysiologic model. *Journal of Alternative & Complementary Medicine, 11*(1), 189–201. doi:10.1089/acm.2005.11.189; Descilo, T., Vedamurtachar, A., Gerbarg, P. L., Nagaraja, D., Gangadhar, B. N., Damodaran, B., …, & Brown, R. P. (2010). Effects of a yoga breath intervention alone and in combination with an exposure therapy for post-traumatic stress disorder and depression in survivors of the 2004 South-East Asia tsunami. *Acta Psychiatrica Scandinavica, 121*(4), 289–300. doi:10.1111/j.1600-0447.2009.01466.x; Ma, X., Yue, Z. Q., Gong, Z. Q., Zhang, H., Duan, N. Y., Shi, Y. T., …, & Li, Y. F. (2017). The effect of diaphragmatic breathing on attention, negative affect and stress in healthy adults. *Frontiers in Psychology, 8*, 874. doi:10.3389/fpsyg.2017.00874.

3 Pinel, J. P. J., & Barnes, S. (2017). *Biopsychology*. London: Pearson.

4 Bonaz, B., Bazin, T., & Pellissier, S. (2018). The vagus nerve at the interface of the microbiota-gut-brain axis. *Frontiers in Neuroscience, 12*, 49 doi:10.3389/fnins.2018.00049; Henry, T. R. (2002). Therapeutic mechanisms of vagus nerve stimulation. *Neurology, 59*(6 suppl 4), S3–S14. doi:10.1212/WNL.59.6_suppl_4.S3; Chen, S. P., Ay, I., de Morais, A. L., Qin, T., Zheng, Y., Sadhegian, H., ..., & Ayata, C. (2016). Vagus nerve stimulation inhibits cortical spreading depression. *Pain, 157*(4), 797. doi:10.1097/j.pain.0000000000000437.

5 Jerath, R., Crawford, M. W., Barnes, V. A., & Harden, K. (2015). Self-regulation of breathing as a primary treatment for anxiety. *Applied Psychophysiology and Biofeedback, 40*(2), 107–115. doi:10.1007/s10484-015-9279-8; Zaccaro, A., Piarulli, A., Laurino, M., Garbella, E., Menicucci, D., Neri, B., & Gemignani, A. (2018). How breath-control can change your life: A systematic review on psycho-physiological correlates of slow breathing. *Frontiers in Human Neuroscience, 12*, 353. doi:10.3389/fnhum.2018.00353; Breit, S., Kupferberg, A., Rogler, G., & Hasler, G. (2018). Vagus nerve as modulator of the brain–gut axis in psychiatric and inflammatory disorders. *Frontiers in Psychiatry, 9*, 44. doi:10.3389/fpsyt.2018.00044; Jerath, R., & Crawford, M. W. (2015). How does the body affect the mind? Role of cardiorespiratory coherence in spectrum of emotions. *Adv. Mind Body Med, 29*, 4–16.

6 Kolb, B., & Wishaw, I. Q. (2015). *Fundamentals of neuropsychology*. New York: Worth Publishers.

7 Lehrer, P. M., & Gevirtz, R. (2014). Heart rate variability biofeedback: How and why does it work? *Frontiers in Psychology, 5*, 756. doi:10.3389/fpsyg.2014.00756; Jerath, R., Barnes, V. A., & Crawford, M. W. (2014). Mind-body response and neurophysiological changes during stress and meditation: Central role of homeostasis. *Journal of Biological Regulators and Homeostatic Agents, 28*(4), 545–554.

8 Bhimani, N. T., Kulkarni, N. B., Kowale, A., & Salvi, S. (2011). Effect of Pranayama on stress and cardiovascular autonomic function. *Indian J Physiol Pharmacol, 55*(4), 370–377; Brown, R. P., & Gerbarg, P. L. (2005). Sudarshan Kriya yogic breathing in the treatment of stress, anxiety, and depression: part I—neurophysiologic model. *Journal of Alternative & Complementary Medicine, 11*(1), 189–201. doi:10.1089/acm.2005.11.189; Marshall, R. S., Basilakos, A., Williams, T., & Love-Myers, K. (2013). Exploring the benefits of unilateral nostril breathing practice post-stroke: Attention, language, spatial abilities, depression, and anxiety. *Journal of Alternative and Complementary Medicine, 20*(3), 185–194. doi:10.1089/acm.2013.0019. Zope, S. A., & Zope, R. A. (2013). Sudarshan kriya yoga: Breathing for health. *International Journal of Yoga, 6*(1), 4–10. doi:10.4103/0973-6131.105935.

9 Mahour, J., & Verma, P. (2017). Effect of ujjayi pranayama on cardiovascular autonomic function tests. *National Journal of Physiology, Pharmacy and Pharmacology, 7*(4), 391–395. doi:10.5455/njppp.2017.7.1029809122016; Mazumdar, I., & Suryavanshi, A. (2010). Effect of Ujjayi and Bhastrika Pranayama on selected physiological variables of physically challenged students. *British Journal of Sports Medicine, 44*(Suppl 1), i69–i69. doi:10.1136/bjsm.2010.078725.229.

10 Weil, A. Three breathing exercise and techniques. *www.drweil.com*. Retrieved 21st November, 2019, from www.drweil.com/health-wellness/body-mind-spirit/stress-anxiety/breathing-three-exercises/.

11 McCloughan, L. J., Hanrahan, S. J., Anderson, R., & Halson, S. R. (2016). Psychological recovery: Progressive muscle relaxation (PMR), anxiety, and sleep in dancers. *Performance*

Enhancement & Health, *4*(1–2), 12–17 doi:10.1016/j.peh.2015.11.002; Nagel, J. J., Himle, D. P., & Papsdorf, J. D. (1989). Cognitive-behavioural treatment of musical performance anxiety. *Psychology of Music*, *17*(1), 12–21. doi:10.1177/0305735689171002; Parry, C. B. W. (2004). Managing the physical demands of musical performance. In A. Williamson (Ed.), *Musical excellence: Strategies and techniques to enhance performance*. Oxford: Oxford University Press; Kim, Y. (2008). The effect of improvisation-assisted desensitization, and music-assisted progressive muscle relaxation and imagery on reducing pianists' music performance anxiety. *Journal of Music Therapy*, *45*(2), 165–191. doi:10.1093/jmt/45.2.165; Parnabas, V. A., Mahamood, Y., Parnabas, J., & Abdullah, N. M. (2014). The relationship between relaxation techniques and sport performance. *Universal Journal of Psychology*, *2*(3), 108–112;

12 Williams, M., & Penman, D. (2011). *Mindfulness: An eight-week plan for finding peace in a frantic world*. Piatkus: Hachette; Kabat-Zinn, J. (2003). Mindfulness-based interventions in context: Past, present, and future. *Clinical Psychology: Science and Practice*, *10*(2), 144–156. doi:10.1093/clipsy.bpg016; Zeidan, F., Martucci, K. T., Kraft, R. A., McHaffie, J. G., & Coghill, R. C. (2013). Neural correlates of mindfulness meditation-related anxiety relief. *Social Cognitive and Affective Neuroscience*, *9*, 751–759. doi:10.1093/scan/nst041.

13 Williams, J. M. G., Crane, C., Barnhofer, T., Brennan, K., Duggan, D. S., Fennell, M. J., ..., & Shah, D. (2014). Mindfulness-based cognitive therapy for preventing relapse in recurrent depression: a randomized dismantling trial. *Journal of Consulting and Clinical Psychology*, *82*(2), 275. doi:10.1037/a0035036; Hofmann, S. G., Sawyer, A. T., Witt, A. A., & Oh, D. (2010). The effect of mindfulness-based therapy on anxiety and depression: A meta-analytic review. *Journal of Consulting and Clinical Psychology*, *78*(2), 169 doi:10.1037/a0018555.

14 Hick, S. F., Segal, Z. V., & Bien, T. (2008). *Mindfulness and the therapeutic relationship*. New York: The Guilford Press.

15 Low, C. A., Stanton, A. L., & Bower, J. E. (2008). Effects of acceptance-oriented versus evaluative emotional processing on heart rate recovery and habituation. *Emotion*, 8, 419–24. doi:10.1037/1528-3542.8.3.419; Kabat-Zinn, J., & Hanh, T. N. (2013). *Full catastrophe living: Using the wisdom of your body and mind to face stress, pain, and illness*. New York: Penguin Random House; Morone, N. E., Greco, C. M., & Weiner, D. K. (2008). Mindfulness meditation for the treatment of chronic low back pain in older adults: a randomized controlled pilot study. *Pain*, *134*(3), 310–319. doi:10.1016/j.pain.2007.04.038; Black, D. S., & Slavich, G. M. (2016). Mindfulness meditation and the immune system: a systematic review of randomized controlled trial. *Annals of the New York Academy of Sciences*, *1373*, 13–24. doi:10.1111/nyas.12998.

16 Lavery-Thompson, T. (2019). *Effects of mindfulness-based stress reduction on flow state and self-compassion during music practice*. Master's thesis, University of Oregon. Retrieved 30th May, 2020, from http://hdl.handle.net/1794/24195; Aherne, C., Moran, A. P., & Lonsdale, C. (2011). The effect of mindfulness on athletes' flow. *The Sport Psychologist*, *25*, 177–189. doi:10.1123/tsp.25.2.177.

17 Williams, M., & Penman, D. (2011). *Mindfulness: A practical guide to finding peace in a frantic world*. Piatkus: Hachette.

18 Williams, M., & Penman, D. (2011). *Mindfulness: A practical guide to finding peace in a frantic world*. Piatkus: Hachette .

10 Pre-performance routines

1 Kremer J., & Moran, A. (2008). *Pure sport: Practical sport psychology.* London and New York: Routledge; Wilson, M. R., & Richards, H. (2011). Putting it together: Skills for pressure performance. In D. J. Collins, A. Button, & H. Richards (Eds.), *Performance psychology: A practitioner's guide.* London: Elsevier. doi:10.1016/B978-0-443-06734-1.00023-7; Moran, A. (2011). Attention. In D. J. Collins, A. Button, & H. Richards (Eds.), *Performance psychology: A practitioner's guide.* London: Elsevier. doi:10.1016/B978-0-443-06734-1.00022-5; Singer, R. N. (2002). Preperformance state, routines, and automaticity: What does it take to realize expertise in self-paced events? *Journal of Sport and Exercise Psychology, 24*(4), 359–375. doi:10.1123/jsep.24.4.359.

2 Wilson, M. R., & Richards, H. (2011). Putting it together: Skills for pressure performance. In D. J. Collins, A. Button, & H. Richards (Eds.), *Performance psychology: A practitioner's guide.* London: Elsevier. doi:10.1016/B978-0-443-06734-1.00023-7.

3 Wilson, M. R., & Richards, H. (2011). Putting it together: Skills for pressure performance. In D. J. Collins, A. Button, & H. Richards (Eds.), *Performance psychology: A practitioner's guide.* London: Elsevier. doi:10.1016/B978-0-443-06734-1.00023-7.

4 Wilson, M. R., & Richards, H. (2011). Putting it together: Skills for pressure performance. In D. J. Collins, A. Button, & H. Richards (Eds.), *Performance psychology: A practitioner's guide.* London: Elsevier. doi:10.1016/B978-0-443-06734-1.00023-7.

5 West, R. (2004). Drugs and musical performance. In A. Williamon (Ed.), *Musical excellence: Strategies and techniques to enhance performance* (pp. 271–290). Oxford University Press.

6 Hays, K. F., & Brown, C. H. Jr. (2004). *You're on! Consulting for peak performance* (p. 64). Washington, DC: American Psychological Association. doi:10.1037/10675-000; Dunkel, S. E. (1989). *The audition process: Anxiety management and coping strategies.* Stuyvesant, NY: Pendragon.

7 Kremer, J., Moran, A. P., & Kearney, C. J. (2019). *Pure sport: Sport psychology in action,* p. 126. London and New York: Routledge.

8 Sinnamon, S. (2008). *Musicians in flow: An empirical investigation of the peak performance experiences in novice and expert performers.* University College Dublin.

11 Putting it all together

1 Ericsson, A., & Pool, R. (2016). *Peak: How all of us can achieve extraordinary things.* London: Penguin Random House; Ericsson, K. A., Krampe, R. T., & Tesch-Römer, C. (1993). The role of deliberate practice in the acquisition of expert performance. *Psychol. Rev., 100,* 363–406. doi:10.1037/0033-295X.100.3.363; Gladwell, M. (2008). *Outliers: The story of success.* New York: Little, Brown and Company.

2 Conway, T. (2016). *Taylor Swift: This is our song.* London: Simon & Schuster.

3 Wilson, M. R., & Richards, H. (2011). Putting it together: Skills for pressure performance. In D. J. Collins, A. Button, & H. Richards (Eds.), *Performance psychology: A practitioner's guide.* London: Elsevier. doi:10.1016/B978-0-443-06734-1.00023-7.

4 Beckett, S. (2009). *Company / Ill Seen Ill Said / Worstward Ho / Stirrings Stil.* London: Faber & Faber.

5 Noone, Eimear (9th February 2020). How to keep your cool in front of 30m people? Be ok with failure. By Horan, Niamh. *Irish Independent.* Retrieved on 9th February, 2020, from www.independent.ie/entertainment/how-to-keep-your-cool-in-front-of-30m-people-be-ok-with-failure-irish-woman-conducting-oscars-38938749.html.

6 Jordan, M. (1997). "Failure". *Nike TV commercial.* www.youtube.com/watch?v= 45m MioJ5szc 26/02/20.

7 Whitecross, M. (2018). *Coldplay: A head full of dreams.* 14th November 2018. Mint pictures.

8 Wilson, M. R., & Richards, H. (2011). Putting it together: Skills for pressure performance. In D. J. Collins, A. Button, & H. Richards (Eds.), *Performance psychology: A practitioner's guide* (pp. 337–360). London: Elsevier. doi:10.1016/B978-0-443-06734-1.00023-7.

9 Duckworth, A., & Duckworth, A. (2016). *Grit: The power of passion and perseverance* (vol. 234). New York: Scribner; Duckworth, A., & Gross, J. J. (2014). Self-control and grit: Related but separable determinants of success. *Current Directions in Psychological Science, 23*(5), 319–325. doi:10.1177/0963721414541462; Duckworth, A. L., Peterson, C., Matthews, M. D., & Kelly, D. R. (2007). Grit: Perseverance and passion for long-term goals. *Journal of Personality and Social Psychology, 92*(6), 1087. doi:10.1037/0022-3514.92.6.1087.

10 Fletcher, D., & Sarkar, M. (2012). A grounded theory of psychological resilience in Olympic champions. *Psychology of Sport and Exercise, 13*(5), 669–678. doi:10.1016/j.psychsport.2012.04.007; Braden, A. M., Osborne, M. S., & Wilson, S. J. (2015). Psychological intervention reduces self-reported performance anxiety in high school music students. *Frontiers in Psychology, 6,* 195 doi:10.3389/fpsyg.2015.00195; Sarkar, M., & Fletcher, D. (2014). Psychological resilience in sport performers: a review of stressors and protective factors. *Journal of Sports Sciences, 32*(15), 1419–1434; Sarkar, M., & Fletcher, D. (2014). Ordinary magic, extraordinary performance: Psychological resilience and thriving in high achievers. *Sport, Exercise, and Performance Psychology, 3*(1), 46. doi:10.1037/spy0000003.

11 Richards, H. (2011). Coping and mental toughness. In D. J. Collins, A. Button, & H. Richards (Eds.), *Performance psychology: A practitioner's guide* (pp. 281–300). London: Elsevier. doi:10.1016/B978-0-443-06734-1.00020-1; Rodgers, S., & Tajet-Foxell, B. (2011). Emotional issues in peak performance. In D. J. Collins, A. Button, & H. Richards (Eds.), *Performance psychology: A practitioner's guide* (pp. 301–318). London: Elsevier.

12 Williams, R. (2004). The Show Off Must Go On. Television broadcast. Channel 4, 16th October 2004. Retrieved on 28th January, 2020, from www.youtube.com/watch?v=iSAUtkqbKi0.

13 Lang, L. (2015). Lang Lang's three secrets for a calm, composed on-stage performance. Classic FM. Retrieved from www.classicfm.com/artists/lang-lang/news/teaching-app on 29th June 2020

Acknowledgements

There are many people to whom I am very grateful for their help and support in writing this book, and without whom, it might never have happened.

I am extremely grateful to editor Christina Chronister for taking on this book and for her encouragement and support along the way. I am also very grateful to Danielle Dyal, editorial assistant, for her wonderful support and help.

I have been privileged to have had Prof. Aidan Moran as my PhD supervisor, my mentor, and friend for 20 years. If I could, I would thank him wholeheartedly for his advice, support, positivity and encouragement over all these years, and particularly in the last two years I so very much appreciated his support of this book and the invaluable encouragement and feedback he gave me. He has been a superbly wise and positive presence and guide, and I have learned a great deal from him.

I am indebted to the professional musicians who took part in interviews and who were, without exception, overwhelmingly honest, open, and generous in the amount of information they were so willing to provide. I was honoured by their giving of their precious time and sharing of their very personal experiences of performance.

Thank you to my violin teachers Loreta Nelson and Hu Kun for their positive impact on my music life. I am grateful to have met and worked with Simon Fischer – he was the first violinist, musician, and teacher I knew to talk 'out loud' about mental practice, visualisation, and the psychological side of practising and performing back in the 1990s in the Yehudi Menuhin School. I send special thanks to my friend Britt Johnson for her amazing graphic design skills and for the time she put into working on the graphic design of the figures in this book. Alan Bennet, thank you so much for your friendship and feedback on versions of chapters in this book. Thanks also to Sinead Reynolds and Rebecca McFadden for reading chapters and talking about flow perhaps for years now. Lola, thank you so much for your beautiful drawings; it's a delight for me to have them in the book.

I especially thank my parents Jen and Des, for your support especially these last few years, and for your proof-reading skills and advice. Thank you, too, for those years of music lessons and playing music together, which have been invaluable.

Tadhg and Lola – I am eternally grateful to you for all that you have given me and taught me; anything that's important, you've shown me. You absorb me, distract me, ground me and challenge me. Thank you for providing me with endless fun and joy.

Index